Anthropology of Contemporary Issues

A SERIES EDITED BY

ROGER SANJEK

"Getting Paid"

YOUTH CRIME AND WORK IN THE INNER CITY

Mercer L. Sullivan

Cornell University Press

Ithaca and London

First published 1989 by Cornell University Press.
First printing, Cornell Paperbacks, 1989.
Fourth printing 1994.

International Standard Book Number 0-8014-2370-8 (cloth)
International Standard Book Number 0-8014-9598-9 (paper)
Library of Congress Catalog Card Number 89-42882
Printed in the United States of America
Librarians: Library of Congress cataloging information
appears on the last page of the book.

⊗ The paper in this book meets the minimum requirements of the American National Standard for Information Sciences—Permanence of Paper for Printed Library Materials, ANSI Z39.48–1984.

Contents

Tables

Acknowledgments

Researching and writing this book have occupied me for several years. I could not have persevered without the support, partnership, and encouragement of many people, to all of whom I offer my thanks.

My first thanks are to those current and past staff members of the Vera Institute of Justice who recruited me for this project and worked with me along the way. James Thompson and Orlando Rodriguez brought me into Vera's Employment and Crime Project and assigned me to collect the ethnographic data that form the basis of this book. Two other members of the project greatly stimulated my thinking on theoretical problems: Richard McGahey introduced me to the problems of labor market theory; and I owe a special debt to Michele Sviridoff, whose pilot studies of the qualitative relationships between employment and crime set the stage for my ethnographic work and whose advice and counsel have been invaluable.

Other members of the Vera Institute have also been very helpful. Jerome McElroy, an associate director, was largely responsible for the decision to undertake the ethnographic research, and his subsequent support, from the difficult first days in the field through the completion of the work, never flagged. I have also profited greatly from the comments and advice of Sally Hillsman, the head of Vera's research department. Director Michael Smith was actively involved in discussing our findings and relating them to current trends in criminal justice policy. And without the patience of Scott Sparks and Judith Woolcock of Vera's clerical staff, the various drafts of the manuscript could never have been produced.

Thanks are also due to the members of the advisory committee of the Employment and Crime Project: Lucy Friedman, Herbert Gans, Kenneth Schoen, Susan Sheehan, Lester Thurow, and Marvin Wolfgang.

Herbert Gans was especially helpful as an advocate and inspiration for ethnographic research.

The work could not have been done without the assistance of Richard Curtis, Pharaoh Russ, and Antonio Valderama, the three fieldworkers with whom I explored the neighborhoods and got to know the young men we studied; Tony Valderama's example to us all will never be forgotten. Because of promises of confidentiality, the youths whose lives we recorded cannot be thanked by name, but our gratitude to them and to their families and neighbors for allowing us into their confidence is no less real.

This work was supported primarily by the National Institute of Justice, with additional assistance from the Ford Foundation. I am grateful to these agencies and to their representatives, particularly Bernard A. Gropper, our project monitor at the National Institute of Justice, who provided patient and consistent encouragement and advice throughout; and Gordon Berlin and Sharon Rowser, our program officers at the Ford Foundation, who generously shared their reactions to our work.

I approached the questions posed by the Vera project in the way I did as a result of my training at Columbia University; I owe many thanks to my professors at Teachers College and in the Department of Anthropology, foremost among them Francis A. J. Ianni, who first interested me in the ethnographic study of crime. Conrad Arensberg, George Bond, Lambros Comitas, and Joan Vincent have also fundamentally shaped my thinking in ways that I can only hope are evident.

Discussions with Jeffrey Fagan as I neared completion of a final manuscript helped me anchor my analyses more firmly in the literature of criminology.

My final debt of gratitude for intellectual advice and encouragement is to the editor of this series, Roger Sanjek, who sought me out to publish this book and whose advice has been extremely helpful.

Finally, I offer my personal thanks to my wife, Ellen Wahl, and my daughter, Laura, to whom this book is dedicated. Laura's birth and infancy during the fieldwork period not only spurred me to complete this task but also opened my heart to the struggles of the children, youth, and families of the ghettos.

MERCER SULLIVAN

New York, New York

"Getting Paid"

[1]

Introduction: Social Theory and Neighborhood Research

Crime rates among residents of inner-city neighborhoods are disastrously high. Inner-city residents also suffer low income levels as a result of low rates of employment and low wages when they do work. For decades, both popular thinking and the literature of social science supported the view that there must be a connection. More recently, however, there has been a sustained assault on the idea that poor employment opportunities cause crime, and both popular thinking and public policy have turned away from the premise that addressing employment problems can help to reduce the high levels of crime which have transformed public life in the cities of the United States since World War II. Most recent changes in crime-control policy have emphasized tougher sanctions in the form of longer sentences for convicted criminals, while efforts to improve employment conditions for purposes of crime control have been widely discredited (J. Q. Wilson 1975).

Yet although tougher criminal justice policies have been and are being tried, crime rates still have not declined dramatically. A modest reduction during the early 1980s was probably due primarily to demographic change: the declining numbers of "high-risk" inner-city male youths. There is little indication that crime prevention programs based on tougher criminal justice measures have been significantly more effective than those based on employment services.[1] Although more people are incarcerated than ever before (Bureau of Justice Statistics 1987), and budgets for jails and prisons are expanding rapidly—though too slowly to keep up with the increasing numbers of people incarcerated for

[1]For reviews of evaluations of employment-based crime prevention programs, see Lipton, Martinson, and Wilks 1975; J. Q. Wilson 1975; Thompson, Sviridoff, and McElroy 1981. For a comprehensive review of the effects of policies to control crime through deterrence, see Blumstein, Cohen, and Nagin 1978.

increasing lengths of time (Rich and Barnett 1985)—crime rates in the United States nevertheless remain much higher than they were a generation ago and significantly higher than crime rates in other developed countries (Currie 1985).

This book reexamines the question of the relationships between criminality and employment opportunities through the analysis of comparative ethnographic data collected in three inner-city neighborhoods of New York City during the early 1980s. My research assistants and I observed life in these neighborhoods and constructed life histories for groups of about a dozen young males in each one, tracing their involvement in schooling, employment, and crime from their early teens to their early twenties.

The connections we found between economic opportunity and criminal behavior shed new light on these questions at a time when traditional theories about such relationships are in considerable disarray. Dissatisfaction with past studies of delinquency, which relied on the concepts of subculture and economic opportunity, has led back to theories based on biology and psychology (Wilson and Herrnstein 1985). These theories tend to see criminals as fundamentally different from other people—less bound by culture and less rational in their behavior. Crime is portrayed as the product of individuals with low intelligence and defective personalities. High crime rates in certain localities are explained as the result of the movement of already deviant individuals and families into those localities rather than as the result of economic and social disadvantages affecting particular groups and areas.

But our research pointed distinctly to economic aspects of criminal behavior. In fact, the young men we studied spoke of their criminal activities as "getting over" and "getting paid," terms that refer directly, albeit ironically, to economic motivation and reflect the perception of a social structure of restricted opportunity. "Getting paid" equates crime with work. "Getting over" means beating the system, a rigged system in which one is unlikely to succeed by competing according to the rules (Bullock 1973).

These expressions indicate both a cultural dimension of shared meanings and an economic dimension of rational cost-benefit calculations. Some of these youths' criminal activities were indeed reckless and thrill-seeking, but others displayed considerable and often successful ingenuity. The assumptions of low intelligence and blind pathological motivation as the chief driving forces of criminality do not square well with such evidence. These youths appeared to be very conscious of what they were doing and why they were doing it, and they usually engaged in these activities in groups rather than as isolated, deranged individuals.

[2]

The fact that so much delinquency is group behavior presents a serious challenge to individualistic explanations (Erickson and Jensen 1977).

The controversy over the relative influence of individual pathology and socioeconomic conditions on criminal behavior is an old one. This study provides a new perspective on the issue by examining variations in criminal participation both within and between three neighborhood-based groups of young males as they aged from their early teens to their early twenties.

Cycles of Explanations for Crime and Delinquency

Theories of crime and delinquency have passed successively through biological, psychological, sociological, and economic modes of explanation. In the face of the intractability of criminality in recent years, the sequence has begun to come full cycle. The scholars who continue to investigate social explanations (Greenberg 1985) are currently on the defensive against new voices calling for a return to a consideration of biology and psychology as the sources of criminal behavior. After decades of seeking the causes of crime in society, it is now suggested that we focus again on individuals (Wilson and Herrnstein, 1985).

The earliest theories about crime portrayed criminals as persons physically and psychologically different from noncriminals (Lombroso 1911). The early biological studies were eventually discredited as unscientific; psychodynamic explanations, usually tracing criminality to family problems, have an equally long but much more durable history. During the 1930s sociologists diverted attention from psychological factors by documenting the tremendous concentration of arrests among young inner-city males (Shaw and McKay 1931; Thrasher 1927). Social area, rather than individual biology or psychology, came to be regarded as the cause of delinquency: delinquents were thought not to have been born with innate tendencies toward deviance but rather to have learned delinquency from others.

Some theorists stressed the cultural aspect of this process, portraying delinquency as learned behavior transmitted within inner-city neighborhoods (Shaw and McKay 1931; Sutherland and Cressey 1955; Miller 1958), and others emphasized social inequality as the driving force (Merton 1938; A. Cohen 1955), but most tended to agree that delinquency was a problem primarily among poor urban youths. The relationship of delinquency to social class and the relative importance of social class over individual factors remained unquestioned for decades, a viewpoint so widespread that researchers neglected to collect data on middle-

[3]

class youths. The culmination of this trend was Cloward and Ohlin's influential study (1960), which combined most of the elements of previous theories and research and posited a close relation between delinquent subcultures and specific local structures of economic opportunity. Their work provided the theoretical basis for many social programs during the 1960s which attempted to reduce delinquency by improving economic opportunities for inner-city youths.

During the same decade, however, this structure of explanation started to unravel. For one thing, theoretical studies began to undermine the dominant concept of "subculture" as the cause of delinquency. Theoreticians questioned the premise that delinquency is the product of lower-class culture by pointing out that the concept of culture, used in this way, explains too much (Matza 1964; Kornhauser 1978). They pointed out that poor people are the most frequent victims of crime and that most of them do not condone crime as part of a general belief system. In addition, the declining rates of crime with age are difficult to explain in terms of culture: if delinquents value their delinquent acts so positively, why then do they stop such behavior as they get older? In seminal formulations of the problem, delinquency was seen as a product of "drift" rather than rational intentionality, and delinquents were said to "neutralize" conventional values in specific situations rather than constructing a perverse and enduring set of alternative values (Sykes and Matza 1957; Matza 1964).

While the theoretical questioning of cultural causality was in progress, empirical researchers had begun to produce new kinds of data that cast doubt on the notion that delinquency was specific to poor inner-city neighborhoods. Previous research had been based primarily on ethnographic studies (Shaw 1931; Whyte 1943) and arrest statistics that consistently showed a concentration of juvenile arrests in these areas (Shaw and McKay 1931). Toward the end of the 1950s, however, sociologists conducting surveys of high school students found high rates of self-reported delinquency in middle-class communities as well (Short and Nye 1958; Hirschi 1969), leading some to raise serious questions about the link between social class and delinquency. Family factors again came under scrutiny and were found to be significant, although the notion that broken homes are the major cause of delinquency was replaced by a new emphasis on neglectful and abusive home environments (Wilkinson 1974). The link between school failure and delinquency also received renewed attention (Elliott and Voss 1974). These new emphases prepared the way for a return from social to psychological explanations.

Further weakening of the presumed link between social class and criminality occurred when economists began to study crime in the 1960s

[4]

and 1970s. The "economic model of crime" proposed to do away with the concepts of both psychology and sociology by showing that the decision to commit crime involved cost-benefit analyses like any other form of economic decision making (G. Becker 1968). Economists set out to correlate aggregate crime and employment rates over time, expecting to demonstrate a strong relationship between the two. Their efforts produced such perverse results, however, that they further weakened the commonsense notion that poor employment conditions produce criminality (Gillespie 1975; Long and Witte 1981; Orsagh and Witte 1981). During the 1930s, for example, unemployment rates were high but crime rates were low; in the late 1960s, employment rates and crime rates rose together. The grand promise of the economic model of crime foundered on the indeterminacy of research results and led to the conclusion that the "moral noxiousness" of criminality could not easily be reduced to economic terms (Block and Heineke 1975).

More recently, quantitative studies using individual-level data have also failed to demonstrate strong relationships between unemployment and criminality. For example, inner-city teenagers who have serious economic problems and are prone to criminal activities do not necessarily commit crimes less often during the times when they are employed (Sviridoff with McElroy 1984; Crowley 1984).

Public policy experiments have contributed further to the disenchantment with theories of crime and delinquency based on the structure of economic opportunity. A number of programs providing social services for disadvantaged youths were tried in the hope of lowering crime rates, but crime continued to rise. Formal evaluations of some of these programs during the 1970s frequently failed to demonstrate significant crime reduction effects (Manpower Demonstration Research Corporation 1980). But aggregate studies of employment and crime rates, self-report surveys, and program evaluations produced conflicting results. For example, not all job programs failed; the most intensive—and expensive—of them, the Job Corps, did show solid results (Mallar et al. 1980). Nor did the finding of extensive delinquency among middle-class youths negate the prominence of severe and intensive criminality and high arrest rates among inner-city youths. More recent studies of the relationship between crime and employment rates have showed a stronger relationship since unemployment began to rise in the 1970s (Chiricos 1987).

For a time, the supposed discrepancy between the results of self-report surveys and arrest rates produced a quandary among social scientists. Even though surveys consistently found high rates of self-reported delinquency in both middle-class and poor neighborhoods, arrest rates

[5]

continued to be much higher in poor, inner-city neighborhoods. It seemed that either the survey methodology must be fundamentally flawed or else the criminal justice system was engaging in massive discrimination against inner-city youths.

Proponents of self-report surveys were eventually forced to acknowledge the inappropriateness of their techniques for the study of serious crimes (Empey 1982; Hindelang, Hirschi, and Weis 1979). High school students, who consistently admit a wide variety of fairly minor offenses on questionnaires, are not so candid regarding major offenses. Also, given the high correlation between being delinquent and not attending school, there is doubt about the extent to which such surveys ever reached the population of serious delinquents. Although the discovery of middle-class delinquency was an important achievement, then, there can be little doubt about the concentration of serious and frequent criminality among poor, minority, inner-city youths (Elliott and Ageton 1980; Elliott and Huizinga 1983).

The most sophisticated recent work with self-report surveys has in fact combined the assumptions of different theories, including "strain" theories that emphasize inequality (Merton 1938; A. Cohen 1955; Cloward and Ohlin, 1960); "social learning" theories that emphasize cultural transmission (Sutherland and Cressey 1955; Akers 1973); and "control" theories that are more psychologically oriented and emphasize lack of attachments to school, family, peers, and conventional activities (Hirschi 1969). These theories, not necessarily logically inconsistent with one another, are found to explain survey data better in combination than separately (Elliott, Huizinga, and Ageton 1982, 1985).

Nevertheless, by the mid-1980s, the stage was set for a rejection of social, cultural, and economic explanations of delinquency and a return to psychological and biological explanations. The conclusions that delinquency, broadly defined, is widely distributed throughout the class structure; that the link between economic opportunity and criminality is more complex than it was once thought to be; and that social programs attempting to reduce crime by improving economic opportunities do not produce quick and easy results have all contributed to a greater receptivity to theories of delinquency not based on social factors. Attention has been newly focused on age, gender, personality, and intelligence—that is, on individual, "constitutional" attributes rooted in biology—as the sources of crime and delinquency (Hirschi and Gottfredson 1983; Wilson and Herrnstein 1985; Gove 1985). The relationship between individual and society has been called into question anew.

Part of the shift in emphasis may be attributable to a shift in research methods away from ethnographic studies toward analyses of self-report

[6]

survey data and of aggregate social statistics on crime and unemployment. The earlier theories that emphasized social causation had relied heavily on such classic qualitative studies as those by Shaw (1931) and Whyte (1943), which related the development of delinquent careers to the specific social environments of inner-city neighborhoods. More quantitative methods do not portray such local-level processes very well. Yet a few contemporary ethnographic studies of life in poor inner-city communities do provide a sense of the social processes whereby such areas come to have high rates of crime and delinquency. Though not based on random samples that would make them precisely comparable to one another or to quantitative studies, they do show how youthful careers in crime develop in specific environments and how crime is both generated and controlled within these communities. While the specific theoretical questions posed in this book derive from recent work by economists and survey sociologists on the relationship between crime and employment, the method of comparative ethnography used here to answer those questions derives from the work of both classic and more recent ethnographic studies, all of which convey a sense of community and spatial organization that has been almost entirely lacking in most recent research on crime and delinquency.

Whyte's classic work on "Cornerville" provided an important beginning, particularly his observation (1943: 273) that what looks to outsiders like the social disorganization of the inner city often turns out to be simply a different form of social organization if one takes the trouble to look closely. Suttles's later study (1968) of Chicago youth gangs reaffirmed this observation and also directed theoretical attention to the importance of physical ecology in analyzing the social organization of urban neighborhoods. The studies of street-corner men by Liebow (1967) and Anderson (1978) have shown the complicated ways in which sporadic employment is combined with other ways of surviving.

More recent ethnographic work has looked specifically at patterns of economic crime among inner-city youths. West (1974) found that "serious theft" served as a "short-term career" among a group of lower-class white youths in Toronto. Sharff (1981) situated youthful drug selling within the household economies of lower-class Puerto Rican families in New York City. Moore's (1978) study of Chicano street gangs in Los Angeles is one of the few that are both comparative and historical; it traces the evolution of gangs in three neighborhoods. Ianni (1974a, 1974b) documented the diverse methods by which New York youths are recruited from the streets to organized crime operations. The work of Preble and Casey (1969) and their successors (Johnson et al. 1985) has demonstrated the redistributive effects of crime by showing how heroin

[7]

addicts in New York City receive a measure of support for their habit by providing a supply of cheap stolen goods for poor neighborhoods. Williams and Kornblum (1985) have compared communities and documented a number of the findings about youthful careers that are presented here, though their results were not published until after our project had been largely completed.

Other ethnographic studies have contributed important knowledge about the economic life of the inner cities. Both Stack (1974) and Susser (1982) have documented forms of economic organization among poor women which are based on reciprocity and help them to cope with poverty and exclusion from the labor market. Finally, Willis's (1977) inspired account of the school-to-work transitions of a group of working-class British youths has shown that the cultural meaning of delinquent behavior to poor and working-class youths is no mere mechanical response to social disadvantage but an active and creative production firmly rooted in the social relationships of their communities.

Although these recent ethnographic studies have demonstrated that the influence of the social processes of community life on patterns of economic crime can be documented and analyzed, they suffer from two kinds of methodological shortcomings. First, they are difficult to generalize to larger populations because they are usually focused on close descriptions of particular behavior patterns within small groups. Second, they sometimes tend to play down differences between individuals within these small groups in favor of descriptions of the common aspects of their experience. As a result, it can be difficult to reconcile the emphasis of ethnographic studies on social process with that of survey studies on individual variation. Paradoxically, small-scale ethnographic studies tend to focus on collective behavior, while large-scale quantitative studies tend to analyze differences among atomized individuals. This methodological divide is the source of much of the current confusion over the relative contributions of society and individual to criminal behavior. The effort to reconcile these differing methods and theories poses a significant challenge (Reiss 1986).

The Research Design: Comparative Ethnography

Very little research to date has attempted to assess both individual and group variation simultaneously, yet this is the approach that seems called for at present, given the tension between social and individualistic explanations of crime and delinquency. This book attempts to resolve that tension by examining variations in criminality both within and between three neighborhood-based groups of young men.

[8]

The concepts both of "culture" and of "economic choice" have been beset by considerable confusion resulting from the conflict between structural and individual levels of explanation. Even among those who remain committed to the proposition that crime and delinquency must be understood in terms of collective behavior rather than individual pathology, there are differences over the extent to which this collective behavior should be understood in terms of culture or of economics. Subcultural theories of delinquency have been found to be overly deterministic, allowing neither for variation between individuals nor for changes within individuals over time or from situation to situation. Economic theories have not accounted well for historical changes in the relationship of crime rates to unemployment rates, nor have they worked very well in the few studies that have examined economic choice at the individual level.

The method of comparative ethnography employed here attempts to overcome some of these controversies by examining the career patterns of young men in three neighborhood groups and the relationships of these young men to other members of their communities. This emphasis on the local community as the unit of analysis provides a perspective on the relation of individual decisions to structural constraints which has been missing from most studies of crime and delinquency and which offers a way out of the theoretical impasses that have beset the notion of "choice" in economics and of "culture" in anthropology and sociology.

Our focus on comparisons within and between local communities grows out of a general interactionist view of culture, society, and economy (Blumer 1969; Arensberg 1972). The values, cognitions, and choices of individuals are seen as embedded in social interaction. The community is seen as a locus of interaction, intermediate between the individual and the larger society, where the many constraints and opportunities of the total society are narrowed to a subset within which local individuals choose. The local community is also the cultural milieu within which the worth of these specific options is defined. The cognitions and values embedded in community context are not so much fundamentally different from those of the wider society as they are more specific to the actual life experiences of local inhabitants. Interactionist analysis portrays simultaneously the reality of differences between groups and the agency and diversity of individual social actors within each group. Culture provides certain parameters for social action; at the same time, individual actions make and remake culture.

The emphasis on the local neighborhood as a partially bounded sphere of interactions in which young males "choose" to go to school, to work, and/or to engage in criminal activities offers a perspective on "economic choice" and "cultural values" which has been missing or incompletely

[9]

applied in previous studies. This book situates the undifferentiated "subcultural delinquents" of previous studies in specific local contexts of economic opportunity and social organization. In this way it portrays an interplay between values and material activity. Because previous research has not been able to capture this interplay very well, it has portrayed delinquent activities either as the product of a set of self-perpetuating deviant values (Miller 1958; Lewis 1966; Banfield 1970) or as the product of purely individual cost-benefit calculations (Kornhauser, 1978). So radical a separation of culture and economy has obscured the explanatory power of both. Moral and economic factors must be considered together in any satisfactory analysis of criminality.

Our research strategy and the language I use to report it were chosen for the purpose of avoiding the pitfalls resulting from the tendency to separate culture from economy and individual from society. Because of the many debates over the meaning of "culture" and "subculture," I reserve those terms for the conclusion of this study, when I relate the findings of our research to the anthropological theories of culture. I use the language of social action theory throughout the presentation of the data. The groups of youths are referred to as "cliques" (Boissevain 1974) in order to present them as individuals doing things together rather than assuming that they share some set of immutable values which drives all their behavior.

By portraying economic choice within socially bounded spheres of interaction, this book attempts to overcome some of the difficulties that have arisen in previous efforts to examine crime as an economic activity. Microeconomic theory, which sees individual careers as the products of the choices of separate and equal competitors in a meritocracy (G. Becker 1975), has not accounted well for the differences in the access to the labor market which we found to be crucial to the career decisions of the young men we studied. At the other extreme, attempts by Marxist criminologists to portray criminality among the poor as a class-conscious form of resistance to oppression (Quinney 1974; Chambliss 1973) have not accounted well for the ambivalence about crime documented in this and other studies. By describing and comparing the criminal careers of young males as these careers develop within three specific community contexts, this book tries to overcome the hazards of assuming either atomized, autonomous individuals or a monolithic, all-determining society.

The theoretical tools I use to develop these comparisons derive from two nonmainstream bodies of economic theory. Both segmented labor market theory (Doeringer and Piore 1971; Gordon, Edwards, and Reich 1982; Bluestone and Harrison 1982) and the concept of redistribution

[10]

drawn from the substantivist school of economic anthropology (Polanyi, Arensberg, and Pearson 1957; Dalton 1969) help to describe and analyze local variations in economic process. Both approaches are attentive to the connections between social and economic process which are necessary to an understanding of the economic aspects of criminality.

Segmented labor market theory informs the portrayal of the different career paths within each neighborhood. Rather than assuming a meritocratic society in which all individuals are equal competitors, segmented labor market theory has proposed that there are at least two labor markets: a "primary" one in which steady employment at relatively high wages can support families, and a "secondary" one in which low-wage jobs, welfare, employment and training programs, informal economic activities, and crime must be alternated and combined because none of these economic activities alone can provide a steady living (Harrison 1972a). The differentiation between primary and secondary labor markets is seen as a consequence of the structure of the economy and society, not simply as the aggregate result of individual investments in "human capital."

This approach does not negate individual choices; rather, they are seen as taking place within socially bounded spheres of interaction. The articulation of the local groups with different sectors of the labor market is the context for the description of the transitions of young males from schooling to the labor market and the relationship to these career paths of involvement in crime for economic gain. This approach asks not just whether different individuals choose to invest in education and training and whether they choose crime or employment as their source of income but also how these choices are conditioned by the social environments of the neighborhoods in which they grow up and by the relationships of those neighborhoods to the education system, the labor market, and the criminal justice system.

Further, the chapters presenting data on criminal activities examine the redistributive effects of youth crime in relation to the social control environment of each neighborhood and show how rewards and sanctions vary according to whether a given crime brings goods and money into the community, takes them out, or merely circulates them within. Crimes are described in terms of who benefits and who suffers, and how victims and offenders are related within the social contexts of the different communities.

This theoretical approach, which attempts to describe and analyze delinquent activity at the local level in terms of specific local structures of economic opportunity, is derived from Cloward and Ohlin's (1960) seminal theory but applied to systematically collected ethnographic data

[11]

with results quite different from those in the original work. Cloward and Ohlin projected an abstract theory onto data collected by others in widely differing times and places. They speculated that different kinds of opportunities at the local level would produce conformist youths in one kind of neighborhood, fighting gangs in another, stealing gangs and drug-using gangs in others. We found all these behaviors in all the neighborhoods, though they were patterned quite differently in each of the three.

The History of the Project

My general interest in both ethnographic methods and the career paths of inner-city youths developed during my earlier research in a New York City high school (Sullivan 1979). There I had examined the differential participation in the school by youths from different class and cultural backgrounds and the ways in which neighborhood-based patterns of association penetrated the informal organization of the school. I had also learned to use life history techniques to reconstruct the personal backgrounds of the individuals whose interactions I was recording.

The further opportunity to investigate employment and crime patterns among inner-city youths arose in the summer of 1979 when I was asked to undertake ethnographic studies as part of the Employment and Crime Project being conducted by the Vera Institute of Justice (a nonprofit corporation in New York City which engages in social research and the development of social programs), and funded by the National Institute of Justice (a research agency in the U.S. Department of Justice). At that time Vera had been engaged for nearly two years in designing and implementing the Employment and Crime Project. The study was originally planned around a survey of the employment histories of a sample of persons who had been arrested. Vera had then decided to hire an ethnographer in order to learn more about what their research design termed the "subcultural and institutional" factors associated with crime patterns in different neighborhoods (Vera Institute of Justice 1979).

The research plan called for me to hire, train, and supervise three research assistants to collect ethnographic data on high-risk youths in three different neighborhoods. The term "high-risk" is widely used among policymakers to designate populations among which the social problems in question are prevalent. Vera had formulated for this project a definition of "high-risk" based on "residence in inner-city areas which offer both relatively low levels of employment opportunity and significant criminal opportunity" (Vera Institute of Justice 1979). Vera's formu-

[12]

lation of the research problem and proposed research strategy offered considerable continuity with my earlier research. My work at the high school had forced me to wonder what happens to those youths who leave school and had begun to suggest the powerful and diverse effects of different neighborhood environments on youthful careers. My involvement with Vera researchers also stimulated me to think systematically about the different kinds of relationships between employment and crime (Sviridoff and Thompson 1983; Thompson, Sviridoff, et al. 1981) and about the structure of labor markets (McGahey 1982). These issues informed the collection of field data over the next three years.

Shortly after I joined the project, Vera decided to conduct a survey among a random sample of arrestees from the borough of Brooklyn in New York City. A boroughwide sample was chosen because all arrested persons from each borough are processed in a central location. Brooklyn was chosen because it contains a broader spectrum of social classes and racial/ethnic groups than any of the other boroughs. Because the arrestee sample was to be recruited in Brooklyn, it was decided that the three neighborhoods for the ethnographic studies should also be selected in Brooklyn.

During the summer and early fall of 1979 I made automobile trips through Brooklyn with Orlando Rodriquez, the deputy director of the Employment and Crime Project, and with Tony Valderama, a research assistant at Vera. Valderama had grown up in lower-class Puerto Rican neighborhoods in Brooklyn and had belonged to street gangs as a teenager. Because of his interest in and knowledge of the neighborhood, we chose "La Barriada"[2] as the first of the three study neighborhoods and asked him to collect ethnographic data there.

We continued to drive through other neighborhoods, recording our visual impressions in field notes and meanwhile also collecting crime and demographic statistics. Our objective was to choose two other neighborhoods that would satisfy the project's definition of "high-risk" yet differ in ethnicity, crime patterns, housing type, and proximity of local businesses and public or private service organizations.

In the fall of 1979, I hired two more research assistants. Pharaoh Russ was assigned to work in "Projectville," which I wanted to study the first time I saw it because it was a poor black neighborhood that differed dramatically from La Barriada in a number of ways (see Chapter 2). The third assistant was assigned to work in a still different area.

Establishing rapport was not easy in any of these neighborhoods;

[2]In order to honor our assurances of confidentiality (described in the Appendix), all names of neighborhoods, individuals, and local institutions such as schools and housing projects have been altered throughout this book.

[13]

several months were consumed in making futile trips to social programs and schools and in driving and walking around the streets and eating lunches in local restaurants. During these first months, we had developed a very strict set of standards (described in the Appendix) for disclosing the purpose of our work to prospective informants. We insisted that anyone cooperating with us be made aware not only that we were researchers but that we wanted to talk to youths who had been involved in income-oriented crime. Tony Valderama was the first to be successful. Despite his familiarity with La Barriada, he had had difficulty at first in establishing relationships, but finally, a social worker introduced him to Arturo Morales. Arturo decided to trust Tony and began to introduce us to his friends, all about eighteen years old at that time.

The research had begun. We visited Arturo's block and also invited these youths into Vera's offices to participate in taped life-history interviews. Tony Valderama collected detailed field notes in La Barriada from the fall of 1979 through the winter of 1981; I also made periodic visits.

Things did not go as smoothly elsewhere. The last neighborhood chosen did not work out at all, and the research assistant assigned there left the project. Pharaoh Russ was encountering considerable frustration in Projectville as well. In the spring of 1980 we finally located a social program there. Even though it served senior citizens rather than youths, we began to spend time in its offices. I helped the staff develop a funding proposal, and eventually the head of the program offered to introduce us to some youths who lived in the housing project building where the program was headquartered.

For the next several months Pharaoh Russ maintained contact with these youths, recording field notes and bringing some individuals into our offices for interviews. Still, rapport developed slowly, and Russ left the project for other work just as we were beginning to get some idea of what the young men were involved in. We knew that several had been arrested and either incarcerated or placed in youth homes, but only the fifteen-year-old Singleton brothers had developed enough trust in us to discuss what was going on. Shortly before Russ left, I visited the Singletons' apartment and spoke with their mother, and I continued to maintain contact with them afterward.

In the spring of 1980 while we were still looking for a third neighborhood, Richard Curtis, a graduate student, joined the project to collect background data on Brooklyn and its neighborhoods. During the summer he invited some white youths he had met at the free jazz concerts in a park near our offices to come for exploratory interviews. These youths were eighteen to twenty years old, and the early interviews I conducted indicated that they had had some experience with both employment and crime. Their descriptions of their neighborhood, "Hamilton Park," portrayed it as a place much different from the other two. Richard Curtis began fieldwork with these youths in the winter of 1981. He moved into the neighborhood for a few months and collected field notes there through the spring of 1982. He also conducted the subsequent life-history interviews with the young men.

Early in 1982 our contacts in Projectville suddenly increased, apparently because of our sustained contact with the Singleton brothers. Several youths who had returned from prison or youth homes responded to invitations to come into the offices for taped interviews. Over the next several months I developed much better relationships with some who had been distrustful of us a year earlier, and a much clearer picture began to emerge. I also maintained contact during this period with three older individuals who were all involved in various levels of the drug trade. They were in their early twenties but acquaintances of the teenage youths.

By August 1982 we had accumulated reasonably good information on the youthful careers of eleven individuals from La Barriada, fourteen from Projectville, and thirteen from Hamilton Park. Each of them had participated in at least one extensive taped interview and had spent time in his neighborhood with one of the researchers. Most of them also participated in at least one additional interview a few months after the initial one, and two or three in each group participated in five or more extensive interviews.

Although this account concentrates primarily on events that occurred prior to August 1982, I have maintained contact with some individuals from all three neighborhoods and discussed our findings with them. Over the years, various transactions of reciprocity have existed between the researchers and the young men we studied. We tried not to rely too heavily on cash stipends in the early days of the research in each neighborhood, but we did pay $5.00 to $20 for formal interviews (cash stipends played a relatively greater role in Projectville than elsewhere). In addition, we have bought lunches, provided automobile trips, made court appearances, and given information and referrals leading to jobs.

Sampling Techniques and Interpretation of Data

At one time, the predominance of inner-city studies obscured the extent of middle-class delinquency and the importance of psychological traits that differentiate delinquents and nondelinquents. More recently, the predominance of self-report surveys of high school students has

[15]

obscured the concentration of serious and frequent delinquency and criminality in inner-city areas.

Given these problems with past research, both the limits and advantages of the methods we used to recruit our research sample should be understood. First, our samples were not recruited at random; we did not knock on every third door or use any comparable sort of randomizing technique. Rather, we worked from initial contacts through networks of friendship and acquaintance. The particular cliques we sampled in each place did not necessarily represent all youths in the area. Second, we actively looked for youths who were criminally involved; thus, our descriptions of crime patterns must not be taken to imply that all youths in a given area were similarly involved in crime.

The shortcomings of these recruitment techniques are apparent. Without large, random samples, for example, it is not possible to make direct analyses of factors that differentiate delinquents from nondelinquents. These techniques do have compensating advantages, however. Though the samples are not random, they are interactive. We recorded not just individual patterns of participation in crime and delinquency but also the social context of that participation. Our data are not simply intensive self-reports but also reports by members of these cliques about one another and about their relationships.

Further, both the comparative design of the project and the addition of supporting data from census and police statistics make it possible to generalize somewhat more from our data than is often possible with small, nonrandom ethnographic samples. The analyses that follow are both holistic and comparative; that is, we are looking not only at participation in deviant activities but also at how those deviant activities fit into the rest of the lives of these youths and others in their neighborhoods. In addition, we are comparing these patterns of deviant and nondeviant activities across three neighborhood environments.

Though we were studying the criminally involved in each place, our findings identified neighborhood-specific processes that led to criminal involvement. The development of delinquent behavior among those youths who did become delinquent was strongly influenced by their particular neighborhood environments. The environmental features that affected delinquency also affected the lives of both delinquents and nondelinquents in other ways. The youths we studied did not share their criminal activities with all their local peers, but they did share many other characteristics, including their families' means of support, the kinds of housing they lived in, and their orientations toward the labor market, the schools, and other institutions—factors related to both amounts and types of criminal activity.

[16]

Within each neighborhood there was a distinctive range of variation along each of these dimensions, evident both in the ethnographic data and in local census and police statistics. By comparing these ranges from one neighborhood to another, this book attempts to overcome some of the limits on generalizability that are an inevitable aspect of ethnographic studies. We collected and analyzed the data to answer two questions: "What is the relationship between crime and employment in the careers of young urban males?" and "What role does the community environment—including school experiences—play in the development of their careers?" The close focus on intensively studied individuals within different environments makes it possible to examine both individual and structural factors simultaneously. This is a comparative study of how individual choices take place within locally specific ranges of alternatives.

[2]

The Neighborhoods

The three neighborhoods were located in Brooklyn, a large area that was an independent city before becoming incorporated as a borough of New York City in 1898. If Brooklyn were a separate city today, it would be the fourth largest in the United States. It has its own downtown business district, and despite the continued loss of manufacturing from the region as a whole, Brooklyn remains a major manufacturing center, the largest in New York City.

Brooklyn has long been known for its many distinct ethnic enclave neighborhoods. In recent years their composition has changed dramatically as many white residents, the descendants of European immigrants earlier in the century, have moved out to the suburbs. They have been replaced by more recent immigrants to the area from southern states, the Caribbean, and Latin America; more than half the residents of Brooklyn now are black or Latino. Despite this succession of population groups, however, many of the same geographical boundaries still define residential concentrations of various racial and ethnic groups. As it has been since the beginning of the century, Brooklyn remains a patchwork of ethnic enclave neighborhoods.

The neighborhoods we studied are referred to here by pseudonyms. When we contacted, observed, and interviewed the young males who are the subjects of this study, we made specific promises concerning the confidentiality of the information we were collecting (see the Appendix). We promised not to reveal either their names or the names of their neighborhoods, streets, and other identifying features. These promises were crucial both for gaining their cooperation and also for protecting ourselves and our data from possible compromising inquiries from the police or other authorities. As a result, my descriptions of the neighbor-

[18]

hoods are written so as to convey what needs to be known about them without making them precisely identifiable.

Data from the 1980 census are used throughout this book to characterize the neighborhoods and to provide a basis for comparison with the ethnographic data. Since our data were collected between 1979 and 1982, the fit with the census data is good. The cliques of youths we studied were so localized that they lived within a very few census tracts. In two of the neighborhoods, most of the youths studied lived within a single census tract: those from La Barriada lived or spent most of their time within a single city block; those from Projectville lived or spent most of their time in and around a single building of a public housing project. The Hamilton Park clique was slightly more dispersed. Though they shared a common recreational area in a local park, their residences were located throughout four separate but contiguous census tracts. Census data used for Hamilton Park, therefore, are averages of the four tracts.

This chapter introduces the neighborhoods, describes their ecology and demography using both census and ethnographic data, and compares them systematically in terms of specific variables.

La Barriada is a mixed Latino and white neighborhood, though all the youths we studied here were Latino, either first- or second-generation migrants to New York from Puerto Rico. They were all bilingual. They were all around eighteen years of age when contacted. They lived near a heavy concentration of factories and warehouses in housing that consisted of old but otherwise sound tenements, most of which burned down during the research period. Their area was physically isolated from the wider neighborhood by a large highway and constituted a pocket of poverty within the wider neighborhood. Their parents either received public assistance or worked at unskilled jobs. Average family income in this group was the lowest among the three groups studied. During the research period the neighborhood was served by a variety of government- and church-sponsored social programs. Crime rates in this section were high, particularly those for auto theft.

Projectville is a predominantly black neighborhood in which there is a large concentration of public housing. It is physically distant from major centers of employment; what remained of a once busy commercial section continued to dwindle as a result of fires during the research period. Most of the youths studied here were around the age of sixteen when first contacted, although three were in their early twenties. Their families represented a somewhat broader range of income and occupational levels than the families in La Barriada. Many Projectville families

[19]

also were very poor and relied primarily on public assistance, but others were supported by government, health, and clerical jobs. Relatively few social programs with services for young people reached this group, with the exception of summer youth employment programs. Crime rates were high, especially for crimes of personal violence.

Hamilton Park is a predominantly white neighborhood in which most families are supported by relatively high-paying, blue-collar jobs; none of the youths studied here lived in households supported by public assistance. Most of them were between the ages of eighteen and twenty when first contacted. Their families were third- and fourth-generation descendants of European immigrants and retained a certain amount of ethnic identity. Catholic churches and schools provide much of the organizational infrastructure of the neighborhood. Like La Barriada, it is located near a heavy concentration of factories and warehouses; in addition, it contains a thriving retail section serving local residents. The housing consists of old, attached frame houses, many of which were owner occupied. Official crime rates in the neighborhood were much lower than in the other two neighborhoods, among the lowest in New York City.

Income

The economic strategies of these young males—their decisions about investing in schooling or other training and seeking income through legitimate work or crime—did not develop in a vacuum but began at a point defined by the resources of their families.

The two high-crime minority neighborhoods differed sharply from the low-crime white neighborhood in levels of family income. Table 1 shows that household incomes in Hamilton Park were slightly higher than the average for Brooklyn as a whole and markedly higher than those in the two minority areas, even though its income levels were among the lowest for predominantly white neighborhoods in all of New York City and were far below the median and mean for the Standard Metropolitan Statistical Area. Note that 12 percent of families there were below the poverty level (all percentages are rounded off), and 10 percent received public assistance (see Table 2 below). The fact that Hamilton Park incomes were slightly higher than those for Brooklyn as a whole reflects the general economic advantage of non-Latino whites over minorities in a borough more than half of whose population comprised low-income minorities.

The census data in Table 1 indicate that La Barriada's residents had

Table 1. Family income: SMSA, borough, and neighborhoods

	Median	Mean	% below Poverty level
SMSA*	$25,249	$30,359	14
Brooklyn	14,664	17,654	21
La Barriada	8,086	12,647	43
Projectville	6,932	8,960	52
Hamilton Park	16,997	18,586	12

Source: U.S. Bureau of the Census 1983.
*Standard Metropolitan Statistical Area, the U.S. Census designation for the region comprising New York City and its immediate suburbs.

higher income levels than those in Projectville, but this was not true for the particular groups of families that we studied. Projectville is a fairly homogeneous area in which most of the housing is public housing and most of the population has low income. The public housing was subsidized at different levels according to the income of individual residents, however, and a few families supported by relatively well-paying jobs did live dispersed throughout the projects; these families paid higher rents, and some of them are represented in our ethnographic sample.

La Barriada was a more economically mixed neighborhood than Projectville, but the poor families were more concentrated. Even within the single census tract represented in the table, there was a marked contrast between the block that we studied and the next block over. Very low-income families dependent on public assistance predominated on the block we studied. The next block was populated by a combination of older, retired white families who owned two-family houses and young, Latino families headed by working males who tended to rent the other halves of these houses.

We conducted an informal census near the end of the research period during which we ascertained which families on our study block were supported by wages and which by public assistance. The results of our survey are compared with official census statistics on household income type in Table 2. It is readily apparent that while Hamilton Park families were primarily supported by wages and/or Social Security income, the two minority neighborhoods were heavily dependent on public assistance.

The comparison between La Barriada and Projectville, however, differs considerably according to whether one looks at figures for the whole census tract or the results of our ethnographic survey. Census figures

Table 2. Sources of household income: SMSA, borough, and neighborhoods

	Households with earnings (%)	Households with public assistance (%)	Households with social security (%)
SMSA	75	13	26
Brooklyn	69	18	26
La Barriada (census)	57	46	10
La Barriada (study block)	26	72	7
Projectville	55	50	18
Hamilton Park	67	10	35

Source: U.S. Bureau of the Census 1983 and ethnographic data.

show La Barriada families as considerably better off than those in Projectville, and, in fact, some of them were. But these better-off families did not live on the block we studied; there, public assistance was even more concentrated than in Projectville. Consequently, throughout this book I refer to the families we studied in La Barriada as even poorer than those in Projectville, even though poverty levels were fairly similar between these two samples and much higher than in Hamilton Park.

The relative economic positions of whites, blacks, and Latinos in this study are representative of the city as a whole. Table 3 shows median and mean family incomes by race and "Spanish origin"[1] for the SMSA and Brooklyn. Although the partial overlap (explained below) between the census categories "white" and "of Spanish origin" must be taken into account, it is still apparent that non-Latino whites are better off than either blacks or Latinos and that blacks are somewhat better off as a group than Latinos.

Family Structure

The greater poverty and welfare dependency in the two minority neighborhoods were associated with higher concentrations of female-headed families. As shown in Table 4, nearly three-quarters of the families in Hamilton Park were married-couple families. In contrast, less than half of the Latino families in La Barriada and only slightly more than

[1]The census bureau uses the phrase "of Spanish origin" to categorize those who identify themselves as having ancestors among Spanish-speaking groups, including those deriving from Latin America and the Caribbean as well as from Spain. The term "Latino" is used in the text of this book, but "Spanish origin" is used in the tables that are taken from the Bureau of the Census publications.

Table 3. SMSA and borough family income
by race and Spanish origin

	Median	Mean
Whites		
SMSA	$22,418	$27,473
Brooklyn	17,563	20,563
Blacks		
SMSA	12,746	15,647
Brooklyn	11,574	14,003
Spanish origin		
SMSA	10,799	13,490
Brooklyn	8,952	11,278

Source: U.S. Bureau of the Census 1983.

a third of the families in Projectville were married-couple families. These numbers need to be interpreted cautiously, given the fact that the undercount of black and Latino men in the census figures has been estimated at levels of over 30 percent for some age groups (Hainer et al. 1988).

The ethnographic data—which do not suffer from undercount, because we visited most of these households and were able to observe whether or not adult men were present—show the same general patterns (Table 5). Adult men were much more likely to be present in Hamilton Park than in either of the two minority neighborhoods and were present somewhat more often in La Barriada than in Projectville.

It should also be noted that family income levels alone cannot explain the higher proportion of married couples in La Barriada than in Projectville. Although the families in La Barriada were even poorer than

Table 4. Family structure: SMSA, borough, and neighborhoods (census)

	Married couple (%)	Female householder only (%)
SMSA	72	23
Brooklyn	66	29
La Barriada	44	51
(Spanish origin only)		
Projectville	35	62
Hamilton Park	73	20

Source: U.S. Bureau of the Census 1983.

[23]

Table 5. Family structure: Neighborhoods (ethnographic sample)

	Mother and father	Mother and stepfather	Mother only	Father only
La Barriada	4	2	4	0
Projectville	3	1	8	0
Hamilton Park	6	0	2	2

Note: Each neighborhood sample included brothers: from La Barriada, one set of two brothers; from Projectville, two sets of two brothers; from Hamilton Park, three sets of two brothers. Thus, the La Barriada sample is made up of eleven individuals from ten families; the Projectville sample, fourteen individuals from twelve families; and the Hamilton Park sample, thirteen individuals from ten families.

One individual from Projectville grew up with both parents as a small child and then alternated his residence between them after his parents separated. He is included under "mother and father."

those in Projectville, adult males were more often present in La Barriada households.

The absence or presence (official or actual) of males in the sample households had important implications for local-level social control (described in subsequent chapters).

Race/Ethnicity and Residential Segregation

Tables 6 and 7 show patterns of racial and ethnic concentration in these areas. These tables must be read together because the census asks people separately about their race and whether or not they are Latino ("of Spanish origin"). Those who identify themselves as Latino may also identify themselves as being white, black, or—as many choose—"other." Less than 1 percent of Hamilton Park's residents identified themselves as black, and less than 3 percent of Projectville's residents identified themselves as white. It appears further that most of those identifying themselves as white in Projectville also identified themselves as Latino. Thus, blacks and non-Latino whites lived almost exclusively apart in these three areas.

Latinos, in contrast, were more residentially mixed with both non-Latino whites and blacks. The census data show that only 86 percent of the residents of the census tract in La Barriada were of Spanish origin, and the ethnographic data identify the non-Latinos as the older, retired, white working-class families on the block next to the one we studied.

Table 6.   Racial patterns: SMSA, borough, and neighborhoods (%)

	White	Black	Asian	Other
SMSA	67	21	3	9
Brooklyn	56	32	2	10
La Barriada	34	4	0	62
Projectville	3	91	0	6
Hamilton Park	94	0	2	4

Source: U.S. Bureau of the Census 1983.

Latinos accounted for slightly under 10 percent of the areas we studied in Projectville and Hamilton Park.

These patterns of race/ethnicity, residential segregation, and income levels appear paradoxical. The Latinos we studied were more residentially integrated with working-class whites than the blacks were, yet these Latinos as a group suffered even more concentrated poverty than blacks as a group. This seemingly paradoxical situation, however, is not unique to our small samples. In New York City as a whole, blacks have been more residentially segregated than Latinos (Rosenberg and Lake 1976). This pattern has also been common in other large cities in the United States (Massey 1979). Despite their greater residential concentration, however, blacks in New York City were also less uniformly poor than Latinos. From the median and mean family incomes shown in Table 3 (although, again, the partial overlap between the categories "white" and "of Spanish origin" must be taken into account), it is apparent that non-Latino whites were better off than either blacks or Latinos and that blacks were somewhat better off as a group than Latinos.

Table 7.   Racial composition of Spanish-origin population: SMSA, borough, and neighborhoods

	Population of Spanish origin (%)	Racial composition (%)*		
		White	Black	Other
SMSA	16	46	6	48
Brooklyn	18	42	9	50
La Barriada	86	28	2	71
Projectville	10	22	22	56
Hamilton Park	8	62	1	37

Source: U.S. Bureau of the Census 1983.
*Racial percentages refer only to those persons who *also* identify themselves as being of Spanish origin, not to the total populations of these areas.

[25]

Age and Immigration

The single most dramatic demographic difference between neighborhoods is in the age of residents, as shown in Table 8. The median age of
Hamilton Park residents was somewhat higher than that for the SMSA
and nearly sixteen years older than those in the other two neighborhoods.

Age differences were largely the result of immigration patterns, although these were complex and could not be ascertained entirely from
census data. The census category "foreign born," for example, did not
include either the immigrants from southern states who lived in Projectville or the Puerto Ricans who predominated in La Barriada, but it
did include a number of adult immigrants from Europe who lived in
Hamilton Park and whose presence is noted in our ethnographic data.

Nearly one in four residents of the Hamilton Park area were foreign
born, but the ethnographic data indicate that these were a very specific
group: chiefly adult males who had immigrated from Poland, many of
them illegally. These men lived several to a room and worked at low-
level factory jobs. Most other residents of Hamilton Park were third- and
fourth-generation descendants of European immigrants. Nearly half
were of Polish origin; the others were of Irish or Italian or other European ancestry. Only one member of our sample from this neighborhood
was part of a family of recent immigrants; he was himself a Polish
national. All the other members of our sample were several generations
removed from immigration.

Most of the Latino residents of La Barriada and the black residents of
Projectville were either first- or second-generation immigrants to this
area; they or their parents had come as young people. Many of the
grandparents of the youths from La Barriada and Projectville continued
to live in Puerto Rico and the South. Most of the parents of the youths in
the Projectville sample had been born in southern states, particularly
South Carolina and Virginia, though a few had been born in New York
City. The parents and several of the youths themselves in La Barriada
had all been born in Puerto Rico, but all the young men we interviewed
had grown up in New York City and spoke English as much as or more
than they spoke Spanish.

Another migration pattern apparent in the ethnographic data distin-
guishes Hamilton Park from the other two neighborhoods: younger
people from this neighborhood appeared to be leaving for the suburbs or
for southern and western states. This out-migration may account for the
fact that the census data showed Hamilton Park's residents to be, on
average, three years older than the average for the SMSA.

[26]

Table 8. Median age of population: Area, borough, and neighborhoods

	Years
SMSA	33
Brooklyn	31
La Barriada	20
Projectville	20
Hamilton Park	36

Source: U.S. Bureau of the Census 1983.

Housing Tenure

Differences among the three areas in patterns of housing tenure reflect differences in both income level and housing type. Table 9 shows proportions of owner-occupied housing in these areas. Projectville's residents tended to be poor, and most lived in public housing. As a result, less than 1 percent of the housing units in their area were owner occupied. In La Barriada, just under 11 percent of the housing units were owner occupied. The ethnographic data identify these units as belonging to the retired white residents on the block next to the study block. In Hamilton Park, in contrast, where income levels were much higher and the housing consisted primarily of small multifamily houses, nearly one in four dwelling units were owner occupied. The ethnographic data suggest that many people also occupied apartments in houses owned by other members of their families. Thus, it is possible that as many as a third or a half of the units were occupied by either owners or relatives of the owners.

Table 9. Residential ownership and tenancy: SMSA, borough, and neighborhoods

	Owner-occupied housing units (%)	Renter-occupied housing units (%)
SMSA	31	69
Brooklyn	23	77
La Barriada	11	89
Projectville	1	99
Hamilton Park	24	76

Source: U.S. Bureau of the Census 1983.

By every measure, the residents of Hamilton Park were more advantaged economically and socially than the residents of Projectville and La Barriada. Despite their generally similar levels of poverty, the two minority neighborhoods differed in demography and physical ecology. The following chapters trace the influences of these varying background conditions on the careers of young males in schooling, employment, and crime.

[3]

Schooling

Any study of the relationships between employment and crime among adolescents must also examine patterns of school involvement. The decision to leave or remain in school is closely intertwined with decisions to seek work or to engage in property crime. Since many street crimes are committed by youths of school age, the linkages between school, family, labor market, and the criminal justice system during the teenage years are of particular interest. Leaving school is a crucial event in the careers of high-risk youths, one that constrains their future options for both crime and employment.

The consequences of adolescent school experiences and of leaving school can be seen differently from two broad theoretical vantage points, the economic and the sociocultural—both of which may be applied to our ethnographic sample. Microeconomic theorists treat schooling as a source of "human capital" (G. Becker 1975) which determines subsequent labor market position by setting the level of a worker's productivity. School achievement, particularly for younger people, constitutes the largest component of their human capital when they enter the labor market. The fact that a large proportion of urban poor and minority youth do not complete high school thus marks them early for low-paying and insecure jobs. Economists of the secondary labor market school partially dispute this view, however, by pointing out that structural factors such as discrimination distort this process. Harrison (1972a) has shown, for example, that the labor market returns attributable to schooling are less for minority and inner-city youth than for majority and suburban youth.

Sociocultural theories treat schooling as a multifunctional process that not only prepares young people for later work but also performs custodial and socialization functions. Writers following the work of Albert

Cohen (1955), in their investigations of the origins of delinquency, have focused on such matters as the conflict between the norms of school organizations and the norms of life in lower-class neighborhoods. Others such as Hirschi (1969) and Elliott and Voss (1974) have studied the connection between delinquency and school-leaving, a connection stronger than that between delinquency and unemployment (Crowley 1984). From these points of view, schools shape attitudes toward authority and adaptations to life in organizations as much as they imbue individuals with productive skills.

Regional Schooling Trends and Programs

Most of the youths contacted in the neighborhood studies had attended or were attending public schools in Brooklyn, which are part of the New York City public school system, the largest in the country. New York City's public schools, like those of many large cities in the country, have seen the withdrawal of large numbers of white, middle-class students over the past generation, resulting in part from the "white flight" to the suburbs of the middle class. Even within the city, however, the public school population has much larger concentrations of minority students than does the general population. This disparity has developed partly because the minority population, generally comprising more recent migrants to the area, is much younger than the general population. Further, poorer families must rely on public education. City-dwelling, white, middle-class families with school-age children have turned increasingly to private schools, and Catholic parochial schools have long served many middle- and working-class families, thus contributing to the concentration of minority children in the public schools.

As a result of these patterns, the New York City public school system is now more than 50 percent black and Latino, though the racial/ethnic ratios vary markedly by school and by borough. At the time of our research, Staten Island's public schools were more than 80 percent white and those in Queens about 50 percent; they were about 25 percent white in Brooklyn and approximately half that in Manhattan and the Bronx. Even within Brooklyn, however, there were great disparities between the largely minority schools in the north and central parts of the borough and the predominantly white schools in the more affluent southern half.

These racial/ethnic ratios are often correlated with income levels, school attendance rates, and school achievement: schools with large minority enrollments are often also schools that serve poor families and schools in which attendance rates and achievement levels are low. More than half of all students who enter high school leave school without receiving a high school diploma.

Most students in the city and most of those in our ethnographic sample do reach the high school level, and high school leads them into a career path in one way or another. The student about to enter public high school in New York City faces a bewildering set of alternatives. Students from a given locality are zoned to a particular "academic-comprehensive" high school unless they apply for one of the specialized schools or programs, which are many and diverse. The distinctions between the major categories have been blurred somewhat in recent years, and none represents a rigid, exclusive track. In theory, students who finish any of the courses of study or training offered should be able to enter college or the job market. In practice, however, these different kinds of schooling are intended for very different kinds of labor market preparation.

Academic-comprehensive high schools, as their name implies, are supposed to offer a full array of college preparatory, business, and vocational programs. These are the most numerous schools in the system, but they vary widely in quality: they include a few nationally known honors schools that admit only by special examination, as well as many schools that are disorganized and dangerous and have very low achievement levels. Although they do provide some vocational programs, their curricula are chiefly devoted to college preparatory and business courses.

Vocational-technical high schools generally admit students by special application and are designed to produce skilled manual workers. Students completing these programs are supposed to be ready for entry-level manual jobs.

Business education courses are offered in both academic-comprehensive and vocational-technical high schools. Their standards, curricula, and intent are quite different from those of the older and more established vocational programs. Students completing a business education curriculum are supposed to be prepared for entry-level jobs as skilled clerical workers. Since the clerical labor market is so important in New York City, the business education programs now enroll more students than do either the college preparatory or vocational programs.

Independent alternative high schools within the public school system offer smaller classes and individualized programs for students who, for various reasons, do not like or cannot get along in the regular high schools.

Schools for the emotionally handicapped serve mainly students who are considered too dangerous to remain in the regular school population.

[31]

They include both day schools for those who have not been deprived of their liberty by the courts and also schools within jails and training institutions. Though they are no longer officially so designated, these are often referred to as "600 schools."

Finally, both schools and community organizations offer preparation for the General Equivalency Diploma (GED). This diploma is technically the equivalent of the high school diploma but requires no set course of study and is awarded on the basis of passing a single examination. Many students who have interrupted their schooling or who are too old to remain in high school find themselves funneled into GED programs.

The potential contributions of schooling to labor market outcomes include the provision of basic skills, including literacy and computation, and job-specific skills, such as typing or auto repair. Schools may also provide credentialing by granting diplomas and other official certification that may be required for entrance to certain jobs; direct job connections through their placement services and ties to local employers; and finally, socialization into relations with authority and a daily work routine.

Our comparative ethnographic data, by tracing neighborhood-specific patterns of schooling for three local cliques, helped us examine the specific ways in which schooling provided both human capital and socialization that affected the youths' short-term and long-term involvements in employment and crime. The data show how schooling served as a developmental link between their family backgrounds and their eventual entry into the labor market—including the criminal labor market.

La Barriada

As a group, the youths from La Barriada were the earliest to leave school and had the lowest levels of educational attainment among the three neighborhood groups. Although some sought out vocational programs in the hope of learning job-specific skills, most of them never finished high school. Schooling provided them with relatively few basic or job-specific skills, credentials, or direct connections to jobs. Despite this general lack of school achievement, there was considerable variation among the individuals in this clique in their ability to read, and some of them remained involved with schooling until their late teens.

Their troubles with school achievement derived initially from their status as members of a recent immigrant group and members of a

[32]

bilingual culture. All of them either were born in New York to recently migrating parents or had come from Puerto Rico with their parents when they were small children. Their parents, besides being nonnative speakers of English, also had lower levels of education than the parents in the other two neighborhoods; many were from rural areas of Puerto Rico, where few people obtained more than an elementary education. Nevertheless, the parents did expect their children to go through the mainland school system.

> *Mario Valdez:* My father couldn't go to school 'cause he got kicked by a horse when he was young. In Puerto Rico the school was far away and he couldn't walk it. But he always told me, "Go to school, try to be somebody." He always wanted me to be a doctor.

Most La Barriada youths went through the New York City public elementary schools with fairly regular attendance and were usually promoted every year, even though some did not learn to read. Some did well in elementary school, including Mario Valdez, Octavio Del Rio, Carlos Hernandez, and especially Arturo Morales.

> *Arturo Morales:* I was supposed to be a little genius, according to one of my teachers in the third grade. He was talking to the assistant principal about me. They were going to put me in a special class, "IGC."
> *Interviewer:* Intellectually Gifted Children?
> *A.M.:* Yeah, that's right. Thanks, I forgot what it was.

Despite the conventional aspirations of their parents and their relatively uneventful passage through the elementary grades, these youths began to leave school as early as the sixth grade, and most never went past the tenth. Even when they were still officially enrolled, they often attended very irregularly. During the period of irregular attendance leading to withdrawal from school, they were struggling both with immediate financial need and with doubts that the schools were providing anything that would lead to later success in the labor market.

Two interrupted their schooling in order to earn household subsistence. Gaspar Cruz left his mother's apartment at the age of fifteen after a fight with his stepfather. He supported himself through stealing for a few months, went to jail for six months when he was sixteen, and combined work and crime thereafter throughout his teens. Mike Concepcion, who lived with his disabled mother, left school at sixteen for a year to work full time loading trucks.

[33]

Mike Concepcion: I was out of school for a year; I was working. That was when things were real bad. We had a lot of money problems with the rent and food and all that. At that time the city was going bankrupt, and they were cutting down a lot of financial aid to all the people on welfare.

All the others who left school in their midteens were still depending on their parents for basic subsistence but nonetheless felt pressure to earn money. Miguel Tirado said that he was ashamed to go to school because "my mother couldn't afford to buy me new clothes." During this period he and his peers were all trying to earn enough to pay for clothes and recreation that their parents could not provide. Sometimes they earned spending money through short-term jobs, but more often they did so through crime.

Irregular attendance and school-leaving were related not only to their short-term needs for income but to these youths' skepticism about the relevance of Fillmore High School, their zoned local academic-comprehensive high school, to their future in the labor market. Fillmore's enrollment was about one-third white and two-thirds black and Latino. Daily attendance was under 60 percent of those enrolled. Nearly one-third of its students received free lunch (a proxy measure of income levels). Two-thirds never graduated. Several members of our sample described the school as offering poor-quality education:

Carlos Hernandez: Most of the classes are huge, and everybody's always clowning around.

Mario Valdez: I know a lot of people who went there . . . they pass you without teaching you nothing . . . when you're graduated out of there you don't know nothing.

They were also skeptical of the worth of a high school diploma alone in helping a person to obtain a job:

Mario Valdez: I know this friend of mine. He graduated from Fillmore. He's working in a factory making $3.10 an hour. A guy with a high school diploma he don't know nothing, so, what trade's he got?

Rather than go to Fillmore, both Mario Valdez and Gaspar Cruz made special application to and were accepted by Webster Vocational-Technical High School, reputed to be one of the best in the system. Webster's enrollment was nearly all black and Latino and four-fifths of the students received free lunch. Daily attendance, however, averaged more than 80 percent, and half the students received diplomas.

> *Interviewer:* Tell me why you didn't want to go to Fillmore?
> *Gaspar Cruz:* They don't show you electrical installation, something you could have a future with. They show you little simple things like math, social studies. I don't wanna hear that. I just want electrical installation, something that could give me a career.

Mike Concepcion, when he returned to school after dropping out to work for a year, also sought vocational training by enrolling in Fillmore's auto mechanics program. Though they were dubious about the value of a high school diploma by itself, these youths did have hopes that a diploma plus training in a "trade" would lead them to good jobs. To most of them, desirable employment meant skilled blue-collar jobs. They had little interest in the college preparatory or business curricula at Fillmore, though they did think that the business courses might be useful to females.

> *Interviewer:* Is your girlfriend learning something at Fillmore, or is she just going to get a diploma?
> *Gaspar Cruz:* She's learning 'cause she's taking up secretary.
> *Int.:* So you think that Fillmore could teach a woman something she could make money from, but not a man?
> *G.C.:* Not a man. Fillmore is for secretaries, bookkeeping, stuff like that, that's what the school is really for. And they got automotives, but I'm not interested in automotives. I'm not gonna take up secretary or automotives.

Even though most of these youths never finished high school, they remained involved in schooling to some extent for several years after they had begun to attend irregularly. Because their parents expected them to be in school, they concealed what at first was truancy and later became official withdrawal. Although many were staying out of school in an attempt to make money, their opportunities for both crime and work during their midteens were generally sporadic, and they frequently alternated work, crime, school, and inactivity. Despite their doubts, they did not totally discount the value of a high school diploma. Many of those who admitted irregular attendance also claimed that they would eventually return to school and finish.

[35]

School offered them social rewards apart from training for jobs. Mike Concepcion and Arturo Morales, for example, were both stars on the Fillmore baseball team before they began to withdraw from school. Others hung out around the school, even when they were not attending, in order to be near females. Still others, like Mario Valdez's younger brother Esteban (not a member of the core clique), maintained school enrollment in order to protect the family welfare budget.

Interviewer: Are you going to school now?
Esteban Valdez: Well, I usually go the first few days to sign up.
Int.: But you don't go to class after that?
E.V.: No.
Int.: Why do you bother to sign up?
E.V.: Well, see, they might cut my mother off welfare, so she makes me go.

School and welfare records are systematically cross-checked in this manner to enforce school enrollment, if not attendance.

Their parents also exerted continuing, it often ineffective, pressure on these youths to do something productive, either to attend school or to find a job. Arturo Morales reported that his parents would buy clothing and provide spending money for his younger brother and sister, who were attending school, but not for him because he was not. Other parents, with limited resources for supplying job connections or manipulating spending money, would not go so far as to throw their sons out of the house but were quite clear in their expectations that they should either go to school or work.

It appears that the failure of parents to supervise their children's school attendance had less to do with their values than with their resources. Arturo Morales and Mario Valdez, for example, both told us how they kept their parents from finding out that they were not attending school. Valdez started playing hooky very early, in the third grade:

Interviewer: Third grade? Wow, your folks didn't know about this?
Mario Valdez: Nah, they [the school] used to send letters home, but I used to grab them out of the mailbox. I had books and I would pretend to do my homework. My father used to check my notebook every day.

Morales became a truant in the eighth grade:

Arturo Morales: You say "let me take one day off," then you take another, then you go the whole week. . . . The mailman used to come,

[36]

I'd sneak to the mailbox and take out the mail. Half the year in the eighth grade I was following the mailman.

The ease with which these youths could deceive their parents illustrates the lack of any contact between parents and school except through the mail.

After several years of irregular involvement with school, most La Barriada youths found themselves so far behind that they withdrew completely. Those who withdrew earliest were those who had never learned to read; for example, Julian Acosta, Gaspar Cruz, and Jorge Padilla went no further than junior high school. Those who could read fairly well—Mario Valdez, Arturo Morales, Octavio Del Rio—maintained at least their enrollment through the tenth and eleventh grades.

In addition to their general lack of academic success, their gradual estrangement from school was hastened by the involvement of these youths in fighting and crime. Some reported getting into fights in school; others claimed that they had trouble attending school because they had to cross the territory of hostile youth gangs in order to get there. Their fighting did not lead directly to expulsion from school, however, and none reported having been in the 600 schools for violent students. But when arrests began to follow serious income-motivated crimes, their school difficulties worsened. After six months in jail, Gaspar Cruz did not return to Webster Vocational-Technical High School:

Gaspar Cruz: When I came out of jail, the school thought I had just been playing hooky, and they didn't accept me. I didn't want anyone to know about that [jail]. I told my mother not to spread the word. So they discharged me.

Before terminating their school involvements once and for all, however, several of these youths went through one final effort to obtain educational certification. After a year or more out of school, they began to reconsider their earlier skepticism and to enroll in programs designed to prepare them for the General Equivalency Diploma. Arturo Morales did so while awaiting adjudication of his court cases when he was seventeen. Gaspar Cruz attended the courses regularly for several months after he had been out of school for nearly three years. Chucho Rivera took part in such a program while confined to a youth home by the Family Court. Octavio Del Rio expressed his intention to sign up for a GED program that would also have paid him a stipend, though he never did so. Despite this last effort to obtain a diploma, none of them actually

[37]

passed the GED examinations, although Gaspar Cruz did dramatically improve his reading.

Of the eleven youths we interviewed from La Barriada, only two eventually obtained diplomas, both from Fillmore High School. In both cases this success came only after interruptions and difficulties. Mike Concepcion graduated at the age of twenty-one, shortly before he would have become too old to remain enrolled in a regular high school. He had been in and out of school several times, and when not attending, he was variously engaged in work and crime. At one point, around the age of nineteen, he was working full time, going to school in a special night program, and also stealing cars with some frequency. He hoped that his high school diploma would help him obtain work as a legitimate auto mechanic, but he remained skeptical as to whether it actually would pay off. He kept returning to school because he considered education intrinsically worthwhile.

> *Mike Concepcion:* I wanna try to get the most out of school, whatever I can. Even though I don't graduate, it still means something to me. I don't care what it means to anybody else.

The other youth from La Barriada who had finished high school was Carlos Hernandez; he had also finished college and was working for a master's degree in construction management. He was a few years older than the others but had grown up on the same block and recognized that he was quite unusual. His older brothers and sisters had all left school and had been involved in crime. Carlos attributed his own success in school and his staying clear of crime to the fact that when his parents started to make some money from a small business, the whole family wanted their youngest to make good. He was also helped along by a special "College Bound" program in Fillmore High School:

> *Interviewer:* Do you think you got better courses in high school because you were in College Bound?
> *Carlos Hernandez:* I know I did.
> *Int.:* We've interviewed other guys from your neighborhood, and they say there's a lot of fooling around in that school.
> *C.H.:* Definitely.
> *Int.:* What was the main thing that made it better?
> *C.H.:* Smaller classes.
> *Int.:* And did you have classes with the same people from one class to the other?
> *C.H.:* Most of them, not all of them.

[38]

Except for Carlos Hernandez and Mike Concepcion, none of the youths from La Barriada entered the labor market with job-specific skills, credentials, or direct connections provided through the schools. Even Mike subsequently worked mostly in low-level auto mechanic and maintenance jobs not requiring a high school diploma. Among the others, those who remained in school longest and who were more literate did move into clerical jobs, which required that they be able to handle documents. The rest eventually took unskilled manual jobs in factories, warehouses, hotels, and auto repair shops, none of which required educational credentials or a high degree of literacy.

Projectville

The youths from Projectville sought high school diplomas primarily as general credentials for getting jobs or getting into college. Like their counterparts in La Barriada, they began to attend school irregularly in junior high or the first years of high school, and most of them were not able to complete the regular high school curriculum. The Projectville youths, however, were more persistent than those from La Barriada in their efforts to gain educational credentials, and several of them managed to earn their equivalency diplomas after a period of interruption in their schooling.

The parents of the Projectville youths were more highly educated than the parents in La Barriada. Some had grown up in the New York area and had completed high school. Others had migrated to New York from southern states as adults and had lower levels of education. In general, the Projectville parents all encouraged their children very strongly to pursue education, at least through high school and, if possible, to college.

As reported both by the youths themselves and also by those of their parents whom we interviewed, the Projectville parents all stressed the need for a high school diploma in order to get jobs. Larry Jefferson's mother said, "I told my kids that without no education you can't scrub a floor around here." Despite their strong desire for their children to stay in school, these parents too lacked the resources to keep them there. The mother of Johnny and Tommy Singleton reported that her sons never got into trouble until they began junior high school. At that point she had taken a full-time job:

Singletons' Mother: Before, I worked in a way that I could always pick them up, until they got into junior high. Then I found they could go by themselves, and that's when I started having problems.

[39]

Interviewer: What about Tommy? Has he been going to school every day?
Mother: Sometimes he goes, sometimes he doesn't. I can't make him go. I figure the best thing is to keep talking to him. He knows how I feel.

Zap Andrews reported that his father had tried to discipline him when he first stayed out of school, but his parents' attitude changed after he began to get occasional employment: "They used to be on my back hard, then they slacked up."

The Projectville youths themselves generally shared the attitudes of their parents, but some expressed skepticism about the value of the high school diploma. Juice Baker, a respondent in his early twenties and a few years older than the others at the time of the interview, had graduated from high school and earned some college credits.

Juice Baker: What do I need a high school diploma for? To mop a floor? Look in here [*pointing to newspaper employment ads*], you don't see anything there says high school grads. It's all college.

Baker's friend and contemporary Sky Wilson said that he had dropped out in the eleventh grade because "I couldn't see how it could help me."

As in La Barriada, this skepticism was accompanied by a perception that females could benefit more than males from high school education because they could move directly from the high school business curriculum into secretarial jobs.

Juice Baker: Everything in here [*still pointing to newspaper ads*] is jokes, unless you happen to be a typing clerk or a bookkeeper.
Interviewer: Did you ever think of learning how to type?
J.B.: Nah, I'm not into that. It's not . . . natural. It's something that's just not . . . a man's not gonna do that now.
Int.: Do you think there are more jobs for women with high school diplomas than for men?
J.B.: Yeah, and with higher pay.

In contrast, Ben Bivins, four years younger than Baker and Whitney, came home at nineteen and sought work as a typist, having earned his GED and a thirty-five-word-per-minute typing certificate in prison.

Despite their skepticism and irregular attendance during their middle teens, most of the Projectville youths retained their belief in the value of a high school diploma. Tommy Singleton aspired to go to college like his older brother. Zap Andrews needed a diploma in order to get into the Navy. Jerry Barnes wanted one because a friend of his who had just returned from prison told him that without it, all he could get would be a factory job. Their belief in the value of the high school diploma came into conflict with their school experience, however. Fights in school caused problems for some, and almost all of them interrupted their schooling at some point in order to seek income.

For two Projectville youths, trouble in school began with fighting during the earlier grades. Both Larry Jefferson and Johnny Singleton were transferred to 600 schools as a result of violent confrontations.

Interviewer: Tell us something about the problems you say you've had in school.
Johnny Singleton: I got in trouble once . . . you know, once you get blamed for something, my mother told me, they always come to you for the next thing. I happened to be walking by and a whole bunch of dudes was acting crazy feeling up this girl. They pushed her down and she happened to be looking up at my face. The cops went to my friend's house and the girl was going to press charges. I don't know what finally happened, but they dismissed the case. I know I got blamed for something I didn't do and I got kicked outa school and I lost a lotta time. Then I got a reputation, everybody said, "Johnny did this, Johnny did that."
Int.: Then you say you were accused of snatching a teacher's purse?
J.S.: Yeah, the teacher. She happened to be walking in the door and somebody bumped into her, and she said I tried to snatch her pocketbook, but she didn't have no proof and the courts wouldn't accept it. Then they had me taking tests to go to a 600 school, only I didn't know it was a 600 school.

Interviewer: When you were in fifth grade, they moved you to a 600 school?
Larry Jefferson: Yeah, 'cause I did something I wasn't supposed to do, so they transferred me to a 600 school, and then after that I said I couldn't stand it with no girls and they saw I was trying my best so they transferred me back.
Int.: Did you get in a fight or something?
L.J.: No. It was really 'cause of the teacher. I got in a car accident and I hate for people to twist my ears.
Int.: You hurt your ear in a car accident?
L.J.: Yeah. And she twisted it, so I got mad, but I didn't really hurt her. I just pulled her wig off and that was it. And I started getting in trouble.

The rest of this group all managed to complete elementary and junior high school without failing a grade or getting into serious trouble.

None of the Projectville youths aspired to either skilled or unskilled manual work. When it came time to attend high school, none of them applied to vocational-technical schools or programs. They all went to the academic-comprehensive high schools to which they were zoned. The zoning for their neighborhood was peculiar, however, and subjected these youths to a variety of stresses. The New York City public school system had for some years tried to overcome racial segregation by moving students from poor minority neighborhoods into schools in more affluent white neighborhoods. In Projectville, a poor and largely black neighborhood, this policy affected only high school zoning. As a result, Projectville youths attended very segregated and disorderly local elementary and junior high schools and then were scattered among seven different high schools. In six of these the student body was more than 50 percent white; they had attendance rates of about 75 percent; and some 60 percent of their students received diplomas.

When they entered high school, the Projectville youths found themselves separated from their friends and facing racial violence. Lucky Giles was the only one who was assigned to a predominantly minority high school in a nearby minority neighborhood. Those who went to schools serving predominantly white working-class families all reported racial confrontations:

> *Zap Andrews:* I had so many fights there. Not because I started it 'cause if it was up to me, color, it don't make no difference, really. I had a lotta white boy friends. I had a lotta white friends, girls too, I never thought I was gonna touch a white girl until I went to that school. But I had a lot of fights, comin' outa gym, comin' down the hallway and a whole gang of them, and I only had a couple of homeboys.

Tommy Singleton cited his troubles to the Family Court when he was arrested at fifteen for burglary:

> *Field Notes:* Tommy Singleton then said, "The judge asked me if I was having any problems in school and I told him yes that I was having racial problems." He then said that he went to a school that was 90 percent white and that he had liked junior high school better because his friends were there. Now he has to cut school to see his friends and he considers that a terrible thing.

One female whom we interviewed, the wife of Steve Johnson, told how she had gotten into trouble in high school.

[42]

Steve Johnson's wife: They used to bus us out there and that's the first time I ever saw anything like this. On Halloween white people came around the school with bats and things. All the blacks used to hang around in a gang, and that's when I first started getting in trouble.

Most of the Projectville youths attended irregularly during high school, and all of them had seriously interrupted their schooling before the eleventh grade. They left in pursuit of short-term income even more than as a result of fights in school. Zap Andrews explained his decision to drop out in the ninth grade, even though he sensed that he might be sacrificing long-term opportunities.

Interviewer: When you quit going to school, was this because of all the fights?
Zap Andrews: Not really. It was just the money problem. I didn't have the things I wanted, like new clothes and stuff like that.
Int.: OK, you quit going to school because you wanted some money now, but did you ever think, "If I quit going to school now, it's going to keep me from making more money when I get older?"
Z.A.: All my life I was thinkin' 'bout that. I had it good back then [when I was in school] 'cause my mother used to work in the hotel, my father had a good job, you know, but then she quit that, things went bad then. . . . My moms and pops wasn't uppin' no money you know. My father says, "All right, I'll give it to you next week." Later for it, I need some money now. Like, the girls, you know, I wasn't lookin' cool enough. But it's not the girls. If it wasn't no girls, I still would've did what I did.

Other Projectville youths left school because they were about to become fathers and wanted to find full-time jobs to support their new families. Stan Williams was one of these who regretted the necessity.

Interviewer: Did you decide that getting a high school diploma was not going to get you anywhere?
Stan Williams: Yeah, it would have gotten me somewhere, but I just could not take the time off to sit around and wait for it. My old lady told me she was pregnant.

Steve Johnson left a GED program when his girlfriend became pregnant. He was getting a small stipend as part of the program but found a factory job that paid more. When Zap Andrews also found himself facing impending paternity after being out of school for two years, he cut short

[43]

his thoughts of returning to school or of joining the military and completing his education there.

As they began to leave school, in reaction to trouble and in pursuit of income, the Projectville youths sought work without much success. Programs that recruited through their schools in fact supplied most of the employment available to youths in their midteens in this neighborhood; separation from school thus partially cut them off from their chief source of jobs. Most of them were involved in crimes for money before they had much access to employment. Both participation in crime and subsequent involvement with the criminal justice system interrupted their education further.

During this period they were all cut off from the regular high schools. Johnny Singleton and Larry Jefferson, who had been placed in 600 schools before they reached high school, later entered residential institutions outside Brooklyn after they were arrested for stealing. Jerry Barnes, Lucky Giles, and Ben Bivins all spent time in jail or prison before they were seventeen. And even before they were convicted, several months of frequent court appearances made it impossible for them to attend school regularly. Tommy Singleton was never given any penalty by either the juvenile or adult courts, but his single arrest made it impossible for him to continue in his regular high school. He was put into a special program for students with court cases and then switched from one school to another for months.

> *Field Notes:* Tommy Singleton said that his court case had caused all of his problems. "That's when they started assigning me to all these different schools." Most of the schools he was assigned to informed him that he was unqualified to go there before he even got there. At one point, he was assigned to a special program in a vocational school, but the program closed shortly after that.

The process by which the Projectville youths left school during their mid-teens partially resembled that of youths from La Barriada. Both groups left school partly as a result of trouble, failure, and dislike; most members of both groups left in pursuit of income. The process differed between the neighborhoods in that more La Barriada youths left as a result of academic failure and dislike of school, and more Projectville youths as a result of getting into trouble.

A more striking difference between the two groups is the extent to which the Projectville youths managed to renew their schooling after these mid-teen interruptions. Like their counterparts in La Barriada, the Projectville youths still considered themselves "in school" as long as they were still of school age, even when they were not attending regularly. They still enrolled each fall, in some cases to protect the family welfare budget but also because they planned to resume schooling and in fact did attend classes occasionally. They still hoped to finish, and they were also drawn to school by social attractions such as athletics and girls.

As they approached graduation age, however, most of them realized that they would not be able to finish high school in the conventional manner. Either they were distracted by the need to make money, or they were too involved with court cases and jail, or they were simply too far behind in their work to complete school on time. Some, including Stan Williams, Zap Andrews, Larry Jefferson, and Jerry Barnes, withdrew from school completely at this point. Those who persisted moved into educational programs outside the regular high school structure: alternative high schools, residential institutions, and several GED programs.

Tommy Singleton was finally assigned to an alternative high school that had opened very close to his neighborhood. Lucky Giles soon joined him there but did not remain long, because he was sentenced to prison shortly thereafter. Tommy Singleton continued in the alternative school for the next three years, attending steadily for periods of months and then not attending while he pursued short spells of both legitimate and underground employment. He received his GED at the age of twenty and subsequently enrolled in a local public college. His college career also proceeded irregularly, as had that of his older brother, who was then in his mid-twenties and had been in and out of college for several years.

Johnny Singleton spent two years in a residential program suggested by a social worker associated with the Family Court. He entered the program voluntarily, feeling that he needed to make a complete break with his former environment in order to stay out of trouble: "I knew I just couldn't make it in these city schools. I knew too many people." He attended the regular schools in the suburban town where he was placed and eventually earned his GED.

Two others in this group also managed to earn GEDs. Reggie Hawkins, even though he had always done fairly well in school, chose to enter a GED program in order to finish high school early.

Reggie Hawkins: I learned about it through my high school. I told them "I don't feel like staying, going one more year, gettin' up every morning in the snow." They said, "Well we got a GED program." I said, "All right, I'll take that." I only had to go three hours a day, so I took it.
Interviewer: This was the start of eleventh grade for you, right? How long did it take you to finish?

[45]

R.H.: I got my high school diploma in January, right before the new term started.

Hawkins went on to earn some college credits.

Ben Bivins earned his GED at the age of eighteen while he was in state prison. Lucky Giles also studied for the GED in prison and missed passing the test by only a few points. He was scheduled for a second test but was released the day before that test was given.

The various educational achievements of the youths from Projectville and La Barriada carried over into their work experiences. More of the Projectville youths had high school diplomas, and most of them could read. Their academic problems were usually with math, and the math portions of the GED test were the ones that gave them trouble. Most of these youths, both with and without diplomas, moved into clerical and service sector jobs that required more literacy than did unskilled manual labor. Some attempted college in the hope of becoming professionals. Those with diplomas were somewhat vindicated in their persistence by obtaining slightly more and better-paying jobs than their peers who did not finish school. Those who did not finish found themselves restricted mainly to messenger and guard jobs. Their skepticism about the worth of the diploma seemed justified, however, by the fact that most of the group, with or without diplomas, were still frequently unemployed or employed in undesirable jobs. Schooling provided most of them with basic literacy and some of them with a credential. Schooling did not give them job-specific skills or direct connections to jobs. The irregularity of their schooling seems to have preceded careers of irregular work.

Hamilton Park

The Hamilton Park youths treated schooling as one possible path into the skilled blue-collar jobs to which they aspired. All of those who entered high school enrolled in vocational programs designed to give them job-specific skills in addition to a high school diploma. Half of this group did not finish high school. A few left because they had been expelled for fighting or assigned to 600 schools or drug programs. Most of these found jobs, usually through family connections, soon after leaving school. Those who finished school generally found better jobs than those who did not.

Most of the parents of the Hamilton Park youths had themselves grown up in this neighborhood and attended the same schools as their children. Many of them had not finished school, either, but had gone to work while they were still of school age. The parents generally encouraged their children to finish high school, but their attitude was quite pragmatic. They thought little of the public schools and, if they could afford it, sent their children to Catholic parochial school in the early grades. Boys were then expected to go on to public vocational-technical high school. Some families tried to keep their daughters in parochial schools through high school. When some of their sons began to leave school before finishing, the parents' attitudes were quite flexible. If the young men went to work, the parents relinquished pressure to finish school.

When they did urge their sons to finish, they emphasized not only the intrinsic value of schooling for getting a job but the need for a minimal credential, the high school diploma, in order to benefit fully from family and neighborhood-based connections to jobs. Teddy Haskell had dropped out of his vocational-technical high school at sixteen and started working in a part-time delivery job in his cousin's business. At eighteen he enrolled in a GED program because he was tired of the kind of work he was doing and his father had told him of a specific way in which the diploma would pay off.

Field Notes: Teddy told me that his father is an engineer. I asked what kind. He said his father operates heavy construction equipment. His father wants him to go back to school because he can get him into the union, but only if Teddy has a diploma.

Some of the Hamilton Park youths had attended public elementary schools, and others had gone to local parochial schools. Most people in the neighborhood thought the parochial schools were much better. John Gutski said that he would have gone to parochial school, but his parents could not afford to pay. Otto Deutsch's girlfriend, Bonnie O'Brien, said that Otto's friends who had gone to public elementary school were having serious literacy problems. Pete Calderone said that his younger brothers had learned more in parochial elementary schools than he and his older brother had learned in public school.

Interviewer: How come you went to different schools? Did your parents start making more money?
Pete Calderone: I guess, maybe, or saved up or something.
Int.: I heard the school in your neighborhood is a pretty wild place.
P.C.: I know. I wouldn't send my kids to that school. I think public schools are the worst thing. I have nephews, I wouldn't want to see them go to those schools. Catholic schools are a lot better, they teach

[47]

you a lot. Public schools, the teachers don't seem to give a shit, they don't have any control over the kids. In Catholic schools it's still pretty strict. They teach you a lot, they really drill it into you. Public schools . . . I never learned my times tables in the third grade. All my friends who were going to Catholic school, man, they knew all the times tables. Same thing with reading, all these guys in Catholic school, third, fourth grade, they were great readers. I couldn't read. I can now.

Int.: And how are you on your times tables?

P.C.: No, I'm bad in that. Something I should study. I'm not a total dummy.

As they entered high school, the Hamilton Park youths all moved into the public school system. Those who left during their middle teens usually did so as the result of getting into some sort of trouble, either with drugs or by fighting with teachers or other students. Most went to work very soon after leaving school, whether or not they left with a diploma. Those who did graduate had access to better jobs not only as a result of the diploma itself and of having learned job-specific skills but also because of direct connections to jobs through the school as well as through their families.

Some of the Hamilton Park youths never made it into regular high school. Brian Deutsch left school after the eighth grade and never returned. Brian Grady and Teddy Haskell got into serious trouble for fighting in junior high and were assigned to a 600 high school.

Brian Grady: Then they shipped me out of that school to a 600 high school. It's really strict. You do something wrong, they fuckin' punch the shit out of you. Kids just don't fuck around over there.

Interviewer: That's when you quit fuckin' around in school, huh?

B.G.: No, that's when I quit school. . . . They was givin' me all easy work . . . fuckin' twenty-three-year-old dudes in there, they don't know how to spell their name. I'd tell 'em it's too easy and they'd say, "You gotta do it anyway, we got to know what level you're on." I'm doin' this for how long, three months? I'd rather go out and work. That's why I went to work.

Brian Grady never did return to school. Teddy Haskell also left the 600 school, although he later enrolled in a GED program. Peter Murphy withdrew from school as a result of drug problems in his middle teens but later managed to earn his GED in a residential drug program.

Most of the other Hamilton Park youths entered Burdock Vocational-Technical High School, located in an industrial area adjacent to their own neighborhood. Like all vocational-technical high schools, it required a special application and entrance examination. Students from Hamilton Park had been going to Burdock for years, however, and these youths had routinely applied to the school and been accepted.

Burdock High School did not have a reputation for being one of the better vocational-technical schools in the system. The student body at the time of the study was nearly three-quarters white. Like the Hamilton Park youths, many of these students were from low-income families; about a fifth of them received free lunch. The school's attendance rate was over 75 percent, but less than half its students graduated. The youths we interviewed all described the school as a disorderly place where many students cut classes, got into fights, and used and sold drugs.

John Gutski: That's the worst school. They call that school "the pot school." Everybody goes to get high, hang out.

Otto Deutsch: I went to Burdock, my biggest mistake. People from my neighborhood go there. They were all goofing off.

Field Notes: Then he [a youth not a member of the core clique] told me that he had gone to Burdock Vocational. He said it was mostly a hangout place where a lot of kids go just to party.

Otto Deutsch and David Henry both withdrew from Burdock under pressure from their parents. When Otto Deutsch fathered a child, he said, his mother "told me to go to work right away." David Henry's mother blamed the school for her son's wild behavior.

David Henry: My mom made me drop out 'cause I was gettin' in too much trouble. She thought I was takin' heavy drugs. I wasn't though. It was just too much drinkin'. It was about thirty or forty kids, meet every day, you know, just buy half-gallons of liquor. You had to be in school eleven-thirty. We'd meet like eight o'clock in the morning. Liquor stores open up, we'd be standin' there.
Interviewer: So this was the ninth grade, tenth grade, something like that?
D.H.: Tenth grade. Then I got a job with my brother-in-law right after that.

The others who left Burdock Vocational without finishing had all gotten into fights. Jim Osinski (not one of the core group) punched his guidance counselor and was expelled. John Gutski also hit a teacher. He

[49]

was in twelfth grade at the time but did not have enough credits to graduate. Carl Pollini was expelled after his second fight with another student. He and Gutski both regretted not having finished, and Carl Pollini expressed resentment toward the school.

Carl Pollini: I had a fight with a guy and they asked me to leave. I shouldn't have done it, but they never should have asked me that either. That wasn't right, I don't think. You don't pull a cat out of school for fightin', you know. Try and help the guy, you know. No matter whose fault it was. But we had a fight and we fought again and that was it. I just left after that.

John Gutski felt that his job prospects had been impaired:

Interviewer: Did you study a particular trade?
John Gutski: Electricity and some plumbing.
Int.: Did you ever try to get a job doing that since you were there?
J.G.: From school I could have, but my shop teacher, I had a fight with him.
Int.: How many kids from your part of the neighborhood graduated?
J.G.: Only a few graduated, three or four I know of got diplomas. They went to college.
Int.: Is that ever a problem for you in getting a job?
J.G.: Half of us don't know how to read and write. Like sometimes I help this guy learn how to count, he's sixteen years old.
Int.: But you seem to have had a lot of jobs, the bakery, construction . . .
J.G.: Well, I have a hard time too. I can't get a job once in a while too. But it don't matter what you know—it matters who you know.

The school-leavers in this group expressed considerable ambivalence about the value of the high school diploma in the labor market. They felt that their job prospects had been impaired by their failure to finish school, but at the same time they expressed considerable skepticism about the importance of the diploma in and of itself for getting a job. Teddy Haskell enrolled in a GED program after having left school not because he thought that a diploma alone would get him a better job but because he needed it to make use of his father's connections to the construction union. John Gutski felt that he had sometimes missed out not only because he didn't have a diploma but also because his shop teacher might have connected him directly to a skilled job. The Hamilton Park youths perceived the credentials and skills symbolized by the high school diploma—"what you know"—as being valuable for getting jobs only in the context of personal connections to jobs: "who you know."

This linking of "what you know" to "who you know" was even more apparent in the attitudes and experiences of the Hamilton Park youths who did finish high school. Both Peter Calderone and Charlie Gaberewski got their diplomas from Burdock, in spite of erratic attendance and barely passing grades, but neither believed that a diploma had helped him or his friends to get good jobs.

> *Interviewer:* Most of your friends finished high school?
> *Pete Calderone:* Yeah . . . the thing that surprises me . . . all my friends who have no diplomas have good jobs . . . maybe not good jobs as careers, for the future, but they're loadin' up trucks, makin' nine or ten dollars an hour. Here I am with a diploma, what they say I need, and I got nothing.
> *Int.:* How do they get these jobs?
> *P.C.:* They just fall into them through people they know or advertisements in the *Hamilton Herald.*
> *Int.:* But the various jobs you've had—do you think it mattered that you had that diploma or not?
> *P.C.:* I don't think so, because the work had nothing to do with school.

Charlie Gaberewski reported that he had just "squeaked by" in Burdock. He failed the physics and computer automation courses that were required for his vocational certification but had enough credits to get his diploma. He got full-time work as a messenger right after he finished school. He thought the diploma might have helped him get that job, but he did not consider it a desirable job in the sense of offering any chance for advancement.

> *Interviewer:* Most of the guys you used to hang out with, did they finish school?
> *Charlie Gaberewski:* Yeah, most of them . . . like, a couple of guys that got jobs around that time, they're still doing it, still making the same shitty wages. It's like they never finished school.

Two other Hamilton Park youths who graduated from Burdock were more optimistic, but they too considered the diplomas alone of dubious use for getting jobs. Teddy Haskell's brother Barney received both his diploma and his vocational certification from Burdock. Instead of seeking a job in the skilled trade for which he had been trained, he enrolled in college. Of all the youths we contacted, only Pete Calderone's

[51]

younger brother Tony made full use of the vocational education system in which most of them had enrolled. Tony Calderone studied plumbing at Burdock and went directly into a unionized plumbing job. Besides getting his high school diploma, he had learned job-specific skills and earned his vocational certification in plumbing. Moreover, his shop teacher also provided him with a direct connection to the firm that hired him.

> *Interviewer:* Did your little brother go into plumbing because you had done it?
> *Pete Calderone:* Yeah, partly. He's a little smarter than I was, he got into it. He had the highest grades in the class. He studied hard.
> *Int.:* How much does he make?
> *P.C.:* About six dollars an hour. He's been doing it for about four years now, working in the same place. His union is pretty decent. They give you a dollar raise every year, so next year he'll be making seven. . . . If he stays he'll be making more and more.

Most of the Hamilton Park youths enrolled in vocational education programs even though these programs fulfilled their mission—providing a high school diploma and job-specific skills—in only a few cases. Both those who finished and those who did not expressed doubt about the value of the diploma and the quality of their school. Perhaps Burdock's most valuable aspect for them was that it was located in an industrial neighborhood and that many of the teachers had ties to local industry, but only Tony Calderone managed both to finish school and to make use of his teacher's connections. John Gutski regretted the loss of his shop teacher's connections even more than his lack of a diploma. Carl Pollini never finished but still managed to get a job through the school indirectly: a friend from his electrical installation class finished school, got an electrical job through the school, and then managed to get a job for Pollini.

Comparison of Ethnographic and Census Data

The census reports the proportion of high school graduates among persons aged twenty-five and over, and of civilians aged sixteen to nineteen who are not in school. Comparisons of these figures for the three neighborhoods (Table 10) generally show the same patterns as the ethnographic data. La Barriada's residents, both adults and those of school age, show far less involvement in schooling than residents of

Table 10.   Schooling patterns: SMSA, borough, and
neighborhoods

	H.S. graduates among persons over 25 (%)	Civilians age 16–19 not in school (%)
SMSA	64	25
Brooklyn	55	29
La Barriada	29	43
Projectville	40	17
Hamilton Park	45	37

Source: U.S. Bureau of the Census 1983.

either of the other two neighborhoods. A slighter higher proportion of
Hamilton Park adults than Projectville adults have completed high
school, 45 percent versus 40.2 percent. The census data for civilians in
their late teens who are not enrolled in school show more contrast between these two neighborhoods than do the ethnographic data. Roughly
similar proportions of each ethnographic sample managed to finish high
school, albeit through different routes: GED programs for the Projectville youths, and regular vocational diplomas for those from Hamilton
Park. In the census data, however, Projectville residents actually report
more school enrollment among youths of ages sixteen to nineteen than
do the Hamilton Park residents: only 17 percent in Projectville are not
enrolled in school, compared to 43 percent in La Barriada and fully 37
percent in Hamilton Park.

Two factors must be considered in interpreting these census figures
on school enrollment. The first is that some eighteen- and nineteen-
year-olds may not be in school because they have already graduated.
Both the ethnographic data and the census data on high school completion rates among adults, however, cast doubt on this possible explanation for the greater reported school enrollment of Projectville youths. All
these data sources indicate that a very high proportion of Hamilton Park
residents do not complete high school.

It is very possible, however, that the disparity in school enrollment
rates reported to the census is greater than the actual disparity in school
participation between Hamilton Park and Projectville. Projectville residents are much more dependent on public assistance than are Hamilton
Park residents. If a child receiving public assistance benefits does not
enroll in school, the welfare budget of that family can be jeopardized.
Therefore, Projectville residents have a very strong incentive to make

[53]

sure that their children are enrolled, whether or not they actually attend regularly. The ethnographic data, though based on small samples, suggest rather similar patterns of troubled and erratic school attendance among both groups, but the perceived value of schooling appears to be much greater among the Projectville youths. Despite their troubles in school, they do see schooling as crucial to their prospects for advancement, whereas Hamilton Park youths are more contemptuous and tend simply to endure school.

Continuities and Variations between Neighborhoods

The schooling patterns of high-risk youth in the three study neighborhoods show similarities and differences both in terms of their provision of human capital and in terms of their provision of socialization into work and/or crime.

We found considerable ambivalence among respondents in all three study neighborhoods about the value of schooling as human capital that would lead them into desirable jobs. They saw their fathers and older brothers working in jobs that did not require school credentials. They saw the schools providing more occupational training for women's employment than for men's. They rated the schools they attended as inferior and unlikely to provide them with substantial skills. Yet they still tended to consider themselves in school even if they were not attending. Part of this ambivalence can be traced to a perception that school could indeed provide human capital but might not pay off for them. From their point of view, a high school diploma was a risky investment: it might pay off but could turn out to be wasted effort.

In fact, the fit between schooling and work was fairly loose in all three neighborhoods. Among people from each neighborhood who did get diplomas, some were seen to profit from having done so, yet it was also clearly evident in each neighborhood that some people who had diplomas were stuck with bad jobs anyway. Under these circumstances, the effort to remain in school was too costly for many respondents. All of them felt pressure to gain income while they were still of school age. Forgoing present income to stay in school in the hope of better money later required faith as much as rationality.

The particular fit between schooling and work did vary between neighborhoods, however, and these variations were closely related to the differences in the amount and types of schooling and employment that characterized each neighborhood group. La Barriada youths participated in schooling the least, and most of them subsequently moved into unskilled manual jobs that required the least education. What they

[54]

needed most from the schools was basic literacy, which only some of them achieved. A few also sought vocational training for entrance to skilled blue-collar jobs, but they failed to complete the programs that might have provided these skills.

Projectville youths, despite their high rates of interrupted and uncompleted schooling, valued schooling more than the other groups. Their perceived need for school credentials anticipated their subsequent paths into the labor market. They most desired clerical and service sector jobs, which require more education and also employ bureaucratic recruitment methods that respond better to abstract credentials than do most blue-collar jobs. As the next chapter shows, the Projectville youths had the fewest family and neighborhood-based connections to jobs. As a result, the difference between having and not having a high school diploma made more difference in labor market returns in Projectville than in the other two neighborhoods.

The Hamilton Park youths' attitudes toward and use of the school system were heavily influenced by the fact that they did have many family and neighborhood-based connections to desirable blue-collar jobs. The high school diploma was valuable to them not in the abstract but as a minimum credential that would allow them to make use of these personal connections; when such connections could pay off without the diploma, these youths often left school to go directly to work. They also valued the schools as sources of job-specific skills and of direct connections to jobs. The long-standing relationship between their neighborhood and the nearest vocational high school in fact constituted an important source of neighborhood-based job connections.

The patterns described in this chapter cannot all be accounted for in terms of schools' perceived and actual functions of providing or not providing human capital. Schooling also produced differential socialization into the legitimate and criminal labor markets, quite apart from its direct provision of skills and credentials that could lead to employment. In the short term, the status of being of school age affected the youths' relations with parents, employers, courts, and welfare agencies. School attendance, more than employment, was the criterion by which their social worth was judged and according to which they received rewards and punishments. Their families were more likely to support them while they attended school and expected them to get jobs if they did not. Many jobs, however, were automatically closed to young men of school age. Family welfare budgets were endangered when school-age youths did not enroll. When they went to court, they received more lenient dispositions if they could show that they were attending school, dispositions that frequently included mandates for further schooling.

The significance of being of school-age and its effects on patterns of crime and employment also varied among the three neighborhoods. Parents in all three neighborhoods expected their sons to go to work when they left school, but the Hamilton Park parents were far more able to provide connections to jobs than parents in the minority neighborhoods. Lacking resources either to enforce school attendance or to provide connections to employment, parents in La Barriada and Projectville often had little choice but to accept the out-of-school, out-of-work status of their sons. Arrest rates and welfare dependency rates were also much higher in these neighborhoods. Crime and court involvements were a more serious source of disruption in the schooling careers of the minority youths. Extensive court involvement, with its attendant disruption of schooling, usually came as a result of systematic stealing, which was more prevalent in these neighborhoods. Youths from all three neighborhoods reported problems with school as a result of fighting, and some individuals from both Projectville and Hamilton Park were expelled because of fights. La Barriada youths were not expelled for fighting, mostly because they left school so early.

Schooling experiences also had socialization effects, apart from the direct provision of human capital, which lasted beyond the school-age years and affected adult patterns of crime and employment. Fighting in school provided early socialization into violent behavior and hostile relations to authority. When these youths eventually did enter the job market, many were handicapped not only by their lack of skills or diplomas but also by their lack of a productive daily routine; years of irregular schooling prepared them for careers of irregular work. This continuity was characteristic of both individuals and institutions: that is, the individuals' irregular commitment first to schools and then to jobs matched both the disorganized nature of the schools that enrolled them and the insecure, poorly paid jobs they entered.

As provider of both human capital and socialization, schooling competed with both employment and crime during the school-age years. Most of these youths who left school did so in the pursuit of income. Immediate financial need precluded their investing in a high school diploma, an investment that might turn out to be useless if not combined with a job-specific skill, a college education, or a personal connection to a good job. Youths who left school for work did recognize that they might be impairing their long-term employment prospects, but in the long run the trade-off between crime and schooling was much more injurious than that between employment and schooling. The Hamilton Park youths who left school for work were sacrificing educational credentials but gaining work experience, whereas the youths from the minority neighborhoods who left school had access only to criminal income at first; they were sacrificing both forms of human capital, schooling and work experience.

Schooling is more than mere technical provision of human capital; it provides a social identity for an age-grade. In the eyes of these youths, their parents, employers, and institutional officials, their primary activity during these years should have been schooling. When crime interrupted their careers, as it did for many, it was schooling rather than employment that was primarily affected. The looseness of fit between schooling and economic success is apparent in the anomalous relationship between the schooling patterns described in this chapter and the family income levels outlined in Chapter 2. Although Hamilton Park's residents had only marginally higher levels of education than the residents of Projectville, their family income levels were double those in Projectville. The following chapter explores further the career paths of youths in these neighborhoods and the ways in which schooling and other factors contributed to success or failure in various sectors of the labor market.

[4]

Employment

The prominence of employment problems among young people since the early 1960s, particularly in inner-city areas, has called forth a number of attempts at explanation by economists. Human capital theorists (G. Becker 1975) have acknowledged the difficulty of modeling the extremely volatile labor market behavior of the young and have frequently tried to explain this behavior in terms of the "school-to-work transition." The age period from the teen years into the early twenties is described as one in which labor market entrants explore various job possibilities, moving rapidly in and out of the labor force or from one job to another as they seek employment that suits their abilities and tastes and decide whether and how to invest in education and training (Adams and Mangum 1978).

Economists of the segmented labor market perspective (Doeringer and Piore 1971; Beck and Horan 1978; Bluestone and Harrison 1982; Gordon, Edwards, and Reich 1982) have also pointed to the volatility of the labor market behavior of all young people but have emphasized the disparities among different racial/ethnic and local groups. One source of these disparities, mentioned in the previous chapter, is the lesser labor market return from education experienced by minority and inner-city youth (Harrison 1972a, 1972b). These writers have also drawn attention to the complex legal, institutional, and social barriers to full labor market participation for young people, especially for those still in their middle teens, who are formally barred from many jobs by labor laws, school attendance laws, and union contracts.

The years from the late teens into the early twenties are also problematic and have been described as a period of "moratorium" in which young people are more interested in establishing personal than occupational identity and so are not fully committed economic actors (Osterman

1980). They are involved in a process of "work establishment" (Freedman 1969) in which choices and experiences may be more significant for their long-term than for their short-term returns. Osterman has shown that unemployment during this period, but not during the earlier mid-teen period, has disastrous long-term consequences for minority and inner-city youths.

Cain (1976) has observed that the central issue in most disputes between segmented labor market and human capital theorists concerns the extent of "noncompeting groups" within the labor market. A number of empirical comparisons between the labor market experiences of our different age and neighborhood groupings reveal both differences based on human capital and several strongly suggesting that such social variables as age, race/ethnicity, citizenship status, and neighborhood of residence do define "noncompeting" groups in this regional labor market. Our research explores the processes linking labor market segmentation to the reproduction of the labor force in specific community contexts.

This chapter follows the transitions from schooling to the labor market of the three neighborhood groups and traces the progression from their earliest employment experiences into the period of work establishment. By the end of the data collection period, most respondents in our ethnographic samples were in their early twenties. Though few were securely placed in stable jobs by this age, most of them had had several jobs, and many were working fairly regularly. Neighborhood-specific patterns of employment during their teenage years varied in terms of the family and neighborhood contexts that mediated both their access to job opportunities and their responses to those opportunities.

The chapter devotes a separate section to each of the three neighborhood groups and organizes them similarly to enable systematic comparison of the physical ecology of the neighborhoods, the family employment backgrounds of the youths studied, the labor market structure within which local youths find jobs and become socialized as workers, and the progression of their work experiences from the mid-teens to early twenties.

The physical proximity of residential neighborhoods to centers of employment reflected historical settlement patterns and the development of the labor market. Local factories, warehouses, and businesses are important sources of part-time and temporary employment for young people, especially for those most likely to be still enrolled in school and thus reluctant or unable to travel long distances to seek and hold jobs. Physical isolation from potential jobs results in very different employment patterns.

The experiences of youths entering the labor market in each neighborhood were shaped also by their family backgrounds. The level of family income determined their own early need for income, and the jobs held by members of their own and neighboring families constituted their most important sources of information about jobs and their most direct connections to employment opportunities. Along with the schools, the employment base in each neighborhood was the most important factor in the reproduction of the labor force at the local level. Differences in family income and employment affected the timing of these young men's entry into the labor market and the types of jobs they sought and found.

Different sectors of the regional labor market preferred different kinds of workers and recruited accordingly. These divisions served to create noncompeting groups in the labor force and affected each local group in distinctive ways. Each neighborhood's employment base tended to reproduce itself through networks of job referral. Additional influences were age and citizenship. Factory jobs, for example, were legally restricted to workers at least eighteen years old, and youths under the age of sixteen who wanted to work "on-the-books" in any job had to acquire working papers. Also, some local employers apparently preferred to hire noncitizens, including undocumented aliens, as a more controllable source of labor than citizens, especially youths.

Although school experience and family- and neighborhood-based connections provided initial points of entry into the labor force, the employment careers of these youths began to develop their own trajectories over time. Early work experiences led to subsequent jobs; conversely, periods of time spent outside school and the labor force—and varying degrees of criminal activity—began to accumulate as barriers to finding employment.

La Barriada

Although the block where most of the respondents from La Barriada lived was physically located in immediate proximity to a large industrial area, the nearby factories provided little stable employment for the block's residents. Several factories were actually located on one end of the block, and the tenements filling the rest of the block had originally housed the families of the workers in those factories. At the beginning of our research period most of the tenements still remained, but the factory spaces were no longer fully used and did not provide the same amount of employment as they once had done. Many of the jobs that did remain were held by workers who came in from outside the neighborhood or were only seasonal, temporary, part-time, and/or "off-the-books." A survey of all the apartments on the block conducted a year after the research began indicated that 72 percent of the households were supported primarily by welfare or Social Security (see Table 2).

The owner of two buildings on the block described the changes that had occurred in the sixteen years he had owned property there.

> *Field Notes:* We talked this morning with the landlord who is on the block every day taking care of his buildings. . . . He said that when he first came here most of the residents of the block were Irish, Italian, Polish, and French. He pointed to a warehouse which occupies one side of the far end of the block. He said that this had once been used for manufacturing but that the company had moved to New Jersey seven years ago. When he first came to the block, many of the residents were workers in the factory. Now, that building is used only as a warehouse, and most of the current residents are Puerto Rican. Some households on the block are still supported by men working in the factories, but most of the families here now are on welfare.

During the first two years of our observations the housing stock deteriorated severely. Property began to change hands rapidly, services became irregular, and most of the buildings eventually burned.

The families of the youths we interviewed from La Barriada were the poorest among the three study neighborhoods. All the parents had been born in Puerto Rico and had migrated to Brooklyn as adults; the youths themselves had either been born in New York City or had arrived there as small children. About half of these families were headed by females and were supported primarily by transfer payments (see Table 5). Other families were supported by men working in low-wage jobs that provided an income only slightly higher than that provided by welfare. Although several of the mothers had worked in factories when they were younger or still did some seasonal factory work, most of the working men were not employed in the nearby factories. Only the family of Julian and Sonny Acosta had been supported by an adult male's long-term factory job. Their father had worked in a factory for twenty-one years and had become a foreman; he lost his job over a dispute with his boss and then began drinking heavily. Gaspar Cruz's stepfather worked occasionally as an unlicensed electrician and handyman. The fathers of Mario Valdez and Arturo Morales had worked for more than twenty years in restaurants. Morales's father reported that he was earning four dollars an hour, sixty-five cents above the minimum wage. Valdez's family also received some welfare payments—illegally, although Valdez claimed that they had gotten into that situation unintentionally.

Interviewer: You said your father was always living with you, and he was always working, right?
Mario Valdez: He was a family man, devoted husband and all that.
Int.: Did your mother ever have any income?
M.V.: She used to work in a factory sometimes, but not since my little sister was born.
Int.: Did she ever get any assistance?
M.V.: Yeah, for about the last three or four years.
Int.: Do the welfare people know your father is living there?
M.V.: No. If they did, forget about it.
Int.: Why did you get on? Your father's salary wasn't enough?
M.V.: I don't know, 'cause, let me see, my father one time, he got sick. He has a nervous . . . he gets nervous, so he went to the Veterans Hospital for a couple of months. He couldn't work, so my mother had to go down there to get a little bit of help till my father got himself back up on his feet. And then he went back to work, and, you know, since the money helps . . . they only send us just enough to pay the rent plus $75 in coupons.

Miguel Tirado also lived in a household supported by a combination of wages and welfare: his mother received welfare, and his stepfather had a factory job.

The rest of the households of the youths interviewed were supported primarily by transfer payments, including the Acosta family after the father lost his job. Mike Concepcion lived with his mother, who received disability payments. Jorge Padilla and Octavio Del Rio lived with their mothers, who received welfare, and Chucho Rivera had lived with his mother on a welfare budget until he was fourteen. During the research period he was living with a sister, who received welfare for herself and her children but not for her brother.

The major exception to this pattern of households supported by low-wage jobs and/or welfare was Carlos Hernandez, the respondent who was a few years older than the others and no longer lived in the neighborhood but still returned there to socialize. When his family had lived on the block, they were supported only by his father's job with the post office. Then his mother had opened a beauty parlor, which prospered, and they moved to a nicer neighborhood.

Carlos Hernandez: There was always, like, this cloud over my whole family. I'm the last, right, and all my older brothers and sisters always got in trouble. My parents were always pretty poor, but then they took a gamble and they borrowed money from all their relatives and they opened a beauty parlor. It turned out well and now they own a second one. So now my brothers and sisters feel like they want more and they can't have it because of their past, they wasted their youth, you know, so they're all rooting for me. I was gonna quit college one time, 'cause it was so hard, but they all got behind me. That's the only reason I finished. It took me six years. I was practically the only Puerto Rican in that school, me and one other guy. He didn't make it.

Many of the residents considered their households to be particularly disadvantaged, especially in comparison with those of some of their relatives or their own during other periods in their lives. The Acostas said that their father's family in Puerto Rico had included storeowners and doctors. Their father had gone to business college on the island and had been an army sergeant, a bank teller, and a factory foreman before he lost his job and succumbed to alcoholism. Mario Valdez reported that his cousins in Puerto Rico and New York included small businessmen and police officers. Other families had sons and daughters who were upwardly mobile in the New York area. Carlos Hernandez's career success contrasted sharply with the problems of all his older siblings, but Arturo Morales had an older brother who was a union printer and a sister who was an executive secretary on Wall Street. Octavio Del Rio had one older sister in college and another who was married to a salesman in the suburbs. Mike Concepcion's father had been a truck driver with steady work before he died.

Several families reported that even though they had always been poor, they had previously lived in "nicer" neighborhoods and had relocated to the block only after they were burned out of their previous residences and had been unable to find other affordable housing. Though this block had long provided inexpensive but decent housing to the families of workers in the nearby factory, it served during the period of field research as a temporary refuge for families whose poverty and employment problems surpassed even those of their own peers, extended families, and residents of the rest of their neighborhood.

Most of these youths had left or interrupted their schooling by the age of fifteen in order to seek employment. They met with some success but more failure; even the most dedicated and successful job seekers had had no more than a year of full-time work before they turned nineteen, and most had worked far less than that, whatever the degree of effort they put into finding jobs. Many were forced to modify previously held aspirations. Leaving school to pursue income but unable to find regular employment, they sought income in other ways. Their participation in regular acts of income-producing crime and the resulting involvement with the criminal justice system in turn kept them out of school and forced them to abandon their earlier occupational goals. Gaspar Cruz and Mario Valdez gave up the vocational programs to which they had gained admission. Arturo Morales, Mike Concepcion, and Octavio Del Rio, who had been doing fairly well in school until they reached high school, all terminated or interrupted their education during this period.

All of them were seeking work at some point during their middle teens, though the intensity of their job search varied. Compared with the two other neighborhood groups, this clique included a larger number of youths seeking work during their middle teens for purposes of basic family support. Mike Concepcion lived alone with his mother and needed work to clear debts that had accumulated. Gaspar Cruz had a fight with his stepfather, left his mother's household, and began supporting himself. Julian Acosta married and fathered a child. The rest received basic subsistence from their parental households during their middle teens and did not feel as much pressure to bring in regular income. They needed money primarily to provide their own clothing and recreation.

Most of their attempts to find jobs, however, ended in frustration. Their search during the mid-teen years tended to be confined to their own neighborhood. Many reported going from factory to factory looking for work, but most regular factory jobs were closed to them because of their age. Only three types of jobs were available in this neighborhood to those younger than eighteen: government-sponsored summer youth jobs, part-time building superintendent jobs, and temporary, off-the-books jobs in local factories and warehouses.

The youths we interviewed had surprisingly little access to government-sponsored summer youth jobs in light of the generally high level of program activity in the neighborhood as a whole. Before we contacted the core group, we had conducted a number of preliminary interviews with gang members whom we met through local social workers. Many of the gang members had had one or more summer youth jobs, but only two of the core group members, Octavio Del Rio and Chucho Rivera, had had such jobs. Del Rio had stayed in school longer than some of the others, signed up for his summer youth job through his school when he was fifteen, and worked on a park clean-up crew more or less regularly all summer. Chucho Rivera was signed up by a social worker when he was fourteen, but he stayed at the job only two weeks. The fact that the others in this group had less access to summer youth jobs was probably related to the fact that they were little involved in either school or youth gangs and so were not affected by local efforts to deliver employment services through the schools or through the social workers focusing on the gangs. Chucho Rivera had encountered the social worker who signed him up because he was more involved than the others with the gangs. Social programs were to be more effective in delivering employment to this group at a later stage.

Most of the mid-teen employment among this group was provided by private employers, the local landlords and factory managers. These jobs were generally low-paying, part-time, temporary, and/or off-the-books. The two instances of full-time, on-the-books work for private employers involved falsifying records to satisfy the age regulations.

Several of the youths had had temporary or part-time jobs as superintendents in their own tenement buildings or in others close by. Unfortunately, the availability of these jobs was closely related to the decline of the worth of the housing and the concomitant withdrawal of services. With the buildings changing hands rapidly, new owners tried to keep them going by hiring teenagers who lived there, paying them very little. This process actually seemed to be working at the beginning of the research period: the buildings were relatively clean, and the youths were happy to have the work. Eighteen months later, most of the landlords had completely disappeared, and most of the buildings had burned.

Jorge Padilla reported the most lucrative and longest-lasting job of this type. When he was fourteen years old, his uncle bought a building in the area and paid him $150 a week to maintain the building and also to help out in the small restaurant on the ground floor. But six months later his uncle sold the building, and Padilla was out of work for most of the next four years.

The other jobs for local landlords reported during the research period all involved the building where Arturo Morales lived with his family. When first contacted, Arturo was being paid $40 a week to clean his building. In addition, he was given the use of a basement room and a telephone. (He tried to rent the room out to a friend, but the friend never paid.) He was eighteen years old at this point, and this was his first employment of any sort.

His landlord also hired two of his friends. Gaspar Cruz performed occasional odd jobs, replacing fixtures and painting hallways. To all appearances, both Morales and Cruz were performing the work they were being paid to do. A few months later, however, they had moved on

[65]

to other work, and Octavio Del Rio took over the building, to the detriment of services.

> *Field Notes:* When Arturo was showing us the basement of his building, he said Octavio was now the super, but he wasn't sure that he was going to do a very good job. Later, outside, Arturo was talking to the landlord across the street. The landlord was complaining about the garbage in the lot next to Arturo's building. After the landlord left, Arturo said, "Octavio was probably cleaning out the abandoned apartments and just threw the garbage out the window."

Shortly thereafter, the landlord of this building disappeared, the residents moved out, and the building burned.

The nearby factories and warehouses remained the largest source of work for these youths during their mid-teens, even though most of the jobs there were legally closed to them. They frequently went from factory to factory asking for work but rarely finding it. Gaspar Cruz reported getting tips for bringing coffee when he was as young as twelve. By the time he was fifteen, he could occasionally find a full day's work, off-the-books.

> *Gaspar Cruz:* I used to hang out, nothing to do, watching people load and unload the trucks. One day I was there, I said "You need any help?" "Nah, not now, what's your name?" They take down your name and phone number. Then they would call me, "Hey, we need you today, we got two or three trucks coming in." So we went to the truck, fill 'em up and that's it. The day is over. Go home.

Some of them claimed that their age and U.S. citizenship were both handicaps, because local employers preferred to hire undocumented adult aliens—Spanish-speaking non–Puerto Ricans generically referred to as "Mexicans," although census statistics and experts on this neighborhood suggest that most of these people were in fact Central Americans who may have entered the country through Mexico.

> *Gaspar Cruz:* They don't like to hire us because we're young and we're Puerto Rican. Them guys, they just want to hire illegal aliens, 'cause they can get over on them cheap.

> *Jorge Padilla:* The bosses play it smart. Aliens, they could go work off-the-books. They got, to 'cause they can't work on-the-books. Unless they got a card, but most of them don't got a card, you know. So what

they do is they go look for a job, say if they're going to make $200 a week, he [the employer] stays with $100 and give $100 to the guy. The Mexican [*sic*] can't do anything about it. He can't go to the Board of Work, or whatever, 'cause they gonna send him back to his country. He'd rather get gypped.

Two of the youths interviewed had worked for more than a year in factory jobs by the time they were eighteen, but in both cases they had lied about their age. Julian Acosta was able to do this only because his father was the factory foreman at the time and manipulated the hiring records. By his own account, however, Acosta was unmotivated to work and stayed only a few months. Gaspar Cruz, by contrast, was the most aggressive job seeker of the group. He had been living on his own since he was sixteen and had spent six months in jail. After he got out, he went to a factory with an older friend, lied about his age, and worked there for more than a year. During that time he was promoted to supervisor and received a raise from $2.85 to $3.50 per hour.

The single most important source of jobs for these youths during their middle teens was a warehouse located right on their block. Mike Concepcion, Octavio Del Rio, and Miguel Tirado had all worked there when they were sixteen years old. The company had once used the facility for manufacturing, but at this point half the building stood empty and the other half served only as a warehouse. Because shipments in and out of the warehouse were irregular, the manager would hire several teenagers from the block to load and unload the trucks as needed. This often meant getting the youths out of bed in the middle of the night. The pay was $3.50 per hour—sixty-five cents above the minimum at that time—and taxes were withheld.

Though all three were employed on a part-time basis, they had quite different patterns of work. Mike Concepcion, working for basic household subsistence, put in between five and fifteen hours a day, averaging forty hours a week for a period of almost a year. Octavio Del Rio worked slightly fewer hours a week and, by his own account, much less diligently. When after five months he got into a dispute with his supervisor and quit, Miguel Tirado took his place and worked there for six months. At that point, the company closed down the facility, and both Concepcion and Tirado were laid off. Despite their varying degrees of commitment to the job, it constituted the longest spell of mid-teen employment for each of them; afterward, they were all out of work for more than a year. Three years later, though they had had some other short-term jobs, Concepcion and Tirado were still citing these jobs to potential employers as their most substantial work experience.

[67]

Others in this group had no employment at all before the age of seventeen. Arturo Morales got his part-time building superintendent job at that age. Mario Valdez went to work, washing dishes in the restaurant where his father was employed, at seventeen. Carlos Hernandez, because of his family's new prosperity, never held a job until the summers after he began college. Even those who did have some work during their mid-teens were out of work more often than not. With the exception of Hernandez, they were all attending school irregularly or not at all during that period, and most of them were involved in fairly regular acts of theft—their major source of income during the mid-teen years (see Chapters 5 and 6). Employment opportunities during this time were severely blocked for them. They were effectively isolated from the adult labor market and were competing for a shrinking pool of local youth jobs.

As they began to reach the age of eighteen, their need for income became more pressing. They no longer needed money only for clothing and recreation; either they were starting to set up new households, or their parents began to expect them to contribute money to the family household. Hence, they intensified their job search, and many more job possibilities did begin to open up for them. They became eligible to work in the factories, and they also began to seek and find clerical jobs in the major business districts.

Nevertheless, they still encountered considerable difficulty in finding and keeping jobs. They were entering the labor market with very little in the way of credentials, experience, or personal connections. In addition, they found themselves hampered by their involvement in crime and the criminal justice system and by the personal habits developed during years of being out of work, out of school, and on the streets. Most of them had several jobs in their late teens, but the jobs usually lasted only a few weeks or months. Many were only temporary and ended in layoffs. Some youths were fired, usually as a result of absenteeism and lateness, and others quit either because of disputes over work responsibilities or in order to search for a better job. Few of the jobs they did find offered much in the way of stability, desirable working conditions, or chance for advancement; even when such opportunities existed, these youths were often able to recognize them only in retrospect.

The transition from crime to work as a primary source of income caused difficulties for many in this group. Arturo Morales and Mario Valdez began their first serious search for full-time employment as a direct result of their involvement in the criminal justice system. Morales went through several part-time jobs and finally—just before he was to be sentenced—found a full-time job at the factory where his older brother worked. When he had quit a part-time job obtained through a local social program, his lawyer had urged him strongly to find work before he was sentenced.

> *Field Notes:* Arturo says his lawyer told him, "You told them that you did it for the money. If you go in there without a job, the judge will assume that you're going to do it again and put you in jail."

Mario Valdez's father took his son to his own place of employment after Mario was arrested.

> *Mario Valdez:* I was about sixteen, seventeen, my father used to get on my case, "If you're not going to go to school, work," you know. Then one time I got busted, and when I came out, my father really went off: "You'd better get a job, or do something!"

Experience with the criminal justice system triggered strong pressures for Valdez and Morales to enter the job market in earnest, but similar involvement hampered the employment of many in the clique during this period. Gaspar Cruz lost one job that he had held for a year after his employer found out he had been in jail. A year later he was assigned a new probation officer who required weekly appearances, and this event prompted him to seek a new job in fear that he would lose his current one as a result of absences. Miguel Tirado lost four different jobs in the course of a six-month period during which he had to make weekly court appearances. He did not want to tell his employers that he had to go to court and could not otherwise explain his absences. At one point, Octavio Del Rio cited court appearances as a reason for not looking for work, though his common-law wife did not accept the explanation.

Social programs delivered significant employment services to this group during the work establishment period of the late teens. During the earlier mid-teen period this group of youths seemed to have had less access to program employment services than other youths of similar backgrounds from their own neighborhood. There was a fairly high level of program activity for youths in the neighborhood as a whole, but services did not reach their particular block until a church organization opened a storefront just around the corner. The organization was small and lasted at that location only for a year, but during that time it managed to connect several of these youths to publicly sponsored job programs. After his first arrest Arturo Morales went there for counseling and got a part-time job in a local hospital as a filing clerk.

[69]

Mario Valdez, Octavio Del Rio, and several others not among our primary contacts got full-time jobs in a neighborhood demolition program designed to teach local youths construction skills while they rehabilitated local housing. The program was largely successful in providing employment, teaching skills, and demolishing buildings. When it ended, unfortunately, it failed in its goal of moving participants into private jobs; it placed only three out of a hundred. While it lasted, however, this program had a significant impact on the lives of the participants. The young men themselves rated these jobs highly, not because of the pay but because of the treatment. They also reported curtailing their stealing far more during this period of full-time employment than when they had had only part-time or temporary employment in their mid-teens.

The youths in this group varied considerably in their stated desire and demonstrated motivation to work, but their actual employment experiences were more similar than different and became more so with age. Julian Acosta and Octavio Del Rio were living with women and children in households receiving welfare by their late teens and openly tried to avoid work. Neither was entirely successful in doing so, however, since their wives, families, and financial circumstances kept forcing them to seek paid employment.

The most avid workers were Mario Valdez and Gaspar Cruz. They talked approvingly of work and sought it relentlessly—with only intermittent success. Valdez returned to Puerto Rico when he was nineteen, after being without work for months following the demise of the demolition program. He could not find work there either and returned. Cruz was more successful in finding jobs, but he also lost them frequently: some were only temporary and he quit others in search of better jobs only to find that they were not better jobs. During their late teens most youths in this group averaged about half a year of full-time work, whether they sought it actively or passively. During the rest of the year they collected unemployment only if their jobs had been on-the-books—which they frequently had not been.

The kinds of jobs they sought and found were of two types. Most members of the group preferred and felt most qualified for manual work. Mario Valdez and Gaspar Cruz, who had tried unsuccessfully to complete rigorous vocational education programs before they left school, kept seeking craft skills: Valdez in demolition, Cruz as an upholsterer's informal apprentice a few hours a night. They and others in this group did not obtain skilled jobs or actual apprenticeships during this period; none gained access to the high-paying blue-collar and municipal jobs that most of them considered the most desirable type of employment. The manual work they did find generally required no skills or credentials and paid only slightly above minimum wage. They worked frequently in the factories but at low-paying jobs in which many of the other workers—women and undocumented aliens—did not remain long. They found most of these jobs through local word of mouth.

There were some in the group who preferred clerical work, generally those who could read and had gone furthest in school. These youths worked as stock clerks, mail clerks, and messengers in Manhattan offices. They found these jobs through public and private employment agencies and through female family members who worked as secretaries. Opportunity for advancement was extremely limited, however since they did not even have high school diplomas:

Arturo Morales: I get along OK there. But everybody in the office there keeps telling me, "You mean you never finished high school?" They keep telling me I got to go back if I want to get anywhere.

It was during this period that he and several of the others who wanted office work enrolled in GED programs.

These clerical jobs were also difficult to find and hard to replace. Miguel Tirado found a messenger job when he was eighteen and held it for more than a year. During that time he was promoted to dispatcher and brought in his friend Octavio Del Rio. Miguel quit when he was denied a raise he thought he was due, but he later regretted his decision: "I made a mistake. I thought I could get another job, but it wasn't so easy." Octavio Del Rio lost his job as a result of absence and later sought other clerical jobs, but he had to accept factory work.

Octavio Del Rio: I missed one day one week and they didn't say nothing. Then I missed again the next week and they fired me.
Interviewer: You didn't think they cared?
O.D.R.: Right. I'm sorry I lost that job too.

Others also treated some of their early job opportunities carelessly and later regretted having done so. They confronted their first full-time jobs with very little experience of the workplace, having spent most of their time during their mid-teens out of school, out of work, and on the streets. They were accustomed to keeping very late hours. They found the discipline of the workplace very much in contrast to that of family, school, and the streets. Their employers in both the clerical and manufacturing sectors emphasized reliability over all other aspects of job performance. Firings almost always resulted from absenteeism. Octavio Del Rio and Julian Acosta lost several jobs in this manner because they

[71]

preferred to stay home with their common-law wives. Some showed themselves willing to work hard and consistently whenever they got the chance, however. Mike Concepcion and Gaspar Cruz had done so when they were still only sixteen.

The brief duration of many jobs resulted as much from the kinds of jobs as from the ability or commitment of the youths. Most terminations during this period were layoffs; the next most frequent were quits, with firings a distant third. Many of the quits were reactions to particularly dirty and undesirable jobs that offered little security or chance for advancement anyway. Arturo Morales worked as an office clerk for a manufacturing firm on and off for a period of over two years. During that time he was laid off, was rehired, quit, was rehired, was laid off a second time, was rehired again, and finally quit for good. After he left the first time, he did report learning more about the rules of the workplace:

> *Arturo Morales:* Before, this guy Eddie, my supervisor, I used to think he was on my back all the time. But when they called me back, he sat down and talked to me and explained things. He's all right. I didn't understand before why certain things got to be done a certain way or on time or whatever.

Still, the repeated layoffs discouraged him from maintaining his commitment to his job.

By the end of their teens most of these youths had found and lost several jobs and were definitely if insecurely participating in the labor market. Wages, though irregular, had replaced theft as their major source of income, and their income needs had become much more insistent. They were still frequently unemployed and generally made low wages when they did work. They found more on-the-books work than during their mid-teens, but they seldom stayed long enough to attain union membership; indeed, they sometimes claimed that they were laid off to prevent access to union membership. With experience, they quit and were fired less frequently but still faced frequent layoffs. Some were still trying to get educational credentials, and others were attempting to learn craft skills outside formal educational or occupational channels. Miguel Tirado and Chucho Rivera were removed from the labor market to prison after felony convictions.

Projectville

Most of the respondents from Projectville lived in a single building in the Morgan Houses, a public housing project. The Morgan Houses comprised several similar buildings and were themselves but one of several housing projects in this neighborhood. This large concentration of public housing was physically distant from any major centers of employment. Much of the surrounding land was literally empty, most of the private housing in the area having been abandoned, burned, or razed over the previous twenty years. The neighborhood has always been distant from major centers of employment. Successive development plans regularly noted the large concentrations of land and labor in the area and recommended industrial and commercial development. Each new phase of development, however, brought more housing projects but very few jobs. The only business activity in the area during the research period was concentrated in a rapidly dwindling commercial section where most of the stores were owned by people from outside the neighborhood. Although most of the residents of the projects were black, the store owners were mostly Jews, Arabs, and Hispanics. During the research period these businesses disappeared rapidly, succumbing to fires on an almost weekly basis.

The projects housed many nonworking people. In some, designated for senior citizens, residents were receiving Social Security and other retirement payments; many households supported primarily by welfare payments occupied the others. Yet despite the lack of local jobs and the high concentration of welfare recipients, the projects also housed many working people. Two activists in a local community organization described the kinds of jobs held by people in this neighborhood.

Field Notes: Mr. Dawkins said that he was a bus driver for the city: "People think everybody in Projectville is on welfare, but there's a lot more working-class people here, blue-collar workers, than people realize." I then asked what kinds of jobs they had. Mrs. Waters said, "We have a lot of government workers: postal workers, transit workers."

The households of the youths we interviewed in Projectville included both those supported primarily by transfer payments and those supported by stable government blue-collar jobs. Zap Andrews lived with both parents, and their household was supported by his father's job as a city bus driver. Jerry Barnes's parents were separated, and he moved between them; his father was a transit worker, and his mother worked as a data entry operator for a city agency. Another youth interviewed, the slightly older Sky Wilson, a resident of a different project, lived with his aunt in a household supported by his uncle's job as a hotel manager. Only one respondent grew up in a family supported by factory work: Steve Johnson's father held a skilled job in a factory. These households had the highest incomes.

Four other youths lived in households headed by females who worked in low-wage health and clerical jobs. Tommy and Johnny Singleton's mother worked as a home attendant, caring for a disabled elderly person. Their household was also receiving Social Security benefits following the death of their father, who had worked many years as a cook. Stan Williams lived with his mother, a secretary for the telephone company. Juice Baker, a neighbor and contemporary of Sky Wilson, lived with his mother, who worked in a day-care center. None of these households had ever received welfare payments.

The other youths in this group came from households that were totally or partially supported by welfare. Ben and Harold Bivins and Sly Landers all reported having grown up with their mothers on welfare budgets. Landers, who was twenty-four years old, had grown up in one of the few private houses in Projectville; his mother had collected welfare when he was a child, but he had lived on his own since the age of fifteen. Lucky Giles lived with his mother on a welfare budget for years, though during the fieldwork period she had found a job as a home attendant (through the Singletons' mother) and was no longer receiving welfare. Larry Jefferson lived with his mother, who received welfare payments only for the children; she herself was not "on the budget" because she held a part-time job as an elevator attendant in the projects. Reggie Hawkins was raised by his mother's parents, who received welfare payments; his grandfather was also paid some money by the small church in which he preached.

The first attempts of these youths to find jobs were more delayed and also more unsuccessful than were those of youths in the other two neighborhoods. This pattern of delayed job search was related both to their long-term educational and occupational aspirations and to the striking paucity of jobs for teenagers in this neighborhood. Most of these youths were about sixteen when we first contacted them, and almost the only employment any of them had had or even sought consisted of government-subsidized summer youth jobs. They had much less knowledge of and contact with the private labor market than those in either La Barriada or Hamilton Park. When asked whether they wanted jobs, most said that they did but went on to say that their families were encouraging them to stay in school rather than seek full-time work. Even as they became more involved in the labor market over the next few years, the commitment to schooling continued to influence their attitudes toward looking for and retaining jobs throughout their teens.

As noted in Chapter 3, the influence of schooling on labor market aspirations in this neighborhood group was greater than in either of the other two. They aspired more to white-collar and service jobs than to skilled blue-collar work, in contrast to the youths in the other neighborhoods. Such jobs frequently require more schooling and school credentials than blue-collar jobs. These aspirations reflected in part the kinds of jobs already held by those adults in their neighborhood who were working. Their commitment to schooling was also related to persistent themes in their popular culture, as expressed in the speeches of political leaders and in the "rap" music that was beginning to appear at this time.

Still, these youths did want part-time work and expressed great dissatisfaction with the lack of local opportunities.

Johnny Singleton: There ain't no social programs, no after-school programs, no part-time jobs, no nothing out there that could keep you off the streets.

Some older males from this neighborhood whom we also interviewed, men in their middle and late twenties, spoke of the decline in job opportunities for teenagers. They related this decline to the disappearance of the local retail businesses and to the increasing separation between the owners of those businesses that did remain and the residents of the projects. One such individual, twenty-eight years old, told us how different the situation had been when he moved there as a child.

We were one of the first black families on the block. This was before they had even built some of the projects, and some of the others were brand new. When I was little, there were lots of stores around the subway stop, and all the people in the stores knew all the little kids. I used to work for the newsstand on the corner, running little errands here and there. The guy who ran it knew my mother, and he knew me since I was little, so it was no problem. Now, most of those stores, and the houses where we used to live too, are all burned down. There's thousands of kids in the projects now and no place for them to work.

A twenty-five-year-old related similar experiences:

I used to work in the supermarkets as a kid, but it's harder now. Arabs took over a lot of the stores, and they don't hire community people. A guy around my way got his store burned down just the other day. That wouldn't happen so much if they would hire community people. But everybody's afraid of these kids now. We used to carry people's groceries home for tips, but now they're afraid you'll rob them.

Two youths among our primary respondents recounted their experiences with trying to find work in Projectville's dwindling retail section.

One of Stan Williams's first employment experiences had been sweeping out a small store when he was sixteen.

> *Stan Williams:* I tried to get some jobs, but they wasn't like real jobs. It was like sweeping out a store, like that, not a real job.
> *Interviewer:* How much would you make?
> *S.W.:* Oh, about twenty dollars. They used to pay me by the week. Every day when they get ready to close up, I come by and sweep the place out.
> *Int.:* How did you get the job?
> *S.W.:* I just walked by and said, "Yo, can I sweep in your yard, mop or something?" I said, "Whatever you are willing to pay, I'll take it." So he said it wouldn't be no real job like that, and I said, "Ah, I'll take it." But then the store burnt down.

Larry Jefferson reported that he had tried to get part-time jobs in these stores but could not because hiring usually depended on a family connection.

> *Larry Jefferson:* The only way I could find a job is, like, if I know somebody, 'cause most of these people who work in the stores around there, they know somebody. Mostly they hire Puerto Ricans, like mostly they family and stuff. There's this one store, Lady's, her whole family works there. There ain't nobody who works in that store that she don't know, like they all family, uncles, cousins, and stuff.

The members of this group in fact reported less employment during their middle teens than did the members of either of the other two neighborhood cliques, and the employment they did report was the most restricted in type. Before the age of sixteen, only two of them had had any sort of regular private job. At fourteen, Larry Jefferson had worked part-time for a few weeks sweeping out a flower store in a distant neighborhood where his aunt lived—his aunt had introduced him to the florist—but the job ended when the store went out of business. When Ben Bivins was fifteen, he obtained a job in a factory, also in a distant neighborhood, through a friend who was twenty years old and already employed there. Ben himself lied about his age to obtain the job and worked twenty-five hours a week at minimum wage for three months during the summer. He professed satisfaction with the job while he was doing it but also said that it had been hard physical work that he did not want to do all his life. At the end of the summer his friend was fired for being absent too often, and Bivins then quit to return to school.

[76]

With these exceptions, the employment reported by this group before the age of seventeen consisted either of errands for older local residents or of government-subsidized summer youth jobs. Two youths who reported packing and delivering groceries undertook these errands on their own behalf; they did not have regular jobs with the grocery stores but simply waited in front of the few local supermarkets and offered their services to the customers—often senior citizens and mothers with small children—coming out of the stores. Zap Andrews reported this as his only employment before he was seventeen. He said that he had been able to make about $75 a week this way, working for several hours a day after school and on the weekends. He worked that much only for one three-week period, however, after which he worked only "off and on." Reggie Hawkins said he made at most $45 a week delivering groceries periodically between the ages of fourteen and seventeen.

Larry Jefferson reported having devised a kind of makeshift paper route when he was fifteen. He solicited individual residents of his building—generally elderly people who had trouble getting out—and brought them newspapers, adding a dime or fifteen cents to the price of the paper. He kept this up for a few weeks, however—until he decided that it did not bring in enough money.

These youths also found a few odd jobs. Since they lived in public housing, they did not have access to the kind of part-time building superintendent and repair jobs provided by the small private landlords in La Barriada, but Zap Andrews reported that he occasionally assisted one of the Housing Authority maintenance workers.

Zap Andrews: I used to help the maintenance man. I always helped on payday. They don't really like to work on payday. Like, the day they get paid, he'd say, "You clean this side of the steps and sweep down, I give you twenty dollars." You should see those steps, garbage all around. Take all the garbage and put it in one big bag, take it down, then come back up. Sweep down, then do the back steps, and that's the worst steps, got to take about two big bags, sweep down, then cut out.

Tommy Singleton reported helping an older man in his building to fix up his apartment. The man paid him for the work, and he also gave him money on other occasions just because he was a friend of the family.

Government-subsidized summer youth jobs accounted for most of the employment experiences among this group before they reached the age of seventeen. Half of these youths worked in such jobs during the summers when they were fifteen and sixteen years old—the first jobs most of them had ever held. Tommy and Johnny Singleton found summer youth jobs when they were fifteen, and these remained their only regular employment until they reached seventeen. Lucky Giles and Jerry Barnes held such jobs for two summers, when they were fifteen and sixteen, their only employment up to that time. Giles had no further work until he was eighteen, and Barnes had still not had any other jobs when last contacted at age twenty. Sky Wilson's summer youth job at the age of fourteen was his first, though he had had two other jobs by the time he was seventeen.

Because the last of this government-subsidized work had occurred the summer before we contacted these youths, we did not observe or interview our primary respondents during the period they actually held these jobs. We did observe some other summer youth workers, however, and our observations accorded with our primary respondents' descriptions of their experiences. Most of the work was performed in crews supervised by slightly older residents of the projects, and usually within the local neighborhood. The youths signed up for the jobs at the schools or at the community center of their project.

The summer youth employment programs were in fact the principal services offered to teenagers at such centers, which otherwise provided very little in the way of either recreation or employment services. Many of our observations and interviews suggest that the isolation of these job programs from established workplace settings was also accompanied by widely varied standards of behavior and strictness of supervision. We observed some summer youth work crews engaged in activities that differed little from those of nonworkers. Jerry Barnes reported irregular attendance at his job: "You don't have to show up, but if you want to get paid, you show up." Others reported being paid for hours not worked and explicitly stated their perception that summer youth jobs were not "real" jobs.

Field Notes: I talked to a female member of one of the youth crews. She was talking to one of her friends by the benches and didn't seem to be working, although she said that she was. She said that she was hired as a junior counselor in the manpower center, but she has never performed those duties. Instead, she is asked to pick up paper and sweep. She insists that she wants to work under her job title and not as an orderly.

She boasted about getting paid and not showing at all. No one checks the time cards. She said that no one enjoys working there because it's boring and disorganized. No one knows who is responsible for what. She says that it is known to the individual that he or she can't get fired from the job because the purpose behind giving school kids these summer jobs is to keep them out of trouble and off the streets. She said that summer jobs should have a full seven-hour day doing something worthwhile, getting experience, and, most of all, doing something interesting.

Most work assignments among our primary respondents were of two types: taking care of younger children, and cleaning up the projects and public areas of the neighborhood. The child-care jobs involved taking children, often their own siblings and neighbors, to public swimming pools or simply playing basketball with them right on the same basketball court in the projects where they themselves played every day of the year. They were familiar with these routines, since they had themselves been cared for in this manner only a few years before.

Some youths did report working regularly and learning something. Harold Bivins said that he improved his ability to deal with children during the course of his summer counseling job. Tommy Singleton's summer youth job experience had differed from those of his friends because he had been assigned to work in the offices of a hospital rather than with a youth crew in the projects. He had worked as a file clerk in the context of an established office routine and supervisory structure where his co-workers did not include other holders of summer youth jobs. He said that he had to show up regularly and that his supervisors checked his work.

During the summer of our direct observations of this group, however, most of them were sixteen and seventeen years old, out of school, and unemployed. Some had tried too late to sign up for summer youth jobs and were attempting unsuccessfully to find work. Others were actively involved in street crime and seeking work only occasionally or not at all; by the end of the summer, several of these had gotten into trouble and had been removed from the community. Larry Jefferson, then fifteen, and Johnny Singleton, sixteen, went off to residential youth homes that September and returned only on weekends for the next two years. Ben Bivins and Lucky Giles, age seventeen, and Jerry Barnes, sixteen, had all been sentenced to prison by the following December and were subsequently absent from the neighborhood for periods of eighteen to twenty-four months. During his second year in the youth home, Johnny Singleton worked part time at a supermarket in the upstate community where the home was located. Giles, Jefferson, Barnes, and Bivins had no contact with the private labor market while they were institutionalized.

Those who remained in the neighborhood reported increasing their attempts to find work, with occasional success but considerable frustration. As they began to look for work more actively, they extended their job search beyond the local neighborhood and sought not only part-time but full-time employment. All had interrupted their schooling by this time, though some would continue their efforts to obtain further schooling and training. They had not abandoned their early aspirations to acquire school credentials and go into government and white-collar jobs but were preoccupied at this point with securing an immediate and regular source of income.

These youths entered the period of work establishment with fewer personal connections to jobs than those in either of the other neighborhoods. Theirs was the most physically isolated from centers of employment; many of their parents had no jobs at all, and those parents who were employed tended to work in government jobs that recruited by bureaucratic means more than through personal networks. Both Stan Williams and Juice Baker expressed their frustration over lack of family connections to jobs.

Interviewer: Doesn't your mother have friends at work or somebody in the projects who has a job connection?
Stan Williams: No.
Int.: Maybe other family members, cousins?
S.W.: I wish I did have an uncle or cousins or somebody like that. The only people I got up here, it's only my mother and eight of us. The rest is down south.

Juice Baker: A lot of jobs have labels on them, nobody knows what they do. "We're looking for a GMP." All right, fine, what's a GMP? Nobody knows and nobody gets the job, unless your father works for the company and knows what GMP stands for; then you get in. That's all it is, a family thing.
Interviewer: Do you know people who have gotten jobs that way?
J.B.: Yeah, a few. I've tried for Amtrak and different things. Basically, they're family. The uncle will recommend his nephew, and that's it.

Without family connections even to low-paying jobs, these youths had to rely on more impersonal methods. Their continuing efforts to obtain school and training credentials represented one impersonal means of finding jobs. Another was applying for work through both public and private employment agencies.

The Projectville youths relied on newspaper ads and employment agencies to a much greater degree than youths in the other neighborhoods. Stan Williams, Zap Andrews, Reggie Hawkins, and Tommy Singleton reported going to private employment agencies, which charged a fee—usually $54—to supply a job. The youths generally borrowed the money for the fee from their parents. They referred to this way of finding work as "buying a job," but this method turned out to be expensive and frustrating and rarely led to jobs that they considered desirable.

Stan Williams reported having gotten four separate jobs through private employment agencies during the year when he was eighteen. He had been out of school without actively seeking work for two years before that and had begun to look seriously for work when his girlfriend became pregnant. The agency sent him first to a messenger job. He stayed at the job for six months but then left because he found that he was expected to work ten hours a day for eight hours' pay. After that, the agency sent him to three separate factory jobs, none of which lasted more than a few days: in two cases he was laid off almost immediately (but still forfeited his agency fee), and he quit the third because he felt uncomfortable working in a place where no one else spoke English. Between these jobs he made several trips to other addresses supplied by the agency, only to find when he arrived that there were no openings. These experiences had left him thoroughly dissatisfied with the agency.

> *Interviewer:* You say you only worked one day at that job; you didn't have to pay the fifty-four dollars to the agency, did you?
> *Stan Williams:* Yes.
> *Int.:* So you lost money on the job?
> *S.W.:* Yeah. The agency is crazy. That's why I'm not buying no more job. . . . I wish somebody would investigate them, as much money as they gypped out of me.

The longest-lasting job obtained through an employment agency by a Projectville respondent was reported by Reggie Hawkins. He went to work as a stock clerk shortly after he received his General Equivalency Diploma. He stayed there for six months, found the work acceptable, and left only to move to California to live with relatives and attend a community college.

The Projectville youths generally did not seek factory work, nor did they remain long when they did happen to find it. The preferred jobs in the clerical and service sectors, and employers in those sectors also appeared to recruit them more than did manufacturing employers. These youths knew very few older people in their own neighborhood who worked at manufacturing jobs, and their schooling experiences were concentrated in academic programs that stressed language and math rather than manual skills. Even those who had not finished high school, as most had not when they first began job hunting, were sufficiently literate to read and handle the forms, addresses, and labels that they would be required to manage in clerical and service jobs.

Five youths in this group held factory jobs briefly while still in their

[81]

teens but none for more than six months. Relatively short tenure at most jobs was generally the case for youths at these ages in all three neighborhoods, but the Projectville youths had particularly short and uncomfortable experiences with factory employment. They suffered frequent layoffs from both factory and clerical work, and some lost both kinds of jobs because they were unfamiliar with workplace discipline, especially with regard to lateness and absenteeism. They found themselves particularly unsuited to factory jobs, however, not only because the work was frequently hard, boring, and poorly paid but also because they encountered a variety of exploitative working conditions and a workforce of immigrants whose language they did not share.

The Projectville youths who reported factory jobs were Ben Bivins, Stan Williams, Tommy Singleton, Steve Johnson, and Juice Baker. Bivins worked part time for a summer when he was fifteen; he reported satisfaction with the job at the time but no desire to do factory work in the future. Stan Williams was laid off from two factory jobs and quit a third because the take-home pay was too low—$79 after taxes and check-cashing fees—and also "because mostly Puerto Ricans were there. The foreman was a Puerto Rican, too. There were a few black guys there, but they was like older men."

Juice Baker worked in a factory when he was nineteen. He had left college a few months earlier and first sought office work. Only after he was unable to find clerical work did he take a factory job, which he found through a Latino acquaintance. He quit after six months because the job required him to commute to New Jersey and because of language differences.

Juice Baker: I worked at that about six months . . . minimum wage, two something. . . . Traveling was too much, so I had to let that go.
Interviewer: How long a trip?
J.B.: Two hours each way. They had a bus that went straight to the company.
Int.: Did you have to pay for the bus?
J.B.: Yes, you did. It was a regular bus. Plus nobody in there could understand me. A lot of Puerto Ricans and Spanish work there.
Int.: Did the foreman speak Spanish too?
J.B.: Everybody! It's not funny, you know, they thought I was Spanish. No women, and all Spanish males, so I split.

Tommy Singleton worked for six months loading trucks in a garment factory when he was eighteen. He "bought" the job through an agency but quit the day after he was notified that he had passed his GED examination, because "I figured I could get something better now." Only Steve Johnson reported any satisfaction with factory work. His father got him into the factory where he himself worked. His son was put on as an apprentice to a skilled job, but the factory had to lay him off shortly after he was hired.

Clerical and service sector jobs accounted for most of these youths' increasing but still scarce employment during their late teens. These jobs also paid low wages—minimum or slightly above—and offered little employment security. The youths also frequently quit or were fired for absence. Nonetheless, the Projectville youths generally preferred these jobs and cited them when asked what kind of employment they thought they could get. Other workers there were more likely to be young, black, and English-speaking like themselves.

These jobs included selling food, working on delivery trucks, working in stores, and serving as security guards. Most prevalent were messenger jobs in the downtown business districts. None of these paid much above minimum wage, but they varied considerably in the hours of work they provided and in whether or not they paid on-the-books. Some even evolved from part-time and off-the-books to full-time and/or on-the-books jobs.

Two youths managed to find service sector work in their own neighborhood while they were still seventeen. Tommy Singleton was interviewed several times during the year following his summer of unemployment. He told of repeated attempts to find work through newspaper advertisements and by going to messenger agencies in the central business district. He said, "I want a job so bad right now, I could climb the walls." He heard about one company that was hiring security guards. Even though he was below the minimum age of eighteen, he went to apply for the job with the intention of lying about his age. He withdrew his application when he heard employees in the office complaining about not being paid on time. During this period he was sporadically attending an alternative high school. After more than a year of periodic searching, he finally found a summer job in a local supermarket when he was seventeen; he got it through his older sister, who had started there a few months before. He left the job after the summer in order to return to school. Lucky Giles also found his first nonsubsidized job that summer, between being arrested and being sent to prison a few months later. He got it by the simple expedient of asking the driver of a delivery truck passing through the neighborhood.

Lucky Giles: I met him on the street. He was riding around, going from store to store and he went by my store.

[83]

Interviewer: What store?
L.G.: Candy store, right where I live at. I seen him there. . . . "Can I have a job, you need any help" He said yeah.

Giles held the job for four months. He worked four days a week and was paid $100 a week, off-the-books. When he returned from prison two years later, he had difficulty finding work and remembered this job favorably: "That was an all right job. I wish I could get it back now."

Two others found work in furniture stores located in an adjacent neighborhood that supported more retail activity than Projectville did. Zap Andrews worked there for his cousin for a few months, and Sly Landers got a job through a friend who lived near the store. In both cases they were paid off-the-books and worked only part time on an "as needed" basis. Andrews finally left the job because his cousin's business was not doing well and the work became more and more infrequent. He had been earning at most $72 per week, and he had to wait by the telephone in order to be available when needed. Andrews was still only seventeen at the time and busily exploring different job options, albeit with frequent spells of unemployment. Landers was already twenty-four when interviewed and had been drifting back and forth for years between low-level legitimate work and low-level "jobs" in the street drug trade.

As they began to reach the age of eighteen, most of these youths sought work outside their own neighborhood. Zap Andrews had more personal connections than his friends because his father was the minister of a small church in addition to working regularly as a bus driver. After he left his cousin's furniture store, Andrews found two subsequent jobs that year through members of his father's church. The first of these was delivering clothes for a dry cleaner in an affluent neighborhood. He worked part time and "on call" for a few weeks at this job until they began to offer him a full week's work; then he could earn $135 per week, off-the-books. He stayed at it steadily for six months but was laid off when the business changed hands. After that, he was unemployed for two months before he was hired by another church member to work as a security guard in a newly renovated apartment building. The job paid only minimum wage, but it paid on-the-books, and he was able to work many hours' overtime. He stayed only three weeks, however; he quit after a close call when a burglar fired at him and killed the guard dog which, along with a billy club and handcuffs, provided his only protection.

Zap Andrews: He was trying to kill us. He killed the dog. Then he must have run out of shells. When he got finished shootin', I ran out of there. I said, "I gotta quit. My life is worth more than money."

Several other Projectville youths also mentioned older brothers and friends who held security guard jobs and said that they knew where they could get such work when they reached eighteen. These were the jobs they mentioned most often after messenger work, but they also feared the risks involved. Besides, they themselves had had occasional run-ins with security guards and were accustomed to taunting them as "toy cops."

After that experience, Andrews was again unemployed for several weeks; he did work for one day as a messenger but quit because it was outside work in bitterly cold weather. Then he was called back to the dry cleaning shop by the new owners. They offered him a steady job, full time and on-the-books, and he worked for them during the next three years, delivering clothes from the shop and also working in the plant in an industrial neighborhood.

Other Projectville respondents also reported undergoing trial periods and shape-ups, in which they lined up for work on a daily "first come, first hired" basis. Juice Baker was working for a maintenance company when interviewed; he had to show up each morning by six o'clock to have a chance to work. Sly Landers had worked frequently for a temporary agency that supplied maintenance crews as well as loaders. Both Baker and Landers said that they had to put in a regular appearance for at least two weeks before the agency began to assign them work every day. Landers had become a "regular," getting work daily for a six-month period. Baker never reached that status; because he missed work one day after he had begun to get regular work, he had to start all over again.

As this group accumulated experience in job hunting, they began to develop limited personal job networks, sharing information about employment agencies and jobs. These were most often peer rather than parental networks and connected them primarily to low-paying clerical and service sector jobs, including some of the messenger jobs that were the most prevalent type of work for this group during their late teens and early twenties. Six of the respondents reported working as messengers during this period, although none of them stayed at it very long. Most of them reported initial satisfaction with the work; in good weather they enjoyed being free of a restrictive office or factory atmosphere, but cold weather, low wages, and small chance for advancement cooled their enthusiasm. Reggie Harrison reported the longest period of messenger work, about eighteen months, starting when he was nineteen. He first worked a full year for a company that paid him a regular salary. Then he was fired for stealing a check but immediately found a similar job, which he had held for another six months when last interviewed. Juice Baker was fired from a messenger job because he carried a loud radio into a bank to which he was making a delivery. The others all quit after a few months at most. Lucky Giles left after two weeks because he was getting married and $50 a week was too little. Stan Williams refused to do ten hours' work for eight hours' pay. Zap Andrews found the weather too cold and the pay too low. Sky Wilson worked for the summer and then quit.

Despite his frequent spells of unemployment, Zap Andrews reported the most work during his late teens, primarily as a result of his dry cleaning job. Some had had short spells of nonsubsidized employment; others were institutionalized during this period. When this latter group returned to Projectville, they ranged in age from eighteen to twenty. As they began to seek work, they also relied on impersonal channels, usually public and non-profit employment agencies serving ex-offenders rather than the private agencies described earlier.

These men also preferred clerical and service sector jobs. Ben Bivins earned his GED and a typing certificate in prison. Returning to Projectville at nineteen, he went to an ex-offender employment service for counseling and further skills training. After he increased his typing speed, the agency placed him as a clerk typist, and he worked steadily for the next eighteen months.

Johnny Singleton, who had worked in a supermarket after school while he was living in a youth home outside the city, also returned at nineteen; he found work as a supervisor in a youth program for the summer but had trouble getting work for several months after that. He then enrolled in an employment program run by a settlement house in a distant neighborhood. He attended punctually and regularly and was one of the five of eighteen students in his class to finish the program, which then placed him as a mail sorter in a private company. He did not like the job but stayed at it for several months, longer than most of the workers who started there. His counselor from the settlement house eventually referred him to a job he much preferred; the pay was the same, but he enjoyed making deliveries for a charitable organization.

Lucky Giles also found work through an ex-offender employment program. He returned at nineteen and had no work for several months. He entered the program when he was twenty and was referred to a factory job paying more than six dollars an hour. He was fired for being absent and then went through three different jobs in the next four months: he tried delivering groceries, being a messenger, and doing maintenance in a nursing home. Unable to make more than $50 a week at the first two jobs, he quit because he had gotten married and needed to earn more; the nursing home job lasted only three days during a strike. When last contacted, however, he had been working steadily in a meat market for several weeks.

By the end of the research period this group had made widely varying adjustments to the labor market. Larry Jefferson and Jerry Barnes had found little work after their return from institutions; at age twenty, both were still trying to finish high school and had had very little employment. Ben Bivins was returned to upstate prison after working as a clerk typist during his eighteen months on parole. Juice Baker was given a multi-year sentence for transporting heroin, and Sky Wilson was making $50,000 a year selling cocaine. The others were either seeking jobs or doing clerical or service work that paid slightly above minimum wage.

The most successful of the group in the legitimate labor market were Reggie Hawkins and Tommy Singleton. Hawkins returned from California and resumed steady work as a messenger. Tommy Singleton, after receiving his GED, quit his factory job and entered a public college. Finding that he could not afford the textbooks, he left college and found a clerical job with a prestigious business school. He did well there and was granted free tuition for night study in a business course. At the end of our study period he had been working steadily and attending night classes for several months.

Hamilton Park

The housing stock in Hamilton Park was the oldest among the three neighborhoods studied, predating even the old tenements in La Barriada. Like those in La Barriada, the residences of the Hamilton Park youths were in physical proximity to a large concentration of factories and warehouses. Unlike the section of La Barriada we studied, however, the central section of Hamilton Park also contained a thriving retail section. Moreover, the factories, stores, other businesses, and residences, though densely interspersed, were generally well maintained and had seen relatively little turnover in occupation and management in recent years. The two neighborhoods also differed greatly in the social integration of residents and businesses. Local businesses in Hamilton Park provided significant employment to local residents; in addition, neighborhood-based job networks connected local residents to desirable blue-collar jobs throughout the metropolitan labor market.

Many of the residents were third- and fourth-generation descendants of the original settlers of the neighborhood, labor migrants from Europe.

[87]

Their housing had originally been built for workers in local factories, but the parents of the youths we interviewed generally did not work in the low-wage assembly jobs in the factories; these were held by more recent Latino and also Polish labor migrants.

Most of the families of the youths we studied were among the more established and better employed in the neighborhood. Their households were supported primarily by the earnings of an adult male from a high-paying, unionized, blue-collar job. Many of these men had worked in the factories when they were younger, before they managed to obtain the better jobs they currently held and had held for fifteen or twenty years. The father of Otto and Brian Deutsch and both of John Gutski's parents were unionized office maintenance workers in the downtown business areas. Barney and Teddy Haskell's father was a unionized heavy equipment operator. David Henry's father worked for a major beverage company. Charlie Gaberewski's father had a college diploma in electronics and worked for a communications company. Carl Pollini's father was a unionized mechanic. None of these youths' mothers except John Gutski's worked full time.

Three other youths came from poorer families that did not depend primarily on the income of an adult male. Peter Murphy's and George Peplinski's fathers were deceased. Murphy's mother was a unionized secretary in a local factory; Peplinski's, a secretary in a Manhattan office. Brian Grady lived with both parents, but his father was unemployed at the time of our research and had spent many years in prison; his mother worked in a local restaurant. Nevertheless, in striking contrast to those in the other two neighborhoods, none of these families were on welfare. The only household receiving any form of transfer payment was that of Pete and Tony Calderone, whose father received disability payments after many years of working at a unionized maintenance job.

Although factory employment was not the major source of income in these households, the factories did provide a significant amount of employment to local residents. Women and young people were more likely to work in the local factories than the adult men, who tended to go outside the neighborhood for higher-paying blue-collar jobs. Two of the mothers of the youths we interviewed worked at clerical jobs in the factory offices: Peter Murphy's mother full time; the Calderones' mother part time, at night and seasonally, in order to supplement their father's disability payments. The factories also hired teenage boys and young men in their twenties in jobs that ranged from part-time, off-the-books employment to jobs as supervisors, loaders, and forklift operators, which paid much better than the assembly jobs usually held by recent immigrants, documented and undocumented.

Since these youths generally came from families that were not as poor as those in the other two neighborhoods, their early job search was not prompted by extreme economic need. None of them, for example, sought work when they were teenagers in order to provide for basic household subsistence, as some did in La Barriada. Nonetheless, most of them did begin some kind of work by the age of fourteen. Money was sometimes needed to provide for the child's personal needs. Otto and Brian Deutsch undertook a paper route when they were twelve and thirteen.

> *Interviewer:* What did you do with the money?
> *Brian Deutsch:* At first my mother would say, "Let me hold it for you." And I'd ask for it say a week later, and then she'd say things like "I bought you underwear and socks 'cause you needed underwear and socks," and I'd say, "I hate underwear and socks." She used to always do that.

Even in families that were better off, the sons began work early. The Haskell family owned several pieces of property in the neighborhood, but as Barney Haskell said, "We really don't have to work, but in our family we all do. It's just kinda expected."

In fact, all these youths reported having had at least some employment by the age of fourteen. Most early employment opportunities came to them through their families, though the local newspaper and neighborhood word-of-mouth also helped. Often, the work consisted of a few days' light construction or cleaning for local businesses. Otto and Brian Deutsch and Teddy Haskell all reported a few weeks' work when they were twelve and thirteen years old, removing cobblestones from neighborhood demolition sites owned by a local resident. They simply responded to an ad saying "Boys Wanted" and were paid $35 off-the-books for a six-hour day. Charlie Gaberewski reported making $2.10 per hour off-the-books to stack materials in a nearby factory when he was fourteen. The others all described various jobs at around this age which they referred to as "one-day, temp things" in local businesses. Sometimes the work was in fact quite hard and dirty, and they quit within a few days.

Besides these odd jobs, several reported working steadily on a part-time or even full-time basis in local businesses during the summers and before and after school—or in lieu of school while they were still of school age. The more regular work came to them almost exclusively through family connections. George Peplinski described his first full-time summer job.

> *George Peplinski:* When I was fifteen, I had just started to drink beer with my friends, so my mother says to me, "What are you gonna do,

stay drunk all summer? Why don't you get a job?" So she sent me over
to a factory where a friend of hers worked, and they gave me a job. I
worked there all summer, full time. It was funny, I was the youngest
one there.

This job, like most of the others during this period, was off-the-books.
John Gutski was only thirteen when he started at the bakery where his
brother-in-law worked. He began at $2.00 an hour, part time and off-
the-books, but he worked there on and off for the next four years. By the
time he was seventeen he was full time, on-the-books, in the union, and
making $8.00 an hour. David Henry worked during the summer when
he was fourteen at his father's beverage company, a large corporation.
He worked on-the-books but with no taxes withheld because he was still
in school. He left school when he was sixteen, went to work full time in
an auto repair shop owned by his brother-in-law, and stayed for three
and a half years, during which time his wages went from $2.00 to $8.00
an hour, all off-the-books.

Teddy and Barney Haskell both obtained regular part-time work
through a friend of their father, a man who owned a local warehouse and
was also active in local politics. Teddy distributed campaign flyers for
$2.00 an hour when he was thirteen. Both brothers also worked in the
warehouse before and after school when they were fifteen and sixteen.
Otto and Brian Deutsch reported two off-the-books, part-time jobs
apiece when they were fifteen and sixteen, all in nearby small businesses. Both sets of brothers reported handing down jobs from older to
younger brother: when the older tired of the work or found a better job,
the younger brother inherited the previous one.

Jobs also circulated through friendship networks. Brian Grady began
working at an auto repair shop in the neighborhood at the age of thirteen
and stayed on until he was sixteen. He got the job because the employer
was a friend of his mother. During this time his wages increased from
$2.00 to $8.00 an hour, although always off-the-books and only part time.
After he left, the job went to his friend Peter Murphy.

When jobs were obtained through family connections, employers
sometimes assumed an avuncular attitude toward the young employees.
Barney Haskell reported that the warehouse owner once interceded on
his behalf and obtained his release when he had been arrested. When
Brian Grady worked at the auto repair shop, his employer used to
monitor and insist on his school attendance.

As in the other two neighborhoods, there was considerable variation
in how well the Hamilton Park youths performed as workers. Some
stayed in the same job for as much as three years during their early and

middle teens, but most jobs lasted a few days to a few months at most. As in the other neighborhoods, most youth jobs were offered only on a temporary basis and terminated by layoffs. Several youths in this group were also fired from early jobs. Otto Deutsch lost a factory job because his employer thought he had been bringing his girlfriend in at night. Charlie Gaberewski was fired from part-time work as a stock clerk for sleeping, and shortly thereafter he lost a similar job for dropping a large crate full of fragile goods. Peter Murphy lost his auto repair job after a fight with his boss and later retaliated by burglarizing the shop.

These youths also frequently quit after a day or two because they were not prepared to engage in hard, dirty work. When he was thirteen, Brian Deutsch got a job with a local employer for whom his mother had once worked.

Brian Deutsch: My mother used to work in his donut shop from like two to four in the morning. The same people also own a factory down over there. I worked for them at the time for like two dollars an hour and we'd work like eleven, twelve-hour days. Man, they would bust our asses. I worked like three days. One day we were working all day in the factory, cleaning it up and loading and unloading trucks. It's like seven o'clock, we figure we're done, we've been there since eight o'clock. We leave, right, we always get a ride home in the guy's car. We get in the car and he takes us over to a different factory he owns. It's a syrup factory and we gotta clean the floor. The syrup is like an inch and a half thick on the floor and we gotta clean the floor. It was psycho, man. So the next day was Christmas Eve morning and I'm walking with my brother over to his job at the florist and we stop and smoke a joint and that was it. I never went back.

When these youths quit their jobs, however, they did so with a great deal more security than was possible for those from the other two neighborhoods. Because their families were generally better off, they could more easily afford to be without work. Several reported quitting summer jobs because they wanted to spend more time at the beach, where many of their families owned summer bungalows. They also quit either to take better jobs or with more assurance that they would be able to replace the job when they needed work again. During one period of unemployment Teddy Haskell claimed that he knew "a place where I can get a job paying $4.25 an hour tomorrow, but they bust your balls there." The relative abundance of job opportunities in this neighborhood meant that job-seeking youths, even while they were still of school age and confined to the youth labor market, had a certain amount of latitude to compare and choose between jobs on the basis of wages and working conditions. A few reported periods when they had difficulty finding work, but most of them had had several jobs by the time they reached the age of eighteen, in sharp contrast to the overall experience of the other two neighborhood groups.

The single most striking contrast between mid-teen jobs in Hamilton Park and those in the other two neighborhoods, however, was that the Hamilton Park group did not report a single government-subsidized summer youth job, whereas some of the La Barriada group had held such jobs and the Projectville group had had little other employment before they reached the age of eighteen. Youth work in Hamilton Park was almost completely supplied by private employers. The only employment secured outside localized job networks during the mid-teen years was reported by Peter Murphy; he was heavily involved with drugs and found one job through a special school and another through a drug program. Neither job was subsidized, however.

As they reached the age of eighteen, these youths—like the others— both began to look more intensively for work and became eligible for a much wider pool of jobs. They could work full time and on-the-books in the factories, and some of them did, though they regarded the low-wage assembly jobs as less than desirable. Most were hoping eventually to find their way into the high-paying jobs held by their fathers and older brothers. Entry to these often requires a waiting period, even with personal connections, but some youths found their way immediately into these desirable jobs, while others alternated between lower-paying, on-the-books work and periods of unemployment, during which they collected unemployment compensation. George Peplinski described the variations.

> *George Peplinski:* One friend of mine just went out and got himself a good job on the docks.
> *Interviewer:* Those are pretty scarce nowadays, aren't they?
> *G.P.:* Yeah, but his father took him over and talked to a guy he had been in the Merchant Marine with years ago and got him signed up. He was lucky. That's what most of these guys want, a job like that. A lot of them are just hanging out now, drinking and getting high all summer, or else they're still holding on to their little supermarket job or whatever, just waiting for the day they get into that high-paying union job.

One kind of employment traditional for males of this age in this neighborhood is the military. Many of the men in their late twenties who frequented the same bars as did the eighteen- and nineteen-year-olds we interviewed were Vietnam veterans. Two of our group had joined up at the age of seventeen. Barney Haskell had been in the Marines and Brian Deutsch in the Army, but neither one had finished his tour of duty; both had been discipline problems and were discharged early.

As noted in Chapter 3, school credentials played a limited role in this neighborhood in channeling local youths into desirable blue-collar jobs. Tony Calderone graduated from the local vocational-technical high school with his certificate in plumbing and moved directly into an apprenticeship that carried with it yearly wage increases of a dollar an hour. Teddy Haskell's father kept urging him to go back to school because Teddy would need a high school diploma in order to activate his father's connections into a construction union. Carl Pollini found an electrician's job through a friend who had found the job through his shop teacher.

Charlie Gaberewski was the only one in this group who reported finding any sort of job through an employment agency. He went to a private agency the week before he finished high school and found a job as a mail clerk which paid $5.00 an hour and offered good benefits. He liked the job well enough but soon left for work in a printing company that paid better. He had heard about it because it was located close to his previous job, and he obtained it not on the basis of his school credentials but because he had worked in his uncle's printing business while in school and had learned some printing skills.

Half of this group never finished high school, but most of the school-leavers still aspired to high-paying, unionized jobs. They relied primarily on family connections, in lieu of rather than as a supplement to school credentials. Otto and Brian Deutsch and John Gutski all failed to finish high school yet managed to get unionized building maintenance jobs before they were twenty years old. Gutski found his job through his parents, both of whom were already union members. The Deutsches' father was a member of the same union, but their direct connection came through an older brother, who brought them to work in the luxury apartment complex where he had been working for several years. None of them performed especially well in these jobs at first. Brian Deutsch was fired after a few weeks because he failed to show up regularly. His brother Otto got several reprimands as a result of spending all day on the beach and then performing erratically during the night shift, but Otto had a reputation for being very concerned with money and managed to hold onto this job. John Gutski was fired after a few weeks for fighting with his supervisor, but when we last contacted him, he had arranged an interview for another job of the same type.

Some of those who could not find their way immediately into the skilled trades did take on-the-books factory jobs paying only a little over the minimum wage. Their experiences were similar to those of the youths from the minority neighborhoods who took such jobs in their late teens; they too felt out of place working in settings where most of the other workers were recent immigrants, documented or undocumented. Pete Calderone took a part-time, on-the-books factory job paying minimum wage a few months before he finished high school and then started working full time after he graduated. He stayed at the job for a year and left after a dispute with a Spanish-speaking co-worker.

> *Pete Calderone:* I quit, just walked off the job one day, because. . . . I'm not too prejudiced, but there was a lot of Puerto Ricans, very few white people who didn't speak Spanish, you know, and like, because you're white, you're the dummy, you couldn't have a conversation with them. I used to always have trouble getting on the elevator. I'd say, "Take me here, I'm going here" and they'd say, "No, you first" to the other guy. It wasn't just one time, it happened a lot, and one day my barrels fell over or something. I said, "Shit, man" and I went to the office and said, "I quit." It wasn't a good job so I didn't care.

Although Pete Calderone referred to his co-workers as "Puerto Ricans," they may have included undocumented aliens from Central and South America as well. Other youths in this group were more explicit in drawing attention to the presence of undocumented aliens in the factories and to employers' practices of paying these persons below minimum wage and maintaining fraudulent records. Otto Deutsch described a clothing factory where he worked for six months until the business closed.

> *Otto Deutsch:* There was a lot of women, you know, machine operators, immigrants, like Polish, Portuguese, Puerto Ricans. I think a lot of them were illegal aliens, who knows? He was paying them dirt cheap, that's what I heard.

John Gutski was himself a legal resident alien who had come to Brooklyn from Poland with his parents. He spoke both Polish and English and worked for a time supervising very recent and undocumented labor migrants from Poland.

> *John Gutski:* After the bakery, I worked construction six months. It was only five dollars an hour so I took a cut, but it was better hours. I didn't

[94]

have to work at night, I could go to the beach, hang out. There was about four Polish people there, illegal aliens working on the side for cash. They were using different Social Securities, this and that. I was the boss of all of them. They couldn't speak English, I was their translator. I used to drive them around in a truck. That was an easy job. I liked it.

Nevertheless, Gutski left the job and collected unemployment for several months until he found his first union maintenance job.

The local neighborhood also offered some factory work that was considered less desirable than the skilled trades but much better than low-wage assembly; it involved heavy physical labor but paid much better than the assembly jobs. None of the youths in the core group we interviewed held such jobs, but they knew of them and treated those who held them with respect. After leaving his first factory job, Pete Calderone had spent a year and a half hanging out, drinking, and doing very little work. Tiring of that life, he then held a succession of low-paying factory jobs and had begun to yearn for better work. He envied his younger brother Tony's school success and place in the plumbers' union, lamented the fact that he had not done as well at his vocational studies, and wished that he could find a job like those held by several of his friends.

Pete Calderone: Some of my friends, they never graduated high school, some of them can't even read, a newspaper maybe but not good, and they're making decent money, nine or ten dollars an hour. These places like the freight company over here, if you can get in, they pay real good. It's hard work, ten dollars an hour, man, what I make in one week they make in a day.

Interviewer: You had some loading jobs when you were younger, didn't you?

P.C.: Yeah, but not like that, mine didn't pay like that.

Int.: What's the difference between a loading job that pays ten dollars an hour and one that pays less?

P.C.: All you do over there is load and unload trucks eight hours a day. That's all they do, and they got guys on top of you watching you all day long. Mine, you weren't working all day long. When the trucks weren't coming in you could take it easy, the boss wasn't always on your back. You need to know somebody to get into one of these trucking outfits. Very rarely you can walk up the street and they'll hire. Really, you got to know somebody to get in.

Int.: Would you take one of those jobs if you could get it?

P.C.: Yeah, I would. I'd break my back for a while for that kind of money, ten dollars an hour. I'd do it.

Although the Hamilton Park youths as a group had much richer employment histories and prospects than the other two neighborhood groups, they still found themselves facing uncertain careers due to the rapid exodus of skilled blue-collar jobs from the region. These were the jobs that had sustained the neighborhood for generations and that most of them considered the ideal type of employment. Yet Pete Calderone was not the only one who encountered difficulties in obtaining a high-paying unionized job. One of the Deutsches' older brothers complained that local factories had lately been hiring young men and then laying them off just before they had worked the six months necessary to become eligible for union membership. Others spoke of friends who had moved south and west in search of work. David Henry had gone to California, where his older brother in the Navy was stationed, though after a year working in a supermarket there, he returned to the neighborhood. John Gutski spoke of friends working in Texas and expressed a desire to join them.

The criminal involvements of the Hamilton Park youths are described in subsequent chapters, but some aspects of their crime patterns affected their patterns of employment. First, since they had more employment both in the middle teens and during the work establishment period than the other two groups, they also had much greater opportunity for theft from the workplace. Several described such activities, but none of them reported being discovered or penalized by their employers for job-related theft. They also had far less involvement in street crime and consequently far less protracted involvement with the criminal justice system: none of the Hamilton Park youths had their careers and jobs seriously interrupted by court appearances or periods of incarceration.

Several members of this group sold drugs, primarily marijuana and pills, but most did so to supplement rather than to replace legitimate employment. Toward the end of the fieldwork period, however, Teddy Haskell and Brian Grady were becoming very active in their drug sales, spending much of their time doing business in one of the local parks and either keeping other sellers out or demanding a cut. Teddy Haskell also worked during this period with a relative whose business had both a legal and an illegal side: it supplied restaurants and other small businesses but also served as a pretext for stealing cash from its customers. Teddy Haskell still expressed a desire to finish his GED and gain entrance to his father's construction union, but his increasing involvement in illegal activities and dependence on illegal income offered the possibility that he might never return to the legitimate labor market.

At the end of the fieldwork period, a few of this group had already found their way into high-paying, unionized, blue-collar jobs. A few more were working at jobs to which they were not committed and which they hoped eventually to replace with good blue-collar jobs. About half of them were unemployed, although most of those had not been out of work long and expected to be employed again soon.

Comparison of Ethnographic and Census Data

Census statistics on employment levels and occupational categories of employed persons in these three neighborhoods show many of the same patterns as those described in the ethnographic data, although allowance must be made for the fact that La Barriada was more mixed by race/ethnicity and income level than Projectville (see Chapter 2).

Table 11 compares labor force participation, unemployment rates, and employment-to-population ratios. The higher employment levels of Hamilton Park's residents are evident. But La Barriada's residents appear in the census data to have significantly higher employment levels than those of Projectville, whereas the ethnographic data indicate employment rates in La Barriada similar to those in Projectville. Table 2, for example, shows even higher welfare dependency rates on our study block in La Barriada than in Projectville. Among our small, intensively studied samples we found roughly similar proportions of families headed by working adults, about half in each case.

Part of the difference between the census and the ethnographic data is due to the greater economic heterogeneity of the study area of La Barriada. Although the families on our block were heavily welfare-dependent, the families on the neighboring block had much higher employment rates. The study block, therefore, was a pocket of concentrated poverty and joblessness even within this one census tract. It is also true that even within this block we found a tendency for young people to enter the labor force earlier than did those in Projectville. Given the relative youth of the population, this tendency may also have contributed to the differences in employment rates between La Barriada and Projectville recorded by the census. Teenagers in Projectville were more likely to remain in school and out of the labor force; teenagers in La Barriada left school and entered the labor force earlier.

It should also be noted that our research took place during the early

Table 11. Labor force participation and employment rates: SMSA, borough, and neighborhoods

	Persons age 16+ in labor force			Employment-to-population ratio (%)
	Total (%)	Unemployed (%)	Employed (%)	
SMSA	59	7	93	55
Brooklyn	54	9	91	49
La Barriada	49	13	87	43
Projectville	38	19	81	31
Hamilton Park	56	8	93	52

Source: U.S. Bureau of the Census 1983.

1980s, when U.S. unemployment rates reached their highest levels since the Great Depression. Unemployment rates for teenagers are also typically twice as high as those for the general population (Osterman 1980), suggesting that employment to population ratios for young people in these local areas were in fact much lower even than those indicated in census figures for the total population of the areas.

Table 12 compares occupational categories reported to the census from these three neighborhoods. These are somewhat difficult to interpret and to compare with the ethnographic data, since the categories are very broad and include a wide variety of jobs paying very different levels of wages. Nevertheless, the census figures show patterns that are generally similar to those suggested by the ethnographic data. The skilled manual jobs represented in the category "precision production, craft, and repair" account for a larger proportion of jobs in Hamilton Park than in the other two neighborhoods and also are slightly more common in La Barriada than in Projectville.

The unskilled manual jobs represented under "operators, fabricators, and laborers" are more common in La Barriada than elsewhere, accounting for over 40 percent of all employment. These patterns of concentration of skilled and unskilled manual jobs are similar to those found in the ethnographic data.

Over half of all jobs in Projectville are in the categories of "service" and "technical, sales, and administrative support" (this latter category includes clerical jobs), and the census shows far more service jobs in Projectville than elsewhere, thus agreeing with ethnographic data that indicates a high proportion of clerical and service jobs in this area. The census data also show more managerial and professional jobs in Projectville than in the other two neighborhoods, though it is likely that most of those are low-level jobs in government service or fast food restaurant management.

Table 12.   Occupational categories of employed persons: SMSA, borough, and neighborhoods

	Managerial and professional (%)	Technical, sales, and administrative support (%)	Service (%)	Precision, production, craft, and repair (%)	Operators, fabricators, and laborers (%)
SMSA	27	36	14	9	14
Brooklyn	20	38	15	10	17
La Barriada	—	43	6	10	42
Projectville	13	34	26	8	19
Hamilton Park	10	37	14	15	24

Source: U.S. Bureau of the Census 1983.

Table 13 compares proportions of government jobs in the three areas. Fully 40 percent of all jobs in Projectville are in government service, a far higher proportion than elsewhere, even higher than in the borough as a whole. This finding also parallels the ethnographic data, which show a high proportion of government-subsidized summer youth jobs in young people's employment and also a high proportion of government jobs among employed adults.

Some of the categories in Table 12 mask substantial differences in wage levels and job security. The "service" category includes both the minimum-wage restaurant and guard jobs so prominent in the work histories of the Projectville youths and the much higher-paying and more secure unionized building maintenance jobs held by a number of the family members of the youths from Hamilton Park. Similarly, "operators, fabricators, and laborers" includes both the unskilled factory production jobs evident in La Barriada and the unionized construction jobs obtainable in Hamilton Park. The "technical, sales, and administrative support" category, which represents similar proportions of jobs in the three areas, includes the clerical jobs and retail sales jobs that are most commonly held by women in all three areas.

Table 13.   Government jobs as percentage of all jobs: SMSA, borough, and neighborhoods

SMSA	17
Brooklyn	20
La Barriada	8
Projectville	42
Hamilton Park	9

Source: U.S. Bureau of the Census 1983.

Despite the complexities of interpreting these broad categories, the occupational patterns shown by the census data are remarkably similar to those in the ethnographic data.

Continuities and Variations between Neighborhoods

This chapter has observed how motivations and opportunities for gaining income through employment were sequenced with age in three different neighborhood environments. Both human capital and segmented labor market perspectives have shaped the presentation and analysis of the data, in order to allow for due consideration of individual and structural influences on the patterns described and to portray the interplay of local opportunity structure and individual behavior.

Several aspects of these employment patterns, primarily related to age, were similar among the three neighborhoods.

All three neighborhood groups experienced legal and social barriers to nonsubsidized, full-time, on-the-books employment during the early and middle teen years. Before they reached the age of seventeen or eighteen, they found themselves defined by others and by themselves as of school age and not old enough to go to work; many jobs were closed to them simply on that basis. Their families generally wanted them to go to work if they were not attending school—as most were not at some point before the age of high school graduation—but also acknowledged the difficulty of finding employment and hoped that their sons might go back to school while they still could. All these youths did enter the labor force at some point during this period, but the only ones who sought and found regular full-time jobs before the age of seventeen were the two La Barriada youths who lied about their age in order to do so.

Youths from all three neighborhoods usually sought and found their first jobs within the local neighborhood. This was a common pattern despite the fact that the amounts and types of early employment varied considerably. The youths from Hamilton Park and La Barriada began with part-time, off-the-books work for local private employers. The Projectville youths found their first jobs through public summer youth job programs that were also offered and performed locally.

Though most youths from all neighborhoods did enter the labor market at some point during their mid-teens, their participation fluctuated during these years; most withdrew at least once after initial entry. Each neighborhood group exhibited considerable internal variation in the extent to which its members desired and sought work. Even the poorest families managed to provide their sons with food and shelter during this period; hence, joblessness at this stage was not considered socially deviant by relatives and neighbors or by institutional officials, especially given the acknowledged difficulty of finding jobs and the expectation that young people would be in school.

As they reached their later teens, youths in all three neighborhoods greatly increased their labor force participation. Some at the age of seventeen and all by the age of eighteen increasingly felt the need for income and encountered social expectations that they provide for themselves. During this same period many more jobs became available to them as legal and institutional barriers fell away. By the age of twenty, most respondents from each neighborhood were unequivocally in the labor market, working or seeking work. Some still sought education and training but usually in combination with work. Involvement in income-producing crime was generally perceived as a supplement to rather than a replacement for wages.

Joblessness was common throughout the middle and late teens. Although differences in unemployment between neighborhoods were striking, finding jobs was difficult in all three places, and the brief duration of most jobs led youths back out of the labor force or into renewed job search.

Most jobs throughout both the mid-teen and work establishment periods lasted no more than a few months, whatever the individuals' degree of commitment or ability. The more ambitious and able changed jobs frequently in order to find better work or to reinvest in education and training. Quitting was the most frequent form of job termination among both more and less committed workers. Most firings were occasioned by absenteeism rather than incompetence; in fact, absence was frequently a way of quitting. Layoffs were nearly as frequent as quits. Most jobs reported among all groups were only temporary to begin with, whether offered by private employers or by public programs. Most jobs did not pay very well and offered neither long-term job security nor direct chances for advancement. This was true for all three groups during the mid-teen period but became less true for those of the Hamilton Park group who began in their early twenties to find their way into desirable and potentially long-term jobs.

Youths from each neighborhood reported encountering many recent labor migrants at workplaces where they themselves failed either to find or to sustain employment; they often referred specifically to "illegal aliens." All the youths associated production jobs in factories with such workers and found it difficult to coexist with these workers in such jobs. Some claimed that employers actually preferred undocumented aliens, on whom they could impose a variety of exploitative working conditions

[101]

that youthful citizens would not accept. The only noncitizen among the youths studied was from Europe, had lived in Hamilton Park most of his life, and carried a green card; the rest were citizens and had lived in Brooklyn most of their lives. Two respondents, one from La Barriada and one from Hamilton Park, reported working as supervisors of crews of undocumented workers and serving as translators; they considered undocumented alien workers a "noncompeting group" in the labor market with whom they competed openly only infrequently and without success.

Despite the foregoing more or less common patterns, the three neighborhoods varied considerably in the amounts, types, and sequences of employment experience that characterized the process of labor market entry during the period from the middle teens through the early twenties.

The single most striking difference was the greater amount of employment in Hamilton Park than in the two poorer, minority neighborhoods, a contrast especially pronounced during the mid-teen years of the youths we studied. During their late teens the contrast began to shift from a difference in job quantity toward a difference in job quality. By their early twenties the youths in the minority neighborhoods had greatly increased their labor force participation and employment but still suffered more joblessness than their age peers in Hamilton Park. The Hamilton Park youths, however, were finding their way into jobs that offered better compensation and security than those found by the minority youths.

The contribution of human capital differences to these disparities between neighborhoods appears to have been minimal, although differences within a given neighborhood were significant. Of the two major components of human capital, education and work experience, the latter contributed more than the former to differences in labor market success.

As a group, the Hamilton Park youths did not have much better educational credentials than the other two groups: only half of them finished high school, and some reported literacy problems. One member of the clique did finish a conventional public vocational training program in high school and went on to work at a good job in that trade; another was still hoping to obtain an equivalency diploma in order to join his father's union. The rest, however, either left school without diplomas or squeaked by with low grades and then went on to jobs that were similar to those obtained by their nongraduating friends.

Because the Hamilton Park youths found far more work than their minority peers during the middle teens, however, they had a clear advantage in work experience by their late teens. The labor market advantages of this mid-teen work experience were manifested not so much in their greater ability to find jobs (since they found jobs more plentiful at all ages) as in their ability to hold on to jobs because they had become more familiar with the discipline of the workplace. By their late teens, fewer of them reported losing jobs that they wished they had kept, primarily because they had already been through that experience.

Human capital differences, especially the attainment of educational credentials, appeared to make more difference within the neighborhood cliques than between them. Those individuals within each local clique who had more educational success did benefit in the labor market. This was especially true for the Projectville youths, several of whom obtained equivalency diplomas after interrupted schooling and were better able to find clerical and service sector jobs as a result. Even in La Barriada, where most youths did not have any sort of diploma, those who had gone farthest in school found access to a broader range of jobs than their peers who had left school earlier and were less literate. Those in La Barriada who had attended school through the tenth or eleventh grade were able to find more clerical and service sector jobs; the others were confined almost entirely to the low-wage, insecure, arduous factory jobs disliked by all the youths in the study. In Hamilton Park the high school diploma made a difference for one youth by providing him the minimum credential for making use of personal job networks.

Personal networks, not human capital in the form of either education or work experience, accounted for most of the disparities between the neighborhood groups. The personal networks derived from existing patterns of articulation between the local neighborhoods and particular sectors of the labor market. These effects of labor market segmentation were important for youth jobs both in the middle teens and during the ensuing period of work establishment. The Hamilton Park youths found a relatively plentiful supply of temporary, part-time, almost always off-the-books work through relatives, friends and local employers during their middle teens, most of it in the local vicinity. As these youths reached their late teens, they employed these same networks to gain access to a substantial if diminishing supply of desirable blue-collar jobs characterized by high pay, strong unions, and job protection. The minority youths suffered during both periods from their lack of comparable job networks.

Although both minority cliques had much worse labor market difficulties than the Hamilton Park clique, there were a number of differences between these two cliques as well. These differences were influenced both by the physical ecology of each neighborhood and by the orientation of local residents toward particular sectors of the labor market. The youths from La Barriada had slightly more work in their mid-teens than those from Projectville; the Projectville youths showed some signs of gaining an advantage over those in La Barriada with increasing age.

The two minority cliques sought and found different types of work. The youths from La Barriada, who lived close to a major concentration of employment, managed to get some work in local factories and from small landlords. As they grew older, they moved into jobs that were more often full time and on-the-books but still more likely than not to be unskilled manual jobs, although some also worked in clerical jobs. The Projectville youths suffered the most joblessness during their middle teens. Their neighborhood's physical isolation from centers of employment limited the work opportunities of residents, especially those of youths in their mid-teens, for whom job search is often confined to the local area. Government-subsidized summer youth jobs played a far greater role in supplying mid-teen employment in Projectville than elsewhere. With increasing age and, for some, educational attainment, the Projectville youths began to move into clerical and service sector jobs. Their experiences with manual work were few and of short duration.

Whatever advantage La Barriada youths enjoyed over their Projectville peers as a result simply of living near many jobs paled in comparison to the superior opportunities open to the youths from Hamilton Park. The Hamilton Park youths also benefited from living near many jobs, but in addition, social ties between residents and local employers reinforced physical proximity to produce a much greater supply of youth jobs than in either of the other two neighborhoods. Although in their middle teens they also worked at unskilled manual jobs, even there they were frequently paid much better than minimum wage, and with increasing age they began to find their way into skilled, unionized, blue-collar jobs.

As the two minority groups reached their late teens, the relative advantage of those in La Barriada over those in Projectville shifted: those Projectville youths who had remained out of the labor market in their mid-teens but had managed to acquire equivalency diplomas faced broader labor market prospects than their age peers in La Barriada.

At the close of the fieldwork period, most of those studied were very much involved in the process of work establishment, yet each neighborhood clique seemed headed for a distinctive niche in the labor market. The youths from both La Barriada and Hamilton Park aspired to high-paying, stable, skilled blue-collar jobs, but those from La Barriada appeared to have much worse prospects. They were beginning to find and stay with unskilled, insecure, low-paying blue-collar jobs and also some in the service sector. Some Hamilton Park youths expressed fear that they might not be able to secure the desirable blue-collar work that had been more plentifully available to their older male relatives, but some had already found such jobs, and others expected to do so eventually. The Projectville youths had little interest in manual work; they aspired either to college and white-collar employment or to good government jobs, and some were actually beginning to find and hold jobs in the clerical and service sectors. Most of these paid little better and offered no more prospects for advancement than the low-level factory work they so disliked, but they preferred the working conditions. They also had readier access to these jobs, although they relied to a much greater extent than the other neighborhood groups on advertisements, agencies, programs, and other impersonal modes of labor recruitment.

Comparative analysis of employment experiences among the three neighborhood cliques indicates several lines of cleavage which appeared to define "noncompeting groups" in this regional labor market. Immigration laws separated citizens and undocumented aliens. Labor laws, school attendance laws, and work rules separated those still of school age from competition with adult workers. In a more subtle but no less effective way, personal networks separated local neighborhood groups in their ease of access to the same sets of jobs. During the mid-teens these personal networks were solely responsible for allocating jobs to some groups and not to others. With increasing age youths did begin to move outside the local neighborhood and to come into more open competition for jobs. Personal networks still maintained a great deal of importance in finding adult jobs, however, and those with effective personal job networks were likely to carry the added advantage of the more extensive work experience that those same networks had already given them.

[5]

Getting into Crime

The involvement in crime and the criminal justice system of the young males we studied has been mentioned thus far only as it affected their schooling and work experience. Many of these youths were seriously involved in criminal activities at some point during their teen years. This and subsequent chapters focus on the development of their exploratory and systematic participation in crime, particularly crime for money, and the factors that led many of them to decrease or desist from criminal activities as they reached adulthood.

The three neighborhood cliques are compared in terms of the specific types, amounts, and sequences of crime in which their members became involved, and their criminal careers are analyzed within the context of their career patterns in schooling and the legitimate labor market. Their criminal careers are presented and analyzed in this way in order to address the problems of explaining delinquency and youth crime discussed in the opening chapter: the relationship of individual pathology to social causes and the relationship of economic factors to sociocultural factors. By looking closely at similarities and differences in criminality among individuals both within and between neighborhood-based cliques as well as between the ranges of experience of the different cliques, the following chapters bring a fresh perspective to these theoretical disputes. They describe both individual and social sources of delinquency and youth crime; in addition, they show how economic decision making is embedded in local-level processes of socialization and social control.

One of the reasons that economic causation of youth crime has been obscured is that social factors are more important in decisions to undertake economic crime than in other kinds of economic decisions. Decisions to undertake crime for money are both similar to and different from other sorts of economic decisions, such as those to invest in education and training or to seek one sort of job or another. They are similar in that there are cost-benefit calculations involved. Time devoted to participation in crime may be time taken away from school attendance or legitimate work. There are risks in investing in human capital or taking one kind of job rather than another just as there are risks in undertaking crimes. Decisions to undertake crime also resemble other kinds of economic decisions in that they involve both an individual and a structural component. Individuals do not all have access to the same set of choices. Social and economic structures limit the range of choices for a given individual.

Thus, the same factors of human capital and segmented labor markets which have been shown to influence careers in schooling and the legitimate labor market also influence careers in crime. More skilled and experienced thieves and drug dealers are likely to be more successful in criminal enterprise than those less skilled and experienced; their criminal skills and experience can be said to constitute a form of human capital. Existing criminal organizations that recruit and train criminal operatives are not necessarily equal opportunity employers (Ianni 1974b); in this sense, there exists a segmented criminal labor market. From these perspectives the analyses of criminal careers resemble the analyses of legitimate careers.

Yet crime as a way of making money also differs from legitimate economic activity because it is both illegal and immoral. Because it is illegal, the risks are not only far greater than the risks of legitimate economic activity but also far more unpredictable. Past attempts by economists to model criminal risks failed partly because they underestimated the risks of crime by relying on measures such as the cost of time out of the labor market due to incarceration (G. Becker 1975). But criminals also risked being maimed or killed by other criminals, victims, or the police; in addition, time in jail is injurious in many other ways than in reducing earnings. The costs and benefits of crime as a way of making money are also hard to fit into economic models because crime is immoral. The failure of the economic model of crime to produce the expected research results has been attributed explicitly to the difficulty of measuring the "moral noxiousness" of crime (Block and Heineke 1975).

Because of the extraordinary risks, the unpredictability, and the moral noxiousness of criminal economic activity, the analysis of decisions to undertake economic crime must take social factors into account to a much greater extent than do other kinds of economic analysis. Considering the segmentation of legitimate and criminal labor markets is one necessary way of bringing social factors into the economic analysis.

In addition, it is necessary to look at the social processes of crime control. The ability of criminals to succeed in crime depends not only on their skill, industry, and rational calculation of costs and benefits but also on the community's degree of effectiveness in controlling crime. Moral noxiousness not only makes crime distasteful to those who might otherwise engage in it but provokes a response from those who might be victimized. In this sense, criminal economic activity is embedded in community context to a far greater extent than other kinds of economic activity. The risks of regular business activity depend primarily on markets and competition. The risks of criminal activity depend on these factors *and* on the relative positions of victims and offenders in the community.

Since the focus of this book as a whole is the process by which inner-city youths choose between employment and crime as alternative sources of income, the emphasis is on crimes that high-risk youths commit for money, designated here as "income-motivated crime" or "economic crime." I do not use the more conventional distinction between "violent" and "property" crimes, because violent crimes for money, particularly in the form of street muggings, constitute one of the primary categories we examine. Since economic and noneconomic crimes were closely intertwined in the lives of those we studied, however, I also look at the intermixture of motivations for crime—violence, thrills, and income—and the transition from the thrill-seeking of early exploratory crime to the more sustained involvement in systematic economic crime.

Previous research, notably that of Wolfgang, Figlio, and Sellin (1972), has found that youths are relatively unskilled and unspecialized in the types of crimes they commit. While our ethnographic research generally confirms these assumptions, the detailed focus on specific local structures of criminal opportunity and the careers of a few cliques and individuals makes it possible to identify patterns of specialization and progression in economic crime which could not be expected to be visible in aggregate statistics. We found that neighborhood variations in crime patterns and changes in crime behavior with age were related to the ways in which each neighborhood environment both generated and controlled different types of crime.

As a result of these variations, distinctive kinds of crime characterized each neighborhood. The major types discussed—street fighting, factory burglaries, residential burglaries, street robberies, snatching of purses and jewelry, auto theft, drug dealing, on-the-job theft, and "errands" for older professional and organized criminals—were not distributed randomly by age or by neighborhood. Differences that affected how they fit

[108]

into a neighborhood or an individual career included the role and amount of violence involved, the amount and type of skill required, how close to the criminal's home they took place, the organization of markets for stolen or illegal goods, the social distance between victims and offenders, and the degrees of recruitment, training, support, and direction supplied by adults or more established criminals.

Gangs, Cliques, Turf, and Violence

Although this book focuses on the crimes that high-risk youths commit for money, whether nonviolent or violent, it is necessary to consider the other patterns of violence which characterize their neighborhoods in order to comprehend the standpoint from which they perceive the costs of engaging in violent crimes for money. Their willingness and ability to employ violence for economic gain, both initially and over time, cannot be understood apart from the context of the noneconomic functions of violence in their neighborhoods.

The most prominent pattern of noneconomically motivated violence in the lives of the study respondents was that of fighting with age peers. Some reported episodes of family violence, but most did not report being seriously abused as children, and the scattered instances of family fights in our data stand in contrast to adolescent street fights in both number and severity. Nearly all respondents, excluding only those labeled "punks" (weaklings) or "*patos*" (Spanish slang for effeminate males) by their peers, reported fighting in both individual and gang confrontations. The fighting was often quite severe, frequently involving weapons. Many had seen companions killed. This adolescent street fighting chronologically preceded involvement in systematic economic crime in most respondents' biographies and provided some of them with experience in the techniques of violence, which they then applied to the systematic pursuit of income.

Patterns of adolescent street fighting differed from patterns of systematic economic crime in two important respects. First, although most respondents in the field study reported both income-motivated crimes and fighting, peak involvement in fighting generally preceded periods of peak involvement in economic crime. Second, although street fighting frequently involved disputes over property, its basic motivations concerned status and territory rather than income (Suttles 1968). Those respondents who became involved in systematic economic crime generally did so after earlier involvement in individual or group confrontations with other adolescents.

The economic crimes characterizing these neighborhoods varied in the role and amount of violence they involved, but all economic crimes— burglary and drug dealing as well as more overtly violent crimes such as street robberies—involved the potential for violent confrontations. By the time respondents became involved in economic crimes on a systematic basis, they had experienced street fights and knew how and when to fight or run and how to procure and use weapons.

We found some variations between study neighborhoods in the social organization of adolescent street fighting, but all three were essentially similar in that any male youth growing up there found it necessary to establish a place for himself in the configuration of adolescent cliques and territories. From the early teens on, the young males in each neighborhood spent much of their time together outside their parents' houses and recognized some sort of attachment to a territory or "turf." Smaller children and adults might pass through unchallenged, but youths from other areas who passed through without invitation or an appropriate display of deference would be assumed to be provoking confrontation.

Local variations in the organization of cliques and establishment of turf included the degree to which adolescent cliques were ritually incorporated as named youth gangs and the significance of ethnic boundaries. La Barriada was the only one of the three study neighborhoods in which there were named youth gangs during our research period, but gangs tend to come and go in cycles; older residents of the other two neighborhoods could remember times when there had been local gangs. Gang ritualization in terms of distinctive names, clothing, and initiation ceremonies did not seem to affect the basic behavior of adolescents in our study cliques. We interviewed some gang members from La Barriada, but the central clique of youths we contacted lived outside the main gang area of the neighborhood. Only two of this core group had been in the gangs; the rest had often had to band together to protect themselves from neighboring gangs, however. Both cliques and gangs were quasi-familial groupings that served to protect their members from outsiders. One youth vividly described the necessity for affiliating with a local clique for purposes of simple self-protection.

Carlos Hernandez: Once we got attacked by a gang . . . it was either Halloween or Fourth of July, one of those things. Someone threw a bottle . . . these guys said they were coming back. The guys on the block went around collecting everybody on the block. When they got to my house, I hadda go outside. I didn't want to, but if I said, "No, I gotta study" . . . well, you could imagine. Not that they would have done anything to me, but I may have needed them some day. I could be getting mugged on the corner and they'll just turn their backs on me or something like that.

Unlike most of the other youths from this clique, Carlos Hernandez never became involved in economic crimes, refrained from drug use, and eventually went on to complete college. Yet even he found it necessary to join with the other youths on his block in street fights.

Youths from the other two study neighborhoods reported similar affiliation into local cliques with loosely defined territory and the obligation to protect one another against outsiders. The territory of the clique from La Barriada consisted essentially of the single city block where most of them lived and where they all spent most of their free time. The Projectville clique, living in a single high-rise project building, treated the benches and basketball court in the immediate vicinity of the building as their territory. Ben Bivins told us what it was like to grow up in this area.

> *Interviewer:* Were there gangs in Projectville when you were growing up?
> *Ben Bivins:* Only when I was real little. There used to be lots of gangs in Projectville, but that's all gone since I was about ten.
> *Int.:* Did you feel you could walk safely anywhere in the neighborhood since then?
> *B.B.:* Well, it depends. If I went more than about a block and a half away, or if I went in somebody else's building, I'd have somebody watch my back.

A Hamilton Park youth, Charlie Gaberewski, described similar processes, even though Hamilton Park was somewhat more affluent than the other two neighborhoods and had a much lower incidence of street crime generally.

> *Charlie Gaberewski:* Some people can't go into different neighborhoods or different blocks. You walk by somebody else's corner and right away they start something with you for nothin'. They grab you, say "What are you doing" . . . "Nothin'" or they grab your radio and run with it. What are you gonna do, do you want to die for a radio? Fuck it, give it up. Or break it, nobody gets it. That's the way it is. I ripped off a couple of radios that way myself.

Many of these kinds of confrontations in Hamilton Park involved ethnic boundaries between a predominantly white neighborhood and the surrounding black and Latino areas. Ethnic factors did not often enter into the confrontations in the other two neighborhoods, because they lacked such sharply defined ethnic borders. La Barriada gangs and cliques were predominantly Latino and fought mainly with each other; Projectville was predominantly black and surrounded by other predominantly black areas.

With or without named youth gangs or polarized ethnic borders, then, all three study neighborhoods were characterized by adolescent street fighting socially organized on the basis of localized adolescent cliques. As the Hamilton Park youth mentioned, such fights might involve the theft of personal items such as radios, bicycles, or clothing, but their primary purpose was the definition of status and territory. As one La Barriada youth put it in describing his involvement in local gangs when he was fourteen and fifteen: "That was about fighting, not stealing."

The distinction between fighting and stealing appeared not only in their own perceptions but also in the sequencing of fighting and stealing activity. Peak involvement in fighting with other youths generally preceded involvement in systematic economic crime, and a developing involvement in economic crime tended to displace involvement in expressive fighting. With the increasing age of the youths fights still continued, but besides being less frequent they were less likely to concern group claims to territory. Fights in the late teens were more often individual confrontations that took place in and around pool halls, bars, and discos.

Despite the noneconomic motivations of such fighting, however, and the fact that it both preceded and overlapped involvement in systematic economic crime, fighting provided some elements of socialization into economic crime. First, as mentioned, fights over territory and status sometimes did involve the taking of another's property; hence, property rights came to be seen as matters regulated by individuals or informal groups as much as by formal authorities. In addition, fighting taught techniques of violence which some participants went on to apply to a more systematic pursuit of income. During the period of field study the fighting often became quite violent. Many respondents reported possessing or having possessed knives and guns. We heard of killings in street fights in each neighborhood. The older respondents particularly perceived an increasing availability of firearms and expressed the opinion that not only were more guns present in their neighborhoods but that they were now in the possession of much younger teenagers than had previously been the case.

Despite the near universality in these neighborhoods of the necessity to fight, however, not all individuals who went through that process went on to become involved in systematic property crime. Further steps were required before recognition of the adolescent clique as a major foundation of social order in the local setting became transformed into reliance on the clique as a support group for participation in systematic economic crime. Some cliques become more oriented toward economic crime than others, or a group of boys who had grown up together might begin to split up as some members became progressively more involved in economic crime and some did not.

One final distinction between patterns of fighting and patterns of stealing concerns the responses provoked by these activities. Except in cases of major gang fights or killings, fights rarely were reported to the police or resulted in formal arrests, whereas systematic involvement in economic crime did eventually result in arrest for most individuals. Though many respondents reported being involved in fights, the only ones who reported sanctions for fighting through the criminal justice system were those who got into fights after they were already on probation or parole as a result of their economic crimes and thus at risk of reincarceration.

The youths from each of the neighborhoods who became involved in systematic economic crimes found that violent confrontations in the pursuit of income incurred costs that they were unwilling to risk on a regular basis. The willingness to risk violence for petty economic rewards is particularly characteristic of youth crimes. This willingness can be understood only in the context of the necessity for youths to fight in order merely to survive in their neighborhoods.

First Explorations into Economic Crime

Noneconomic adolescent violence in the form of street fighting provided early socialization into illegal behavior and the techniques of violence, which some individuals then went on to apply to systematic economic crime. Sustained involvement in economic crime resulted in patterns of behavior which were shaped by neighborhood-specific illegal markets, criminal organizations, and environments of social control.

Early explorations of economic crime, in contrast, were typically undertaken without accurate knowledge of the associated risks and rewards and also typically undertaken at an age at which the individual had little experience with generating a flow of income of any sort. Under such circumstances, these youths' expectations concerning the returns from economic crime differed considerably from the expectations they developed later on when they experienced a need for more sustained

[113]

income and had developed a more realistic perception of the varied legal and illegal income opportunities open to them. More sustained involvements in economic crime were shaped by the structure of both illegal and legitimate economic opportunities within the individual neighborhoods.

A few respondents cited as their first economic crimes incidents of stealing fruit or candy from stores before they were yet teenagers, but most, even though they had committed such acts, did not consider them significant crimes. Those who had become involved in systematic economic crime tended instead to cite incidents that occurred when they were fourteen or fifteen years old as their first experiences with gaining illegal income. These were generally nonconfrontational acts of theft such as picking pockets, stealing car parts, or, most commonly, burglaries of factories or apartments; they were usually conceived and carried out very close to their own familiar territory by pairs or groups of age peers. Violent confrontations at these ages were still almost always fights with other youths for status and territory rather than for economic gain. During their early teens, none of the respondents was willing to risk violent confrontations with adults, even though fighting with other youths was common.

Respondents varied considerably, both within and between study neighborhoods, in the degree of emphasis they attributed to economic and noneconomic motives for engaging in their first crimes for money or property. Their accounts of these experiences differentiate them both from street fights, including those in which radios or other personal items were seized, and also from later and more sustained involvements in economic crime. Such statements as "that was about fighting, not stealing" in accounts of street fights clearly downplay the economic motive. In contrast, the accounts of sustained involvements in economic crime include constant evaluations of the risks and benefits of particular types of crime in relation both to other types and to legitimate jobs.

Between these two extremes, accounts of first explorations of economic crime typically emphasized a certain amount of explicitly economic motivation combined with a search for excitement and the desire to establish a reputation among peers. This admixture of noneconomic motives in early economic crimes is evident in the field material from all three neighborhoods. A Projectville respondent who later became a frequent economic offender described his first experiences with shoplifting and purse snatching when he was fourteen.

Ben Bivins: I used to be with guys a little older than me and we would go stealing.

[114]

Interviewer: What was that like back then? What did you want the money for?

BB: It wasn't so much the money then. It wasn't till I got older, say 'bout seventeen, and I wanted to buy clothes and impress females, that's when I started caring about the money. Back then, it was more like the excitement of it, plus, you got to make that reputation for yourself.

Several of the Hamilton Park youths described a toy factory burglary that they had all participated in as their most significant early experience with economic crime. Although they later sold some of the toys for profit, they had played around inside the factory for a while and were quite boisterous about removing what they stole. Vandalism and rowdyism, as much as economic motives, appear to have motivated this burglary. Some La Barriada youths also reported breaking into factories initially just for fun and then subsequently for profit. Reports of auto theft also reveal mixed motives. Respondents from both La Barriada and Hamilton Park reported stealing cars initially for joyriding; some individuals then went on to strip parts to sell for profit.

The most in-depth example of the mixture of economic and noneconomic motives in early experiences with economic crime comes from the material on La Barriada. It is worth quoting in full, since it seems to exemplify the motivations that underlie many exploratory economic crimes. Arturo Morales wrote the following document; he did so on his own initiative, although he knew that we would be interested in what he wrote. He was seventeen at the time and had already been involved in economic crimes for about two years, but his writing still reveals quite a mixture of motives.

> Let's say it was right before the burglary with a serious armed robbery charge on me and pending. How was I thinking then? If I was to write my thinking about myself in a scale of 1 to 10 it was a 2 if I was lucky.
> 1. Didn't care if I got caught by police, prepared to do any crime. Down to shoot, stab, not fatal thoughts though, mug, rob anybody, burglarize any property.
> 2. No job at all.
> 3. No girlfriend or person to count on.
> 4. School, I gave up on that.
> 5. Family let down.
> 6. Real tight dirty relationships.
> 7. Try to get over on cheap shit (crime in general).
> 8. Thinking to do a job for some money.

[115]

9. Wasting time on absolutely nothing but to think nasty and dirty things to do.
10. Damaging myself physically on a day to day basis without doing any sort of positive thinking for myself.
11. Almost every penny to get high or find dumb pleasures.
12. Didn't handle boredom the right way.
13. Being in the neighborhood 90% of the time.
14. Hanging out with the wrong people 85% of that time I hang out.
15. Thinking that I had authority to rob and steal.
16. Not think about the future at all, or serious thing not to do especially at such a young age.
17. Just falling into hell.
18. Not using nothing at all as lessons.
19. Not knowing all I was doing was wrong and was later going to be punished for it.
20. Letting money problems get to me thinking I was slick, having a let's do it attitude.
21. Nothing to be happy about.

Morales's list reveals many motivations of a social and psychological rather than economic origin: low self-esteem and boredom; isolation from family, girlfriends, and school; and the desire to impress a peer clique already heavily involved in economic crime. Lack of a job and a need for income are also prominently mentioned, however. This mix of motivations appears throughout the field notes and life histories collected in the study neighborhoods.

The relative emphasis on thrills versus economic gain did vary among individuals and neighborhoods, but some mixture of the two characterized most early explorations of economic crime. One example of variations within one neighborhood is the contrast between Arturo Morales, whose motivations at age seventeen were still significantly oriented toward thrills, and Gaspar Cruz, who reported a very businesslike attitude toward theft from the age of twelve on. The most distinctive variation between neighborhoods with regard to the mix of motivations was the contrast between the greater and earlier income orientation of the youths from the poorer minority neighborhoods, Projectville and La Barriada, and the greater importance of expressive motivations for the somewhat more affluent youths in the white neighborhood, Hamilton Park.

Whatever variations, however, the income motivation during early economic crimes appears to have been generally undeveloped; the excitement of doing the crime was at least as important as the profit to be gained from it. This early emphasis on thrills, despite the fact that most of these youths came from poor families, is not surprising when one considers their situation at the ages of fourteen and fifteen. At this point in their lives almost none of them had experienced earning a regular flow of income, legal or illegal. Even the Hamilton Park youths, whose parents were somewhat more affluent and who would themselves have access to a considerable amount of part-time work in their later teens, had not yet had much work. Nor were they expected to provide regular income to support basic subsistence. Even the youths from the poorest households in Projectville and La Barriada depended on their parents for food and shelter; though they knew need and deprivation, they experienced them as the children of impoverished parents.

Under these circumstances, their initial economic crimes must be seen as responses to poverty in a dual sense. First, the income that they did derive was used to satisfy those personal needs beyond basic subsistence for which their parents could not provide. In fact, most of their early income, from whatever source, was spent on clothing and recreation. Second, the actual doing of the crime constituted a kind of recreation (Tannenbaum 1938, quoted in Silberman 1978: 91) in environments with few recreational facilities and lots of boredom. Crime in the early teens was undertaken not as an easier or more lucrative income alternative to employment (which in any case was often unavailable) but rather as an alternative to hanging out day after day with no money at all.

The undeveloped nature of these youths' economic motivations is evident not only in their own evaluations of why they first committed thefts but also in the way they handled the proceeds. Many stole initially in order to enjoy direct use of the stolen objects. Stealing that took place in adolescent street fights, for example, usually involved the appropriation of youth culture consumer items—radios, bicycles, sneakers, coats—which were then as likely to be used directly as to be sold. Initial experiences with stealing cars were often for the purpose of joyriding. Some youths who snatched gold jewelry on the streets and subways did so initially in order to wear it themselves. Because they were usually unaware at this stage of the true worth of what they had stolen, they received only a fraction of what it was worth, even on the black market, if they did sell the merchandise.

After the first few experiences with economic crime, however, their motivations began to change. Few encountered serious sanctions as a result of their initial ventures. Crime proved a viable way to make money at the same time that they were beginning to perceive a need for more regular income. With continued involvement, the income motivation became steadily more important. Stealing for direct use gave way to

[117]

conversion of stolen goods into cash. Once they learned what prices to expect for stolen goods, the risks and rewards associated with specific criminal opportunities were weighed against those associated with opportunities for other types of crime or for legitimate work.

At this point, the specific opportunity structure of each neighborhood environment began to channel exploratory criminal behavior into very distinctive patterns. Although the movement from stealing for thrills to stealing as part of a more sustained search for income was a common process in all three neighborhoods, both the extent of more sustained involvement and the particular types of criminal activity undertaken in each neighborhood were shaped by the local environment.

The Transition to Systematic Economic Crime

The variations between neighborhoods in opportunities for legitimate employment, described in Chapter 4, were one set of factors influencing the extent and type of developing involvements in economic crime. The greater availability of employment for the white youths of Hamilton Park was associated with lesser involvement in systematic economic crime, especially during the middle teen years. The Hamilton Park youths who did commit economic crimes tended not to commit the highly exposed and risky predatory street crimes in which many of the Projectville and La Barriada youths became involved.

Although neighborhood variations in employment opportunities influenced the propensity of local youths to engage in income-motivated crime, their actual participation derived from features of their local environments which combined to produce neighborhood-specific structures of illegal opportunity. The following neighborhood characteristics influenced the types and sequencing of opportunities for income-motivated crime, as reflected in the neighborhood-specific crime patterns of local cliques of youths.

Ecology. The physical ecology of the local neighborhoods defined a certain set of possibilities for and limits on illegal income opportunities for local youths. Since youths tend to commit crimes fairly close to the area with which they are familiar, especially during their earlier stages of involvement, ecology had a direct effect in terms of the sheer physical availability of crime targets—factories, stores, crowded shopping areas, unprotected pedestrian routes to and from transportation—and of empty lots and abandoned buildings to conceal stolen goods or car-stripping and drug-selling operations.

Ecology also reflected the social isolation of poor neighborhoods. The same residential areas that contained high proportions of burned-out blocks and abandoned buildings or were located near noxious industrial and transportation facilities were also characterized by a lack of services and of effective neighborhood organization to demand services. This isolation from municipal government and services affected the ability of local residents to control crime in their areas.

Local Markets for Illegal Goods and Services. Physical opportunities for economic crime do not elicit criminal behavior apart from a social atmosphere that validates and supports economic crime. The most pervasive social supports for youthful economic crime in the study neighborhoods were the markets for the illegal goods and services supplied by youths. Such markets played a crucial role in channeling exploratory ventures into more systematic economic crime. When youths found that they could sell the products of criminal enterprise with ease and virtually no risk, this discovery provided an early and crucial connection between their individual acts of income-motivated crime and a wider, reinforcing social context.

The organization of underground markets varied from one neighborhood to another, however, and this variation contributed to the specificity of local structures of illegal opportunity. Neighborhoods varied in how openly drugs and stolen goods could be sold on the street and in their particular combinations of diffuse and specialized markets. Some neighborhoods contained specialized fences for gold, auto parts, and other goods; all neighborhoods contained diffuse markets, based primarily on personal networks, in which youthful suppliers could sell illegal goods and services to ordinary residents buying for their own use. Certain neighborhoods or sections of a particular neighborhood were also known as marketplaces for stolen goods, drugs, gambling, and prostitution, attracting a large number of both suppliers and purchasers. These relatively open marketplaces were in some cases located on the borders of a residential area in which such activities could not be carried out so openly but which supplied clientele to the adjoining market areas.

Social Organization of Criminal Operations. Few of the income-motivated crimes reported by youths in the study were carried out by one individual alone. Most youths operated with others in some kind of structured relationship, however rudimentary. Several aspects of the social organization of the actual criminal operations had significant implications for the types and sequencing of illegal opportunities within each neighborhood environment.

[119]

First, there were different *patterns of recruitment*. The major distinction was between recruitment by the adolescent peer group and recruitment by older or more established criminal entrepreneurs. Most youthful stealing was conceived within peer cliques and did not involve older people except as buyers of stolen goods. Involvements in such youthful predations lasted from a few weeks to two or three years but rarely continued unchanged once the participants reached their twenties. The pattern frequently reported was one in which youths in their middle teens learned from slightly older youths how to rob and steal just as the older youths were about to decrease or end their own involvement.

Though most youths were recruited into economic crime initially by other youths, some respondents did report being recruited by adults. This kind of recruitment characterized certain types of crime—specifically auto theft, drug selling, and organized gambling—and had much different implications for the career possibilities of the youths involved.

Second, associated with the difference in being recruited by peers or adults were differences in the importance of *vertical and horizontal lines of organization*. Youths working primarily with each other, though they might assume differentiated roles at some points, all faced roughly the same high level of risk and were forced to decrease or discontinue their predations as risks and sanctions mounted. In contrast, youths who worked for adults started off doing the riskiest jobs but faced the possibility of advancing to more sheltered and lucrative criminal roles. Horizontal relationships were also important at higher levels of criminal enterprise, as in the case of drug sellers who shared sources, clients, and information.

A third aspect of the social organization of crime is the *transmission of skills*. Although crimes committed by youths tend to be relatively unskilled and unspecialized, some individuals from each neighborhood clique emerged as more successful than their peers at types of crime that many of them had attempted. The more successful individuals could attribute their success to special abilities and cite specific reasons for the failures of their peers.

Two broad categories of skills were significant: manual skills, which are important in burglary and car theft, and social skills, which are important in drug dealing and in working with others generally. Those who claimed such skills also acknowledged learning them from older or more experienced individuals. Skill acquisition was particularly important in criminal operations that included vertical lines of organization and possibilities for career advancement. Those who aspired to such advancement displayed a keen awareness of the need to learn the requisite skills.

A fourth aspect is *the role and management of violence.* Since the ability to employ violence is a third kind of criminal "skill," both the propensity of an individual to engage in a crime and his ability to continue engaging in it had much to do with that crime's requirements for the use of violence. The kind of crime that a local neighborhood would tolerate also had a great deal to do with the type and amount of violence involved: robbery, which automatically involves the use or threat of violence, was the most universally unacceptable crime in each of the study neighborhoods. Larceny and burglary, however, also involve the potential for violent encounters with the police or with a victim.[1] Some youths started selling drugs because doing so did not involve violent predations, yet the potential for violent encounters with predators or competitors is very high with protracted involvement in the drug world. As noted earlier, all these neighborhoods were characterized by patterns of noneconomic violence, and most males in these neighborhoods knew how to use force. The role of violence in the types of economic crime they undertook and their ability to manage it, however, were crucial factors in determining how long they could continue to be involved in systematic economic crime. The indiscriminate use of violence led inevitably to arrest or retaliation; the ability to employ it effectively without upsetting business required nerve and judgment that most often came with experience. Older individuals who had acquired such experience thus had a broader range of opportunities for economic crime.

Social Control Environment. Besides offering a distinctive set of opportunities for economic crime, each study neighborhood possessed a distinctive approach to the social control of crime. The character of that social control varied both according to the types of crime that local residents were willing to tolerate and according to their resources for controlling the crimes they did not wish to tolerate. Drug selling and traffic in stolen goods occurred in all three neighborhoods, though they varied in how openly these operations could take place. Violent predations committed by a youth close to his own home drew sanctions in each neighborhood, though in some situations the residents preferred to deal with the situation themselves rather than call the police. The kind of police available—regular, housing, or transit—varied, as did the quality of the ongoing relationship between local residents and the local police.

[1]Although the term "robbery" is sometimes used generically in popular speech, it refers technically only to theft accomplished by the use or threat of force. "Burglary" is theft that involves illegal entry into a building. Theft that does not involve either force or illegal entry is classified as "larceny."

Neighborhoods also experienced considerable internal dissension over how to control their criminally involved youths. The particular social control environment resulting from these kinds of variations also influenced the types and sequencing of criminal opportunities available to local youths.

The following chapters examine the three neighborhood patterns of youth crime and how they were shaped by the local combination of the foregoing neighborhood characteristics.

[6]

Crime in La Barriada

Our field contacts in La Barriada were concentrated among a clique of youths associated with a single city block where most of them lived and all of them spent most of their time. This particular block was ecologically well situated to provide criminal opportunities, particularly for burglary of factories and for auto theft. The block was bounded on one side by a large complex of factories and cut off from the rest of the neighborhood on the other side by a major highway. The factories were empty at night, protected only by alarms and irregular police patrol. Abandoned buildings and the easily accessible basements of old tenements provided storage space for stolen goods and refuge from the police. Vacant lots provided sheltered space for stripping cars.

Several social characteristics of the population reinforced these ecological shelters for criminal activities. The families living on this block were, as a group, the poorest of the three study neighborhoods. Many households were headed by females, and most were supported primarily by welfare payments. Those families headed by working adult males were scarcely better off financially, as these men worked in the lowest-paid service jobs associated with local industry. The parents of the youths interviewed had grown up in Puerto Rico, received little education, and spoke more Spanish than English. The residents of the block were generally isolated from local employers, from community organizations and politics, and from the police and other agents of institutional social control. Housing conditions deteriorated rapidly during the period of study as landlords first began withdrawing services, then either let the buildings burn for the insurance or surrendered them to the city in lieu of taxes. The abandoned buildings all eventually burned as the result of arson committed by agents of the landlords, by vandalizing youths, or by older heroin addicts who then stripped the building remains of their plumbing to sell for scrap. By the end of the study period only a few buildings remained on the block. During the preceding few years, however, the block had provided local youths the most regular opportunities for illegal income that we discovered among the study neighborhoods.

Although there were individual variations, the general pattern of economic crimes among La Barriada youths was a progression from exploratory and then systematic factory burglaries during their early to middle teens, to robberies at knifepoint during their middle teens, to a gradual decrease in frequency along with a shift to less risky crimes in their later teens. In the first two phases of this process, crime was their major source of income; the deintensification of street crime activities in the later teens was associated with a rapid increase in income from regular employment. Auto theft activities were intermingled with other crimes throughout this period, but they are discussed separately below because different career patterns were associated with them. Some youths also dabbled in selling marijuana and collecting numbers bets, even though these activities provided less income than the various crimes of direct predation.

Theft

The recruitment of youths into systematic theft and the planning and organization of most theft operations occurred within the context of the adolescent peer group. We found little evidence in La Barriada that adult-controlled criminal organizations directly recruited youths to undertake burglary, larceny, or robbery. Jorge Padilla described the importance of the peer group for the planning and organization of these crimes.

> *Interviewer:* So, you used to go to the next block over to hang out?
> *Jorge Padilla:* Yeah, I found it more better, like these people on the block where my mother lives. They use to hang out and talk about going to school, this and that. Go to the other block we be talking that.
> *Int.:* Do people talk about crime a lot? How do they talk about it?
> *J.P.:* Like they would say, "What we gonna do today?" and all day, "What gueese[1] you got planned for today?" "Me? nothing, man." And

[1]"Gueese" (spelling approximate) was the term La Barriada youths commonly used to describe theft when speaking English. This "Spanglish" term is similar to the Spanish *un guiso*, which can mean crime but also has a broader range of meanings. *Eso es un guiso*, for example, can mean simply "that's a cinch, it's easy" in reference to a perfectly innocent task. *Un guiso* can also have approximately the same meaning as the term "hustle": that is,

like everybody use to say, everytime everybody had a gueese, like if three persons was involved they didn't want nobody else, you know, like them three would go to a corner and "Hey, psss, psss" this and that, they would of talked about it and they would do it, but they don't want nobody else. Like everybody was in a group of three or four, everybody use to hang out together, but if there's gueese going on, about three of them use to cut out and go do it, come back with some money, hang out.

Int.: Would they talk about it afterwards?

J.P.: Yeah, they would talk about it afterwards.

Int.: Beforehand they wouldn't tell anybody else, but : . . .

J.P.: When they got over, they would come and say it.

Int.: Would they buy smoke [marijuana] for everybody or be generous with the money, or what?

J.P.: Naw, that's it, that's the point, that's why people rob because, like, one day we hang out about six of us on the corner, or seven, or nine whatever. From all of us probably three got money. So like they would say, "Let's chip in for something," and I would say, "I don't got no money," and they would like try and push me out to the side, like "You don't got no money, you can't get high with us." So you would say, "Ah, fuck that, I'm getting money to hang out," and that's why people go to get money. They go do crime to hang out with the group that got money. "Now I got money. Now let's go hang out," you know.

Although the adolescent clique is described here as the generating milieu in which many economic crimes were conceived and planned, it should be emphasized that the clique was by no means a specialized criminal organization; it was rather a multi-functional, quasi-familial grouping in the context of which these youths discussed school, jobs, their families, and girlfriends or played handball, raced pigeons, and engaged in many other activities besides economic crimes. Their orientation toward economic crime was definite, however, and contrasted with that of the school-oriented youths on the neighboring block where Padilla actually lived. Two other youths who moved onto the block from other areas, Arturo Morales and Mike Concepcion, also described the crime orientation of the local youths as stronger than they had previously encountered and one that quickly drew them into regular theft.

some kind of job for money, either legal or illegal, which is different from regular employment. A typical example of a legal *guiso* would be a musician's single engagement for a weekend dance. Among La Barriada youths, however, the Spanglish word "gueese" did not cover this broader range of meanings. "Let's do a gueese" spoken in English referred specifically to a crime for money.

The adolescent clique remained the primary source of recruitment and organization as these youths progressed from factory burglaries through street robberies to the decrease in frequency and shift to less risky crimes in their late teens. The relation of these youths to the local social control environment, however, underwent considerable change as their criminal careers progressed. In comparison to the other two study sites, the social control environment of this block was the most isolated from the police and other bureaucratic control agencies. The residents, though not always approving what they saw, were reluctant to call the police unless they felt directly threatened and had no other recourse.

Many illegal activities were carried out in the middle of the street and on the sidewalks, including the selling of soft drugs and stolen goods and the stripping of automobiles. These overtly illegal activities were performed mostly by the youths but also by a group of older males in their twenties and thirties who were heroin addicts. Other illegal activities such as public drinking and gambling were common among a wide range of residents, including the older men who in good weather set up their domino games in front of the corner store. The corner store sold candy to school children in the afternoon and marijuana to older residents in the evening.

Despite these elements of permissiveness, some kinds of activities were not condoned. Heroin sales took place behind closed doors, for example. When violence or theft threatened too close to home, residents did respond, although they still preferred to avoid using the police if possible. This social control environment afforded a certain amount of shelter for the illegal economic activities of the local youths, but the extent and limits of that shelter varied according to the type and amount of criminal activity and the social identity of the criminal. Most of the youths on the block took advantage of the opportunities presented by their situation and decreased their criminal activities only when these activities had saturated the environment.

The earliest and most frequent systematic economic crimes committed by the La Barriada youths were burglaries of the nearby factories. Most were extensively involved in such burglaries in their middle teens. Some began even earlier, as in the case of Gaspar Cruz, who claimed to have engaged in systematic burglaries from the age of twelve. The technical requirements of burglary worked to the advantage of their age and situation. A successful burglary involves no encounter with the victim and no violence, thus making it feasible for youths who are still physically immature. Burglars also profit from advance knowledge of the premises, manual skills, and the means to transport, store, and sell their stolen goods. The physical and social situation of the La Barriada youths and their orientation toward manual work functioned to their advantage in fulfilling these technical requirements.

One major advantage of these youths was that they knew a lot more about the physical layout and social organization of the factories than the owners and managers knew about the youths.

Field Notes: Arturo pointed out several old factories which he claimed he has broken into with several friends. As he pointed to one particular building which has several floors, he told me exactly what is manufactured on each floor. He told me that most youths on the block know what the different factories produce. Arturo says that he himself knows "every factory" and how to break into it. I asked him, "How do you and most guys find out what is manufactured in these factories?" He told me that they know just by observing the delivery trucks when the finished products are taken out. They also find out from people they know that are employed there. "Some of the guys who work there hang out with us," he said. "Sometimes we hear people talking about what is made there." He told me that the method of learning how to break into the different factories is by getting the information from other guys who have successfully broken in previously, or learning about an easy way to break in from someone who works there. Sometimes the youths see for themselves how to get in while they are working there. They can break into these factories successfully and get away with it due to their familiarity with the area. Since the youths live in the neighborhood, they are aware of ways to get away in case the cops show up. Arturo claims that, for the most part, the guys know how to get away.

Other interviews and observations generally confirm Morales's account. Most of the clique's burglaries were directed against factories and warehouses within four blocks of where they lived, including several dozen establishments arrayed in multistory loft buildings. The goods taken were then stored in abandoned buildings and basements on their own block until they could be sold.

The local youths' knowledge of the organization of the factories was not matched by knowledge of the local neighborhood and its people on the part of the factory owners and managers. Very few of the youths had worked in the factories, because they were too young; those who had worked inside had done only occasional odd jobs. At twelve and thirteen, for example, Gaspar Cruz swept up or took orders for coffee; he used this access to study the physical layout and alarm systems and then returned at night to commit burglary. No one in the neighborhood suspected him for a long time because he was so young.

Besides not knowing the youths who were burglarizing them, neither the factory owners and managers nor the police were familiar with the residential part of the block or willing to chase the young burglars through it. Several of the youths interviewed described the ease with which they could escape into abandoned buildings or even the buildings where they lived if they were interrupted in the midst of a burglary. The significance of the fact that the factory owners and managers lived outside the local neighborhood also became clear when we asked how the youths disposed of the stolen goods.

> *Interviewer:* Weren't you afraid of getting caught when you tried to sell the stuff?
> *Gaspar Cruz:* We would go out, wait till, say, seven, eight o'clock the next night. You don't expect the owner of the place to be up here at this time. What are your chances of the owner of that factory walking through here at eight o'clock, nine o'clock at night? Wow, chances are hard, damn. You would not get that guy. You'd find a regular person, "Hey, you wanna buy a nice typewriter, nice calculator," whatever had to be sold.

This separation between the local people and the factory owners also extended to the police.

> *Mario Valdez:* We always know who the undercover cops are. I mean, there's no Spanish cops around here. Once a white lady comes up the street from down that way. We know there's nothing down there, where's she coming from? She's got to be a decoy. Another time a white guy comes around here asking about guns. Arturo really had him going: "Yeah, come back tonight, I'll get you all the guns you want." The guy comes back, Arturo says, "Get out of here, sucker, everybody knows you're a cop."

One police officer who was well known in the neighborhood came down to the block not to stop crime but to buy stolen parts for his own car.

The young thieves could not hide their burglaries from local adults as easily as from the factory owners and police but did not need to; indeed, local adults provided indirect but essential support for their burglaries by buying the stolen goods. This area of La Barriada was characterized by both diffuse and specialized markets for stolen goods which cross-cut almost every segment of the community. Stolen goods were sold openly in the street and through personal networks, as well as to specialized fences.

[128]

Interviewer: So how did you sell the stuff? Do you know a fence?
Jorge Padilla: Nah. Just go up to anybody on the street, or, I got friends who will buy lots of things for the right price.

Mario Valdez: We knew this friend. He had a van. An older guy. He'd be talking to the store owners up on the Avenue. We were young you know, we couldn't negotiate to do stuff.

Arturo Morales: Sometimes we'd sell to anybody. Other times we took it to an apartment.
Interviewer: A fence?
A.M.: Yeah.
Int.: Did all your friends go to him?
A.M.: Nah. Only a couple of us knew him.

Mario Valdez: You should have seen it when we sold those coats. It was right before Christmas. Everybody was coming out of their houses, old ladies, everybody.

Field Notes: Today, I saw two guys selling an electric typewriter and adding machine. Several people on the block saw but did not buy. Later I found out that they sold the typewriter to a factory owner and the adding machine to a store owner. Both businessmen said they would be interested in other things if it was a good deal.

Field Notes: I ran into two of the guys. They offered to sell me a pair of leather gloves. They had at least ten pairs of these gloves. I told them I didn't want them so one of them asked me for a quarter to buy a soda. He entered the store and bought a bottle of juice and stole another one which he hid under his coat. The owner of the store saw the lump under his jacket and asked what it was. Sammy said "a gun" and walked out. The owner came outside but Sammy had already hidden the bottle. Then Sammy offered to sell the gloves to the store owner's wife. She said she didn't want them because she couldn't sell them. She then said, "If you get me Duracell batteries I'll buy them from you, or anything that I can sell here."

As these examples indicate, organized fencing operations did exist but were only one avenue for disposing of stolen goods. The market for stolen goods was so pervasive that it included even the factory owners and merchants who were the most frequent targets of crime.

[129]

The interviews with the youths from La Barriada reveal various levels of technical expertise and planning in the commission of these burglaries. Some individuals, for example, claimed that they did not like to do crimes with certain others because they did not like their methods.

> *Interviewer:* Could you tell me about the time you got arrested with Arturo?
> *Octavio Del Rio:* I should have never went with Arturo. . . . He's a dumb burglar. We broke in, there was a gate, right?
> *Int.:* What kind of place was this?
> *O.D.R.:* Sells guitars, drums, records . . . the door was kind of weak. We could have kicked it in but I wasn't gonna take those chances because the door might have an alarm . . . so we spend time, we made a hole, cut through the tin and everything, got in the place. . . . So I go in there, I go upstairs and I come down and I see Arturo playing with a little box, clicking it. He says, "Octavio, what's this?" Next thing I know the cops are right there. After we got busted, we was inside the precinct, the cop told us, "Which one of you triggered the alarm? You got in the place, you had a chance to get away, who touched that alarm?" I started thinking: Arturo. Then Arturo says, "No, no that isn't the alarm." I just left it like that, but I was really mad.

Gaspar Cruz emerges from the notes as the most meticulous and manually skilled burglar of the group:

> *Field Notes:* Gaspar told me "I always plan everything, that's why I never get caught." He gave me a detailed account of how he rigged up an alarm wire so that the alarm would not go off. He explained that his sister takes out books on alarms from the library and reads them to him because he can't read very well.

Though none of the other youths showed such pride of craftsmanship in their burglaries, most of them did recount a fair degree of planning. Besides gathering information about the layout and schedule of the factory, they also decided in advance what tools to use and ways to break in; they organized lookouts and learned the schedule of police patrols. Carrying out the burglaries also required them to perform a certain amount of semiskilled manual work, and in this their crime patterns paralleled the work orientation of this group toward manual labor. This degree of planning, skill, and labor by youths age twelve to sixteen seems remarkable in light of some stereotypes of youth crime as unskilled and spontaneous. What is even more remarkable is that they progressed with age to crimes requiring more physical daring but *less* skill and planning.

As a result of the physical proximity of their homes to the factories, the physical isolation of both from the rest of the neighborhood, and the curious mixture of social connections into the factory with social isolation from the owners and the police, such burglaries provided these youths with criminal opportunities that were relatively safe and lucrative compared with those available to youths in the other study neighborhoods. It is difficult to estimate their income from these activities, though the topic is often discussed in the notes and interviews. Many individuals claimed that they "couldn't count" the number or frequency of their burglaries.

> *Interviewer:* Would you say you did a gueese every week?
> *Gaspar Cruz:* No, it's not like that. Depends on how much you make. When you run out of money, you have to do it again.

When asked how much they made from an individual burglary, most individuals tended to cite their biggest take. Thus, three different individuals told us nearly identical stories of breaking into a coat factory and selling the coats in the street to all sorts of neighborhood people. They all claimed to have split $1,000 three ways. This claim is not unreasonable, since a field observer once saw about that amount of business being transacted in a similar manner by a group of the older heroin addicts who had stolen a large quantity of towels. The most reasoned estimate we got seemed to be that of Gaspar Cruz, who, when pressed, finally said he thought he had been making about $75 per week in this fashion, and he appears to have been the most active burglar of the group. Despite the difficulty of estimating the profits from these thefts, even with the cooperation of the participants, it does appear that economic crime provided these youths with a fairly regular income during their middle teens, during which time they had very little income from legitimate employment.

The factory burglaries committed by the youths from La Barriada constituted the most sustained and sheltered pattern of youthful theft discovered in any of the study neighborhoods, but even they eventually began to draw sanctions. After periods of a few months to a few years, many of the youths involved began to get arrested. As they overstepped the limits even of their particularly permissive social control environment, their ability to continue burglary with impunity began to run out, either because they had done too much, because they had struck too close to home, or because they had run into a violent encounter.

[131]

In order to understand how they eventually overstepped the bounds of the protection afforded them for carrying out their burglaries in this particular environment, one must examine more closely the interactions between the youths and the adult residents of the neighborhood, who generally did not themselves commit or condone predatory crimes. The attitudes of local adults toward the local youths involved in theft were highly ambivalent. Adults were reluctant to call the police because they had personal ties with the youths, because the youths usually directed their thefts away from those with whom they had personal ties, because the youths sometimes provided them with cheap goods, and, finally, because the youths were not above intimidating or retaliating against someone who "ratted out." On the other hand, many local adults disapproved of crime both out of a general sense of morality and also out of fear that they might become victims.

The field data document these various aspects of the social control environment. Arturo Morales began to experience the generalized moral disapproval of theft after he had been arrested.

> *Arturo Morales:* The good people treat me differently now. Some of those guys have some pretty daughters. Now they're not going to let them talk to me.

The towel incident, which occurred around this same time, illustrates the ambivalence of local residents who disapproved and feared crime even while they benefited from the supply of cheap stolen goods.

> *Field Notes:* Today the junkies were selling towels, lots of them, ten dollar towels, real thick, for a dollar apiece. All the people were down there buying them, even one lady who wouldn't let her son go to the baseball game with Arturo the other week because he had been arrested. Also, the landlord who won't let the junkies in his building told me he bought two and his wife told him when he got home that he should have gotten more at that price.

The sellers in this instance were heroin addicts in their twenties and thirties who lived in groups, moving from one abandoned building to the next. Although these addicts also committed many factory burglaries and provided a local supply of cheap stolen goods, their relations to local people were otherwise quite different from those of the youths and resulted in different patterns of victimization and social control. The addicts, indiscriminate in their choice of burglary targets, were quite as willing to burglarize the residential buildings as the adjoining factories.

[132]

Hence, the residents, even though they might buy stolen goods from the addicts, feared and avoided them otherwise.

Although generally preferring factory burglary as safer and more lucrative, the youths we interviewed reported some apartment burglaries as well but maintained that they did not victimize their own relatives, friends, and neighbors. If they broke into apartments, they either went some distance away or chose a victim whom they did not consider "one of my people." The only two burglary victims we identified on their immediate block, for example, were an elderly Jewish man and a homosexual, both of whom lacked supportive personal networks in the area. The youths contrasted their own choice of victims with the indiscriminate thefts committed by the older heroin addicts.

> *Mario Valdez:* That Frank Feliciano stole the plumbing out of the building where his own daughter lives. Those junkies don't care about anybody.

In contrast to the addicts, the nonaddicted youthful thieves maintained a wide range of social ties, which their crimes often strained but which also served to channel their crimes for the most part away from the apartments and persons of their friends, relatives, and close neighbors.

The ambivalent attitude of local adults to the crimes of the youths on the block was based not only on personal ties but on fear: if the youths felt that someone was "ratting them out," they were capable of intimidation and retaliation.

> *Gaspar Cruz:* Nobody knew it was us for a long time because we were so young they thought it couldn't be us. But then we heard some of the ladies talking about our new clothes. So we messed up their clotheslines, and then they didn't talk about us anymore.

> *Mike Concepcion:* I fixed that guy good, the one who ratted out Arturo. I went up on the roof and dropped a concrete block on his car.

The second of these examples followed the kind of incident in which the youths had gone too far, overstepping the boundaries of the environment that had afforded them a considerable amount of shelter for their crimes. Arturo Morales was "ratted out" by a resident of the block after he had burglarized a small two-man repair shop located right in the middle of the block, much closer to the apartment buildings than to the loft buildings at the end of the block. Although Arturo had previously burglarized many local factories with impunity, he had erred in thinking that the repair shop was as isolated from the local residents as the factories were. In fact, the men who worked there knew the people on the block quite well and quickly learned Arturo's identity. When we interviewed them, they expressed amazement that Arturo had not known better than to steal from them.

> *Repair Shop Manager:* It was that fucking Arturo who did it. He should have known better. It's always the new kid on the block who does something like this. None of the kids who have lived here for a long time would do this, because they know we have friends around here. That's how we found out who did it. We're not like some of these bigger places. We let kids come in here and put air in their bicycle tires or paint their school projects. Every now and then you get one, you see him looking around, I say, "What are you doing? Don't case the fucking joint."

In dealing with the crime, the men from the repair shop avoided involving the police as long as possible. First, they sent out word that they knew Arturo had burglarized them and offered to let him return the tools and merchandise he had stolen. When he did not respond, they began telling people that the stolen merchandise actually belonged to "the mafia" and that Arturo could be in real trouble if they passed on his name to the owners. Finally, as a last resort, they called the police, and Arturo was arrested. Even then they expressed regret at having to use the criminal justice system, because they thought the process too complicated and the results too uncertain.

Although Arturo's arrest was seen by his victims and also by some of his peers as the result of a mistake by the "new kid on the block" who had been "trying to prove himself," other youths who were more experienced at burglary also got caught eventually. Even Gaspar Cruz, the most careful and intensive burglar in the group, was convicted after fighting with police who had followed him while he was carrying stolen goods into an abandoned building. He spent six months in jail. Mario Valdez and two others were arrested after they assaulted a man who returned to his apartment while they were in the midst of a burglary. The very factors that had made burglary so lucrative for these youths eventually raised the costs prohibitively. The convenience of being able to steal so close to home began to work against them when their activities became too obvious and too extensive to be ignored. Violent confrontations resulting from interrupted burglaries led to serious sanctions from the criminal justice system. Stealing close to the area with which they were familiar had provided initial advantages but eventually saturated the environment. Besides the fact that the youths became too well known, the environment itself began to change as the factories increased security, the residential buildings next to them burned down, and the block became depopulated.

Burglaries, then, were the first systematic economic crimes committed by the youths in La Barriada, dominating their income-seeking activities around the ages of fourteen and fifteen. But by the time they reached sixteen, though still involved in burglaries, many were also stealing cars and committing robberies. This was the period of their most intensive involvement in income-motivated crime. At this point in their lives they were developing needs for more regular income. Some were already experimenting with living on their own; others wanted money for recreation and to buy clothes to impress females. Most still had very little access to legitimate employment.

The progression from burglary to robbery was based in part on the fact that robbery provided a much faster source of cash, since the whole process of having to transport, store, and sell bulk stolen goods was eliminated. The other element in the progression, however, was the increase in their capacity for violent encounters. Burglary preceded robbery in their careers in part because it minimized the chances of violent confrontation. Looking back on their early burglaries, several referred to them as "little, sneaky things I used to do when I was a kid." Having been relatively successful at burglary and having learned the techniques of violence from street fighting, they went on to apply the conscious threat of force to the pursuit of income. Robbery, however, though it could yield a quick cash return, proved to be a much more unstable source of income because the confrontations it involved could not only lead to identification but also elicit much more severe sanctions from both neighborhood residents and the criminal justice system.

The robberies they committed during this period were usually carried out at knifepoint against random victims selected at some distance from their local neighborhood. The necessity for going farther away for robberies is apparent in the case of Chucho Rivera, who had the most extensive involvement in muggings. Rivera started out by robbing students outside a nearby junior high school when he was only fourteen. Among members of this clique he was known best by the local police and was in and out of youth homes for years. His tendency to indiscriminate violence also provoked local adults. He had to leave the neighborhood for six months after he had cut a woman who lived on the block and her husband came after him with a shotgun. Although the adults on the block might only grumble about youthful factory burglaries and auto theft, they were not ambivalent in their responses to violence.

[135]

At the other extreme from Rivera's robberies too close to home, Gaspar Cruz reported having robbed stores at gunpoint, going as far away as New Jersey, after he came out of jail. Most of the others operated between these extremes, some distance away from their own block but within the general area known to them. Mario Valdez waited outside subway stations for people coming home from work. Arturo Morales began by threatening drunks outside bars with imaginary weapons and was eventually convicted of robbing at knifepoint a middle-aged businessman who was leaving his house in a nearby but more affluent neighborhood. Most of these robberies were committed with knives against victims chosen more or less randomly. The income gained could range from only a few dollars to about a hundred dollars.

Compared to their burglaries, which lasted over several years and overlapped the period of their robberies, the robbery careers of these youths were fairly brief. For some, this curtailed involvement in robbery was a matter of taste: they tried it and did not like it.

> *Mike Concepcion:* I only did two muggings, with Arturo, and I didn't enjoy it.
> *Interviewer:* Why?
> *M.C.:* I'm a thief with heart. I don't like to see people suffer that much. I'd rather do it behind somebody's back and not hurt nobody . . . rather than inflict any pain. I don't go for that.

Those who persisted found it much more difficult to avoid arrest and conviction for robbery than for burglary. Their own local environment did not shelter violent theft, and when they strayed outside their own area, they found themselves operating in a much more exposed environment of control. Violent confrontations in the form of interrupted burglaries or robberies led most of them into continuing involvement with the criminal justice system around the age of sixteen or seventeen. Gaspar Cruz spent six months in jail when he was sixteen. Miguel Tirado was sentenced to eighteen months in prison when he was nineteen. Most of the others were on three to five years' probation by the time they reached the age of eighteen. Jorge Padilla was the only one of the criminally active youths we interviewed in La Barriada who had never experienced a felony arrest, even though he had accompanied many of the others in numerous burglaries and robberies.

After they reached the age of eighteen, most of these youths decreased or terminated their criminal involvements, not only because of mounting sanctions as a consequence of their saturation of the local environment but also because of their greatly increased opportunities for legitimate employment. Most were on probation by their late teens, and though they still experienced frequent unemployment, they were in the labor market and working more often than not. Moreover, they now needed more regular income than the sporadic profits achieved through crime during their middle teen years. With work more available and providing more regular income, some ceased engaging in crimes completely for long periods of time. For others, occasional crimes provided a supplement to their wages. In addition to shifting crime to the periphery of their income-seeking activities, they also shifted the types of crimes away from the time-intensive burglaries and highly exposed random street robberies of their middle teens toward on-the-job theft and more selective robberies—specifically, robberies of persons known to be undocumented aliens who could not go to the police. These were the people they referred to as "Mexicans," even though experts on the neighborhood suggest that they were Central and South Americans who may have entered this country through Mexico.

An interview with Gaspar Cruz specifies these shifts in the frequency and type of income-motivated crimes during the late teens. At the time of this interview, Cruz was nineteen years old and had been working at one full-time job for more than a year.

Interviewer: Have you done any crimes since the last time we talked?
Gaspar Cruz: Yeah, a couple of little things. Me and some of the other guys took off ten Mexicans at a card game in the park. It was Friday afternoon, we were hanging out, drinking, getting high, and we ran out of money. We wanted to stay high, so we got some sticks . . .
Int.: What kind of sticks?
G.C.: A gun and a knife. We put stockings over our heads and took their money. Then we went around the corner. Fifteen minutes later we walked right by and smiled. They never knew it was us. We robbed another game, too, but that was a lot more dangerous.
Int.: Why?
G.C.: Because this time it was older guys, blacks, Puerto Ricans. Those guys have guns. With the Mexicans, it's better. They don't have guns, and they're illegal aliens so they can't go to the police.
Int.: Have you done any more factory burglaries?
G.C.: Nah.
Int.: Why not?
G.C.: That takes too long. Factories you got to spend days setting it up and it takes two or three hours to do it and you got to wait till the middle of the night, then you got to sell the stuff. To take somebody off in the park only takes fifteen or twenty minutes. If you're high, you want to stay high, you don't wait.
Int.: But it's much worse if you get caught for a robbery, isn't it?

G.C.: You don't think about that at the time. Besides, like I told you, Mexicans can't go to the police. Also, we used the disguises.
Int.: Are there any other reasons you don't do burglaries any more?
G.C.: Well, I used to be littler. I could climb in the bathroom window and just walk into the office. Also, it's not like it used to be when I was younger. Crime keeps going up and up. The factories have more alarms, more gates on the windows, more dogs, and more guards. Plus they understand how we operate. They know how it is we come in, whether it's through the window or the roof or whatever.

In addition to Cruz, both Mario Valdez and Jorge Padilla reported working more regularly, ceasing their burglaries, and occasionally mugging undocumented aliens during their late teen years. The only one of the group who reported any involvement in burglaries during this period was Octavio Del Rio, who was unemployed most of the time, lived with a woman on welfare, and thus still had time to plan and execute such thefts. Even Del Rio lessened the frequency of his burglaries, however, in response to the increased security in the factories. Many of these youths were also removed from physical proximity to the factories as their block burned down.

The other patterns of income-motivated crime during this period were on-the-job theft and sudden reversion to crime as a result of being laid off. Jorge Padilla reported work-related thefts, not at his own workplace but at that of an older friend.

Jorge Padilla: I haven't been stealing too much. The only times are . . . sometimes I go to where my friend works and he throws rolls of material out the window to me.

This pattern of work-related theft also came out in an interview with an older neighborhood resident. Willie Vazquez was twenty-eight years old and had been in jail for theft several times. When interviewed, he was working in a garment factory and reported that sometimes he managed to stuff garments into the garbage containers for later retrieval.

Reversion to crime after being laid off was reported by Arturo Morales and Miguel Tirado. For more than eighteen months after being put on probation, Morales had worked at several different legitimate jobs. But when he was laid off from a clerical job he had held for several months, he committed three muggings during a period of thirty-six hours. He was subsequently rehired at the same job and again refrained from criminal activity. Miguel Tirado committed no crimes during the period of more than a year that he worked as a messenger. When the job ended after a dispute with his supervisor over promotion, he sought but was unable to find new employment and lived for several weeks on his savings. After his savings ran out, he robbed a local salesman at gunpoint of nearly a thousand dollars. Tirado was convicted of that crime and subsequently served eighteen months in prison. Both Tirado and Morales had committed many income-motivated crimes before they entered the labor force decisively, but only the crimes following their layoffs were directly caused by unemployment: that is, specific crimes were precipitated by loss of employment. The most crime-intensive years for them and the rest of their clique were the mid-teen years during which they most often were unemployed or out of the labor force.

Although most members of this clique followed this general progression from exploratory economic crime through systematic factory burglaries to street robberies to decreasing criminal involvement, there were variations and exceptions. As noted, some never became deeply involved in robbery, and two youths in this clique never participated in systematic economic crime at all, even though both had brothers who did so. One of the two was Carlos Hernandez, the youngest sibling in a family that had begun to make money from a small business and had moved to a better neighborhood. He still came back to the block to sit on the stoops and drink beer with his old neighbors, but he himself went on to complete college. The other was Julian Acosta. Although his younger brother Sonny was one of the most active thieves on the block, Julian was never known to fight or steal. Having married and fathered a child before he was seventeen, he attempted to live on his family's welfare payments, avoiding both work and crime. Although the other youths ridiculed him for his extreme passivity, he said that he did not worry about his own masculinity, citing his many sexual exploits as proof of his virility. He did work periodically, at the behest of his wife and welfare officials, but openly proclaimed his desire to live on welfare.

At the same time that most members of this clique were decreasing their involvement in burglaries and street muggings, two of them were becoming involved in illegal income-producing activities of a different kind, activities that made possible intensified reliance on crime as a source of income. Mario Valdez, after returning from his unsuccessful job search in Puerto Rico, worked for a time in a local store that sold marijuana. Mike Concepcion was maintaining a regular involvement in quasi-organized auto theft. Unlike the burglaries and robberies of these youths' middle teens, drug selling and auto theft operations are characterized by the direct recruitment of young workers by older persons and by the type of career ladder they offer. Auto theft patterns in La Barriada are outlined below; drug selling is discussed in the Projectville and Hamilton Park chapters.

Auto Theft

During the same period when members of the clique in La Barriada were involved in various other types of theft, some of them were also making money from stealing automobiles and automobile parts. Unlike most of their robberies and burglaries, their acts of auto theft did not always originate within the adolescent cliques, and not all their careers in auto theft had saturated the environment by their late teens. Though some youths stole cars and parts in a relatively unskilled and spontaneous manner, others were recruited by adults, developed specialized skills, and operated in the context of criminal organizations that offered possible advancement to more sheltered and lucrative criminal activities. One individual in particular developed special skills and was recruited into more organized forms of auto theft.

Both the presence of a thriving auto theft industry in this particular neighborhood and the fact that it was considerably more organized than the youthful robbery and burglary activities described above are closely related to the particular technical requirements and social control environment of auto theft. This crime shares some of the characteristics of burglary in that it profits from the application of manual skills, is usually nonviolent, and consequently does not incur as rapid or severe sanctions as robbery.

The nature of the goods being stolen, however, differentiates burglary and auto theft in their technique and organization. Cars are easy to move but difficult to conceal; an intact car is also easily identified by the serial number on the engine block. Consequently, skilled auto thieves frequently try to dismantle stolen cars as quickly as possible and sell the untraceable parts. Once the car is stripped, risks diminish rapidly, since possession of stolen parts is not as serious a crime as possession of a stolen car. In order to strip cars, however, auto thieves need sheltered space for a few hours' work. La Barriada's abandoned buildings and empty lots provided such space. The practicality of ongoing organization in auto theft operations derives from the need for mechanically skilled individuals to rework the cars and from the possibility of dividing the responsibilities and risks associated with the different phases of stealing, reworking, and marketing. The levels of organization of auto theft in La Barriada reflected different approaches to these technical problems.

Several members of the clique reported stealing cars or parts in a relatively spontaneous manner during their middle teens. The simplest approach was that reported by Chucho Rivera: "If somebody told me they needed a battery, I would just go around the corner and take a battery." Jorge Padilla, Mario Valdez, and others reported stealing whole cars, although they employed very little skill.

> *Jorge Padilla:* One day I was out walking and I saw this car parked right on the street with the door unlocked and the keys in the ignition and everything. I needed money to hang out, so I just took it and parked it in front of my house, took out the radio, the speakers, this and that, put them in my house, then I drove it down the block, took off the tires, this and that, made me a couple of bucks.
> *Interviewer:* Did you know who you were going to sell the stuff to beforehand?
> *J.P.:* No, but in my neighborhood you sell it quick. Everybody buys. I took the tires to a car service. They got a lot of cars, they need tires. You're not gonna sell it for 100 percent what it costs in the store, cause nobody's rich over there, so we give them a nice price, they buy.
> *Int.:* You don't break the lock or anything?
> *J.P.:* Nah, I don't steal cars like that. I just walk around. If it's on, I take it. If it's not, I don't take it with a pulley. I know how to do it, my friend showed me, but I just be walking down the street and people leave their car and I hop in and book [leave].

Padilla went on to relate that he had stolen about eighteen cars in this manner, making $100 to $200 on each and selling to different buyers, including both individuals and small businesses. On four occasions he stole specific models on request.

> *Jorge Padilla:* They would tell me, "Hey, I need two doors for a Monte Carlo; I need this front end," so I would tell them, "Look, I'll bring you the whole car. You just give me $100 and strip it yourself."

Not all of the youths in the clique stole cars, however, even among those who committed other kinds of thefts. Arturo Morales and his close friend Mike Concepcion had gone separate ways about the time Concepcion began to get heavily involved in auto theft. Previously the two had committed many burglaries and two muggings together as well as playing on the same sports teams in school and being constant companions. "I always got along with Mike," said Arturo, "but he's into cars now. I'm not into cars." Mike had his own view of why Arturo was not interested in auto theft: "Some of these guys on the corner, they don't want to get dirty to make money." In fact, Arturo Morales did generally dislike manual work, legal or illegal, and began to move into low-level clerical jobs as he got older.

Mike Concepcion, in contrast, not only did not mind getting dirty but showed a genuine fondness for working on cars. Besides stealing and stripping them, he did occasional legitimate work in local body shops, spent most of his free time and his income working on his own car, and developed an ongoing career as an auto mechanic and thief.

Mike Concepcion stole his first car when he was sixteen years old and had already committed many factory burglaries. He had left school for a year to support himself and his mother, lost his job when the company relocated, and returned to school. He reported having some family background in auto theft: both his father and uncle had stolen cars, his uncle apparently on a professional basis. Mike's parents separated when he was only ten years old, however, and he claimed it was not family influence that led him into theft but the atmosphere on the block in La Barriada where he moved when he was fourteen: "I used to see all these things going on out my back window and I said to myself, 'Damn I want to get into that.'" He was recruited by an eighteen-year-old, who taught him to use specialized tools.

> *Mike Concepcion:* I learned in one day. This friend of mine, Cisco, you could say he recruited me. We went up to a car that was already stripped but it still had the ignition. He showed me how to take off the door cylinder with pliers. Then there's this tool called a butterfly, it's a bad tool, you stick it in the key and you just slap it out in one shot and pull the starter and turn it with a screwdriver.
> *Interviewer:* But you say the car was already stripped?
> *MC:* It was, like, practice, just practice. This was in the afternoon. That same night, I went out and did it by myself.

After this initiation, Concepcion rapidly became involved in systematic auto theft. He began going into middle-class neighborhoods with the person who recruited him and others. He obtained his own tools. He was neither working nor in school at this point and was stealing a car every weekend, selling to a variety of buyers in individual negotiations. After a few months of this, however, he was arrested in a stolen car with his tools.

> *Mike Concepcion:* We got chased by the cops a few times, but we had a Trans Am hooked up real good, it was fast and legal. We got away. Then one time, I stopped for a light in a hot car on my way to Queens. I stole the car in Brooklyn to go get another car in Queens.

Interviewer: You had an order for a certain kind of car?

M.C.: Yeah, and I stole the first one for transportation to go get it, but I didn't notice that one of the back lights wasn't working too good and the cops noticed it. All of a sudden I got about three cops surrounding me and no way to get away.

This arrest, his first of any kind, led to a court case that lasted for six months. Mike's stealing actually increased during that period of time, as he began to work in the context of a more organized operation.

Interviewer: Could you tell me more about how you got into organized stuff?

Mike Concepcion: I was gettin' hooked with, like professional guys. They had some bad tools . . . see, they were experts in alarms, cutoff switches, chain locks, anything. If the car didn't turn on, they would find out what's wrong with it quick.

Int.: Were these older guys?

M.C.: I was the youngest guy there [seventeen at the time]. The others were around nineteen, twenty. One was in his thirties. But they all learned from much older men . . . men like in their thirties and forties who used to do it when they were as young as us. So they showed us the tricks of the trade. Sometimes the old guys put the young guys to drive the cars. The old guys already have records. If they get caught they know they get in more trouble, they got families or they know the consequences are gonna be worse. Now the courts know a young fella might have made a mistake, give him a break. Not the older person. They don't give you no break.

Concepcion's own still-clean record allowed him to take risks for the organization in return for learning skills, working with more professional associates, and having access to more regular buyers for parts. Around this time the car ring rigged up an advantageous workspace for stripping cars, right on Concepcion's block and during the period of field observations. The block had already become a popular spot for car stripping; not only the youths but also some of the heroin addicts stripped cars in the street every week. Concepcion's group, however, found a back yard protected from view and fenced off by the property owner. They installed a gate and put their own lock on it to protect themselves not only from the police but also from addicts and other unwanted collaborators who might try to horn in on the stripping.

The disposition of his court case brought an abrupt change to Concepcion's place in the organization: he was put on probation for three years. The end of his clean record and an incident in which he was shot at during a theft convinced him to quit stealing and confine himself to less risky roles.

Mike Concepcion: We got a little setup in this back yard. Me and two other guys are the only ones who have the key. I let 'em in if he tells me to. I don't do any actual stealing no more. I just do the stripping. I get the customers too sometimes. I get parts or they'll throw me something, fifty or twenty-five dollars for getting them the customers. It's about fifteen cars back there now. They go in, they don't come back out. We take out the motor, the interior, everything.

A further consideration in his decision not to continue actively stealing cars was his perception that the police were becoming more effective in cracking down on auto theft. He described a kind of technology race between car thieves and the police.

Mike Concepcion: People still go to Queens. I don't understand it. They got better cars over there, but Queens is so hot, it's burning. They got an anti-crime unit out there that's real good, they are not stupid. That's one of the reasons also I quit. These guys are gettin' too smart for us. Every time we learn something, they learn something. They know all about the slappers . . .
Interviewer: Slappers?
M.C.: The thing you slap the ignition on with. . . . Some of the thieves are getting police scanners now. . . . You need that little edge over the cops . . . like that corkscrew . . . that's two seconds right there.

While his backyard car-stripping operation lasted, Concepcion also performed other organizational functions. He recruited a fourteen-year-old to help him dismantle the cars. He kept the addicts away from their operation. He also paid some addicts and smaller children and others on the block to keep watch for the police.

Mike Concepcion: Even the ladies used to watch out for me.
Interviewer: Why did they do that?
M.C.: They thought I was like Robin Hood 'cause I used to give their kids a couple of dollars to watch out for me. I used to put somebody on the roof, somebody up the block . . . all the money I was making then, I didn't mind spending a little here, a little there, and everybody would watch out for me. The ladies and the kids would be yelling "la jada, la jada [the police]."

For a period of some months the backyard lot flourished so well that it almost had to be abandoned because it was too full of stripped car bodies. At that point someone placed a call to the city to complain about the lot. City workers appeared and cleared out the remains of several dozen cars, thus unwittingly allowing the operation to resume.

Within a few more months, however, the shelter provided by the back lot had disappeared, along with over half the dwellings on the block, as a result of fires. The addicts began to draw police attention as they increased in numbers and brought in stolen cars indiscriminately. When buildings burned, addicts appeared to scavenge the fixtures and then take up residence in the basements. As more buildings burned, residents of the next building in line began to leave to avoid the fires. Soon the back lot was part of a large open space, which the addicts used for a new source of income: copper prices had soared, and they were bringing in carloads of copper cable from abandoned docks, using the lot to burn the insulation off the copper before selling it.

Concepcion's building was one of the few that did not burn, and he continued living on the block. During this period, though still stripping cars and arranging deals, he was also working and going to school again. He had gone back to school when he was put on probation, transferring to an auto mechanics program. He had also taken a maintenance job that one of his friends had told him about. The job paid only about half the $200 a week that he had averaged stealing cars, but his block had become too exposed to serve as a convenient place for stripping cars. His associates had to move their operations elsewhere.

Mike remained in contact with them, however, and within a few more months he was once more stealing cars. Now nineteen years old, he had left school again but was still working.

Mike Concepcion: I'm working now and maybe once in a while I'll steal. I don't really have the time to do that. You gotta be up late at night and you gotta take chances. Then when you get the car you gotta strip it, that takes time. I ain't got time. I gotta go to work.
Interviewer: Before you said you had quit stealing and you let younger kids take over that part. Why did you go back? What's different.
M.C.: It's more professional now. When I take a chance now, it's for big money, good money.

At this point he was working with another nineteen-year-old and a fifteen-year-old, the person he had recruited to help him strip cars when the back lot was still functioning. They followed the strategy of having the fifteen-year-old drive the stolen car and also minimized their risks by planning in advance which cars to take. Concepcion actually drove stolen cars himself only when they took two or three at a time. They had also made connection with their most discreet and reliable buyer yet, a junkyard with a limitless capacity for parts and an excuse for having them.

At the close of our fieldwork in La Barriada, Mike Concepcion's career in auto theft had gone through several phases in less than three years. He was not at all certain how long he could escape jail, despite the fact that he continued to acquire professional expertise and organizational affiliations that both cut his risks and increased his profits.

Though it was impossible to predict his future career, some further field data give an idea of the possible directions it might take and also help round out the picture of the structure of opportunities for auto theft in this neighborhood: the distinction between levels of organization in auto theft, the types of involvement in auto theft of older men in this neighborhood, and the overlap between legitimate and illegitimate work on automobiles.

Though Mike Concepcion's auto theft activities were considerably more organized than those of most of the other youths and older heroin addicts from his block, still higher levels of organization existed. His uncle had been involved in a more sophisticated operation years earlier.

Mike Concepcion: He was organized all the way, with the mafia. Nobody believes me around the block except Fausto, you know the guy who runs the store on the corner? He knows from those days what my uncle was into. Way back then the cops didn't know . . . my uncle had his own lot, towtrucks, everything . . . they used to steal cars and bring 'em down to Florida and things like that. My aunt didn't like it, but they wouldn't let him go. They wanted him 'cause he was a real professional.

Concepcion's mother confirmed his uncle's occupation.

Access to such highly organized and capitalized criminal operations was thus conceivable to Mike, though two other kinds of career patterns were more immediately visible to him. One was to continue stealing—discreetly and with skill—as a supplement to legitimate wages rather than as a full-time occupation.

Interviewer: You say most of the guys you work with now are around twenty. Do you know older guys in the neighborhood, say in their thirties, who still steal?

[146]

Mike Concepcion: Yeah, there's people like that around, but they're chilling out. People like that know when to do it. They got family so they're real careful. They do it, they chill out, they do it again, then they chill out. It's not like an everyday thing.

Another possibility was to combine legitimate and illegitimate work by holding a regular job in one of the neighborhood "chop shops," which perform a variety of legal and illegal business functions; he had already worked in some of them. In separate field contacts in a different part of this neighborhood we interviewed two young men in their mid-twenties who had gotten involved in illegal operations after starting their careers in legitimate auto repair. One was a mechanic, the other a body-and-fender man, and both had gotten offers to make "big money" working at night on stolen cars.

Mike had also made two attempts to enter auto mechanic training programs—once in school and once after he left school—which would have given him legitimate credentials had he completed them. Thus there was also the option of going completely legitimate, although it would have involved much lower earnings.

Interviewer: Ideally, what would you like to do for a living?

Mike Concepcion: Something to do with cars, I guess. That's what I know about.

Int.: You think you could get a regular job as an auto mechanic around here?

M.C.: Yeah, I got a friend who might open his own place. This one's strictly legitimate. I could work for him. But it's hard, you know. All these little places around here, they don't make so much money. They try to get over on you. There's a lot of guys who want to work on cars, so they try to pay you about eighty dollars a week or something. That's not very much.

[7]

Crime in Projectville

Our field contacts in Projectville were concentrated in one building of a public housing project. Like the block in La Barriada, the housing projects were physically isolated. A massive concentration of low-income housing projects sat amid acres of burned-out rubble relieved only by a few shopping streets, a small section of private houses, and a very few factories. Fire continued to ravage what was left of the retail section. Successive development plans had recommended both housing construction and industrial development in this part of the city, citing the availability of cheap land and cheap labor, but the construction of public housing had never been matched by the commercial or industrial development that could have provided jobs for the many low-income residents of the projects.

The Morgan Houses, where most of the youths contacted in this neighborhood lived, were modern high-rise buildings surrounded by open space with some benches and a few basketball and handball courts. The residents, mostly black, included high proportions of women, children, and elderly people. Some buildings were set aside for the elderly, and female-headed households receiving welfare accounted for much of the nonelderly population. Unlike residents of the study block in La Barriada, however, these people were not uniformly poor. There were moderate-income families as well, paying higher rents than the welfare and Social Security recipients, whose rents were supported by higher levels of public subsidies. Many such families were headed by transit, postal, and hospital workers.

Though the housing was modern and physically sound, other aspects of this environment were quite dangerous. The high proportion of poor teenagers, vulnerable senior citizens, and women and children, combined with some unfortunate design characteristics, led to very distinctive crime patterns. Lacking the opportunities for factory burglaries and auto theft found in La Barriada (though some youths did shoplift in the rapidly dwindling commercial sector), the most available targets for local youths who were tempted to steal were the apartments and persons of their neighbors. Since the apartments were more difficult to break into than the old tenements and factory lofts of La Barriada, the most common crimes around the projects were mugging, and the snatching of purses and gold jewelry. These commonly occurred in elevators and stairwells or in the empty, unprotected open space that separated the project buildings from each other, from transportation stops, and from shopping areas. After practice in the local neighborhood, some Projectville youths went on to commit similar crimes on the subways and in distant downtown commercial areas.

Recruitment to these activities occurred, again, primarily in the context of cliques of age peers. Like the youths in La Barriada, the Projectville youths were frequently out of work and out of school during their mid-teen years. They spent most of their time either in their apartments or, in good weather, hanging out around the basketball court and outdoor benches; in bad weather they congregated in the public interior spaces of the building.

The planning of crimes often occurred in these settings, as Tommy Singleton told us a few months after he was involved in his first and only court case.

Tommy Singleton: To tell you the truth, I don't spend that much time down there anymore. I'm trying to stay out of trouble, so I've been staying up here in the apartment. I go down to play basketball, but you can't play basketball all the time. All they want to do down there is get high. They say, "Come on, let's go get a trey bag" [three dollars worth of marijuana]. Now I won't lie. I like to do that sometimes, but some of those dudes, that's all they ever do, and if nobody got any money, it's "Let's get down; let's go get paid."

The circumstances leading to the planning of crimes among the Projectville youths were similar in many respects to those described by Jorge Padilla in La Barriada. In both cases, out-of-school and out-of-work youths in their mid-teens spent much of their time together and concocted illegal schemes for making money. The differing ecological and social circumstances of the two groups, however, led to very different crime patterns.

The distinctive crime patterns of the Projectville group derived not only from the ecological and demographic characteristics but also from

[149]

the social organization of their environment. The Projectville youths faced an environment that was both more anonymous and more exposed than that of La Barriada. The anonymity derived from the concentration of a large population in multi-story project buildings in which residents could not know each other as well as did the residents of the block in La Barriada. Along with this anonymity, however, there existed an oversee-ing bureaucracy and a group of residents with middle-class values who tried to use that bureaucracy to control local youths. Whereas the adults in La Barriada, either from fear or familiarity, usually ignored groups of youths hanging out together, some Projectville adults engaged in a continual struggle to keep local youths from loitering in the stairways, elevators, and lobbies of the buildings. Unlike the informal methods of social control preferred in La Barriada, social control methods in Proj-ectville were highly bureaucratic, involving the housing police, the housing office, the city police, and tenant volunteer patrol groups.

Though these methods often proved ineffective in preventing crime, they did produce an atmosphere in which local youths experienced constant harassment, especially during the winter months. If they gath-ered in halls and lobbies, tenants would call the housing police, who issued summonses to the youths for loitering or smoking marijuana. If the youths pled guilty, they were fined through the housing office: their parents were notified and had to pay the fine along with the next rent payment. One respondent complained that he was once arrested and fined for loitering within seconds of stepping out of the elevator. Local police also kept a lookout for crime suspects.

> *Tommy Singleton:* Sometimes the cops come in the lobby. They're holding pictures in their hands. They look at the pictures. They look at our faces. If nothing matches, they leave.

Despite the fact that tenants and police constantly attempted to watch and control the activities of these youths, such attempts could only be partially successful; there were too many youths and too many spaces. The efforts of some tenants toward more social control were further complicated by the fact that other tenants sympathized with the youths. As Tommy Singleton's mother put it, "They're big boys. They can't stay in the house all day." There was almost literally no other place for them to go, unless they got on the subways to get out of the neighborhood entirely. The result was a constant struggle between the youths on the one hand and on the other the tenants who feared them, allied with police and housing officials.

[150]

Theft

The economic crimes described by members of the Projectville clique included apartment burglaries, shoplifting, picking pockets, and, most prominently, the snatching of purses and gold jewelry. As these young men aged, they did tend, like the youths from La Barriada, to move from crimes depending on stealth to those involving the direct use of force.

Several youths reportedly were involved in apartment burglaries when they were fourteen and fifteen, devising ways of entering even though the apartments in these modern buildings are relatively secure. In the most notable incident a group burglarized an apartment in their own building, having determined that the woman who lived there was away for the evening, by assigning a small fourteen-year-old the task of entering through a window on the fifteenth floor. Zap Andrews told us the details.

> *Zap Andrews:* These brothers in my building robbed this lady on the fifteenth floor. This little guy crawled in her window. See, the windows are like this, there's one here in the hall and then you got to crawl across the outside of the building.
> *Interviewer:* Did they need a little guy to get through the window?
> *Z.A.:* Yeah. If you're real husky, you can't get through there. I could get in there myself, but I ain't crossin' no windows on the fifteenth floor. Any ol' way, they blamed the whole group of us. The cops came to my house the next morning, wakin' up my father. I said, "I didn't do it," and they said, "You know who did then." I didn't know what was goin' on. A bunch of them finally squealed, and the lady pressed charges against them all. They said Ben Bivins did it and he got time, because he had a record. All of them are home except for him. And the thing is, he didn't have nothin' to do with it. I was smokin' reefer with him downstairs when it was goin' on.

In addition to having a record for shoplifting and snatching gold chains, Ben Bivins was also older than the rest of the group; he was seventeen at the time, and most of the rest were fifteen. Bivins consequently was prosecuted as an adult, while the other cases were dismissed or handled through Family Court. Tommy Singleton, who did participate, described his experience with Family Court.

> *Tommy Singleton:* I heard the cops were looking for me, so I went right down to the station house. They sent me upstairs and I saw all my

friends in handcuffs. They never put cuffs on me, but they arrested me and put me in a special school. The case got dismissed 'cause I had no record and they had no evidence, no witnesses. But they sure messed me up in school. I've been tryin' to transfer into a regular school ever since, but they always find some reason not to accept me.

Though Zap Andrews disclaimed involvement in this incident, he described another burglary that he committed by means of guile rather than acrobatics.

Zap Andrews: This lady in my building used to come see my mom. One day I told my friend, "Hey, I can get the key and go in her house and take what we want and put it in your house. Then I'll take the key and put it back in her coat." It went along just like that. We took a TV, a camera, and a jewelry box with lots of gold bracelets, watches . . . we sold it and made around three hundred apiece.

That particular burglary was successful, but burglaries in general were relatively infrequent for this clique, certainly in comparison to the clique from La Barriada and probably as a result of the superior physical security of the project buildings. More common among the nonconfrontational crimes characteristic of their early to middle teens were picking pockets and shoplifting. Lucky Giles, eighteen when interviewed, reported that he had been a pickpocket when he was younger.

Lucky Giles: I used to dip but I can't do that now, I be scared and shit, 'cause I used to be little. I could just run through the crowd. I'm getting too big for all that.
Interviewer: Were you good at it? Could people tell you were doing it?
L.G.: I used to be with people who knew, then I knew I could do it. This guy who lives in the next building, we used to go out there all the time. I used to be with this girl too. She dipped on a lady, got her Citibank card with the code number right on it. She went to the machine, got about five hundred dollars.

Lucky Giles and Ben Bivins also shoplifted drugstore items.

Lucky Giles: People used to say, "You got a whole lot of heart, going out there in the white people's neighborhood." We used to take the bus all the way to the end, we used to boost, Dristan and Tylenols, get a whole bunch and sell it to stores. Not like going to knock somebody in the head.

[152]

Interviewer: Clothes?

LG: No clothes. Drugstores, like Key Foods, A&P, they have a drug section. We use to go in there and take them and sell them to the stores on the corner. We sell them for half price and they buy 'em. We used to come home, have about fifty dollars in my pocket.

Ben Bivins, who tended to shoplift closer to home, was caught several times and thus made himself visible to the local precinct, setting up his later conviction for burglary.

By the time they were fifteen, some of these youths were already involved in mugging local people in elevators and hallways. The elevators were a constant source of friction in the building. Even young children knew many ways to manipulate them: stopping them between floors, jamming their doors, and frequently putting them out of order, leaving residents stranded in the high-rise buildings. We observed such manipulations during our field visits; none of these involved crimes, though people in the building reported incidents that did. The residents considered the stairways even more dangerous than the elevators. The youths we interviewed reported growing up with the constant worry of being robbed themselves by youths from other buildings.

Zap Andrews described his involvement in elevator and stairway muggings when he was around fifteen.

Zap Andrews: Me and Ben used to do a couple of things before he went to jail. We caught one lady as she was going to pay her rent. We put on stocking caps and then I dived on her as she was walking down the steps. Then we split. Another time, we got on top of the elevator. A lady got on. We cut off the lights, jumped down. That shit is dark. Then we take her money, get back on top, open the door, get on the other elevator. She never knew who did it.

A few months later, however, he was recognized.

Zap Andrews: Another time, I was with this girl, and we tried to do the same thing. I ripped off a lady and she seen my face, and then, one day I tried to rap to her daughter, only I didn't know it was her daughter. Next thing you know we really started getting friendly and she said, "I want you to meet my mother." She knew it was me right off the top. She just pulled me over to the side and said, "I know what you done. Now I ain't gonna do nothing and I ain't gonna mess my daughter up, but do you still do that?" I said, "No, I stopped that now." We the best of friends now.

[153]

This incident in fact proved an abrupt turningpoint for Zap Andrews. Around this same time his whole clique began to divide into two factions with respect both to their interactions and to their involvement in economic crime. Zap Andrews, Tommy Singleton and his brother Johnny, and Stan Williams began to steer clear of theft. Ben Bivins, Larry Jefferson, Lucky Giles, and Jerry Barnes became increasingly involved in confrontational economic crimes, particularly the widely publicized practice of snatching gold chains on the streets and in subways.

To some extent, this divergence seems to have derived from different family situations. The youths who began to avoid crime lived in more nurturing households with higher levels of income. Zap Andrews's father worked as a bus driver; the Singletons' mother both worked as a home attendant and received Social Security. Andrews and the Singletons explicitly attributed Lucky Giles's crime behavior to his family situation. Giles lived with several siblings and his mother, who worked on and off as a beautician and storefront preacher and was often away from home for days at a time.

Tommy Singleton: No wonder Lucky do like that. His mother don't take care of him. You go in his house, it look like somebody's back yard.

Other individuals, however, could not be so readily categorized in terms of family situation. Jerry Barnes, who became a chain snatcher, was the only child of two parents with steady jobs and received more spending money than the others. His parents were separated, however, and he moved back and forth between them, ending up with his mother, who drank heavily. Ben Bivins and Larry Jefferson lived with their mothers and several siblings in households supported primarily by welfare. Their families were close but very poor.

Though family income and socialization may have contributed to the divergence in crime behavior in this clique, these factors did not operate mechanically. Whatever their family differences, all these youths were generally poor and had experimented with economic crime by their mid-teens. Family background is not sufficient to explain which ones decreased or increased such activity thereafter. Their choices were also the product not only of such intangibles as "character" but of their actual experiences of stealing money and their developing perceptions of the risks, rewards, and alternatives. Those who moved away from crime did so when it became clear that they could not continue without being discovered. They began to fear retaliation and incarceration. For Zap Andrews this realization came when he was recognized by the woman he had robbed in the elevator.

Interviewer: After she recognized you, you changed your mind?
Zap Andrews: Yeah, that changed it. Because if I ripped off somebody else it wouldn't be that easy. If I run into their house and all they sons be home and say "that's him" and they all break on me or something like that.
Int.: And did you stop?
Z.A.: Yeah. That played out now. By the time I got to be sixteen, I wasn't even thinking about that no more. I figure if I want something I might as well work for it.

Further, he had seen Lucky Giles encounter retaliation.

Zap Andrews: Lucky act too bad. They don't like him. Matter of fact, couple of times they be carryin' they piece, "Man, I'll blow his head off." I don't wanna go through that.

The Singleton brothers decided to move away from crime after they were arrested in the apartment burglary. Even though the case against them was dismissed, Johnny Singleton and his mother decided to seek residential placement for him away from the neighborhood, which they arranged through the Family Court; he remained for a year and a half. His brother Tommy stayed home, began to dissociate himself from the clique, and finally achieved placement in a new school. Both Tommy Singleton and Zap Andrews increased their efforts to find work at this point, though with little success.

Although the members of the clique had grown up together and claimed to have been very close since they were small children, by the time we met them, most of the incidents described above had already happened, and they had begun to go different ways. They still saw each other every day but, for example, no longer wanted to include Lucky Giles in their basketball games.

Field Notes: I walked some of the guys over to the Center to play basketball. Lucky had a bike which they said he had stolen and the rest of them were walking. They kept trying to shake Lucky. Stan told me that they were not about to go in the Center while he was there. They say he is a bum who takes off neighborhood people.

A few days later, the field observer saw the whole group together but arguing about what to do.

Field Notes: Today when I got there everybody was talking about "getting paid." Only three of seven were willing to "get paid": Lucky, Jerry, and Johnny. Then Johnny became undecided and Lucky and Jerry went off to Central Park. Johnny said he would go in later. Then he told me that he has a different way of "getting paid." He said the other two are probably going to snatch a purse or mug somebody. He has met someone who is going to advance him some marijuana to sell.

Those who continued to seek money by stealing on a regular basis began to move out from the projects to find opportunities on the shopping streets near them, on the subways, and in the business districts of Brooklyn and Manhattan. Like Zap Andrews and the Singletons, they also realized that they could not continue to victimize their immediate neighbors without being recognized. Lucky Giles had gone too far in this regard and encountered consequences: he was partially ostracized by his peers and eventually had to leave the neighborhood to escape the retaliation of his neighbors. After some men with guns came looking for him, his mother sent him to stay for a few months with relatives in South Carolina.

In addition to perceiving the need to take their predations farther from home, these youths had discovered the "new" criminal technique of snatching gold jewelry from the necks of people in the streets and subways, an activity that became profitable and popular very rapidly during the summer of 1980 when the price of gold had risen steeply. Both the rewards and risks of this crime changed dramatically, however, as its implications dawned on the youths, the police, the public, and the buyers of gold.

By the end of the summer of 1980, chain snatching had become a media-certified crime wave. Excerpts from a *New York Times* report ("Gold Chain Snatchers" 1980) provide some background:

The incidents are part of what police officials believe is a wave that became serious less than six months ago. So far this year, two women have been killed in attacks involving chain snatchings.

Most of these thefts take place on subways because of the ease of escape and the isolation of the victims. The crime is now the largest class of transit felonies.

In the first eight months of this year, nearly 2,000 people have reported having had necklaces snatched in the subways alone, and since the warm weather began in late April, the pace has built to nearly 500 a month. . . .

Transit Police Chief James Meehan says of the criminals: "With gold selling at more than $600 an ounce, it's natural they'd turn to this eventually." Young men, teenagers, and younger boys have been arrested with $200 or $300 in their pockets, he said.

But beyond the price of gold, there are other factors that influence these young criminals: It's an easy crime that requires little "muscle"; it affords little danger, since most victims do not bother to prosecute; it offers an easy escape; and because the victims are usually uninjured, judges impose short jail terms or more frequently parole when the thieves are captured.

In addition, gold chains are easy to sell. Many jewelers are happy to offer the novice criminals cheap prices for the gold. In some instances neighborhood gift shops, pizza parlors and coffee shops have acquired jewelers' scales and put up signs: "We buy gold." A necklace with a gold value of $1,500 may be bought from a snatcher for $100 or $200. . . .

A recent tour with two transit plainclothes officers showed why the subways are so popular for chain snatching. . . . "Watch the doors," said Officer Young. He positioned himself in front of a subway door. Next to him, seated, was a young woman with a heavy gold chain, a would-be mark. As the doors began to close, Officer Young wedged his foot into the door to prevent it from closing. His partner moved quickly across the train and out the door as Mr. Young motioned toward the woman.

Had it been a theft, the woman's necklace would have been snatched, the thief out the door, and the train immediately moving out of the station. The thieves would have been up the stairs and into the street by the time the train reached the next station, where the woman could report the crime.

Except for its statement that these novice criminals easily avoid arrest, this newspaper article accords with the accounts of chain snatching in our field notes and interviews. Ben Bivins, Lucky Giles, Jerry Barnes, and Larry Jefferson all operated on the subways and sold their stolen gold to a variety of fences, ranging from jewelry stores and smaller neighborhood businesses to individual entrepreneurs. Our field material places this type of crime within their criminal careers and within the social context that defined this criminal opportunity and its limits.

The spread of chain snatching occurred at the same time that the Projectville clique was dividing into those decreasing and those increasing their involvement in crime. Spontaneous snatching by some individuals in the midst of group outings accelerated the split. Lucky Giles described his quick decision to snatch a chain during a trip into Manhattan with a friend.

Lucky Giles: We was goin' to the movies. I had ten dollars in my back pocket, but it was gone. I had left my pocket open, and somebody took it. I should never have put it back there. I was mad, so I see this old man, he looked all drunk, I didn't have no money so I just snatched it and ran.

Interviewer: Did your friend know you were going to do it?

L.G.: Nah. He was standing by the movie, I was walking down the block, I snatched and ran across the street.

In this case, Lucky Giles was apprehended without involving his friend. Tommy Singleton described another occasion when he was nearly arrested as a result of similar behavior by Jerry Barnes:

Tommy Singleton: Jerry came over to my house with money in his pocket and asked me did I want to go downtown. We got on the train and he starts talking about he's gonna snatch a chain. So we was getting near where I had applied for a guard job before and the man had told me to come back and check it out next time I was around. When we came into the stop, I got off first. Then he snatched this chain and she started cursing at him and the cops started chasing him. I just walked up the steps and went on to see about the job. Then a couple of weeks later, the cops called my house and said he wanted to talk to me about chain snatching. He said witnesses had seen me with Jerry and I better come down there. Then they're telling me, "Just admit you held the door." I told them exactly what happened, that I didn't have nothin' to do with it even if I was with him. Then they talk about, "He's gonna tell when we get in court."

Interviewer: Who's going to tell? Your friend?

T.S.: Yeah. I known him since we was little, then he's gonna go and do something like that? I ain't seen him since.

Int.: You think he gave your name to the cops?

T.S.: He did. Otherwise, how would they know?

Lucky Giles and Jerry Barnes were the two most active chain snatchers in this clique, becoming separated from the Singleton brothers and others as they became more heavily involved. Both eventually received felony convictions and prison sentences following a particular snatching incident on the subway. After serving a year and a half in state prison, Lucky Giles returned to the neighborhood, and we developed a closer relationship with him. We provided him with job placement assistance and conducted some in-depth interviews. During one of these interviews, he showed us a copy of his parole report:

On ———— [date], the subject, Lucky Giles, and several codefendants were on the ———— subway train. As the train pulled into the ———— station, codefendant George Hackett held the door open while codefendant Jerry Barnes grabbed the complainant X's bracelets. Apparently, the complainant was kicked and punched by the codefendants during the commission of the robbery. At the same time, complainant Y felt her necklace being grabbed at. She was able to identify the subject Lucky Giles as the perpetrator grabbing at her necklace. The codefendants then fled the subway train. One of the train's passengers, who had seen what transpired, apprehended codefendant Barnes and handed him over to the police officers. The subject Lucky Giles and codefendant George Hackett were running around the station and were pointed out by the complainant. They were apprehended at this time. All the other codefendants were also apprehended within the station.

Giles's own account differed somewhat from that in the official records. According to him, he, Jerry Barnes, and George Hackett (not a member of the core group) had not gotten on the train with the other three codefendants; they were younger acquaintances from the neighborhood who had boarded the train separately. It was they who had initiated the spree of gold snatching; only then did the others become involved. Giles described Jerry Barnes as the most spontaneous and seemingly irrational of the group.

Lucky Giles: See, the other guys started it, and then Jerry wanted to be greedy so he went for it. He saw them start for this lady's chains and then he tried to beat them to it. There was this off-duty correction officer. He seen me and said, "That's one of them" and then they got Jerry down on the floor. Jerry was crazy. They had a gun in his back and he was still fighting back.

Jerry Barnes's wild behavior was also described by the Singleton brothers and other members of this clique.

Lucky Giles and Jerry Barnes were both eighteen at this time, both had previous arrests for similar crimes, and both received prison sentences. George Hackett, who had boarded the train with them, was acquitted. The three younger acquaintances were all juveniles and had their cases removed to Family Court. Lucky Giles returned from prison eighteen months later, married within a few weeks, and did not experience any further arrests before the end of the research period several months later. Jerry Barnes, however, was rearrested and reconvicted for a similar crime within weeks of his return from prison.

A closer analysis of some of the technical aspects of chain snatching helps contextualize this activity within these youths' criminal careers. These technical considerations include the relative lucrativeness of the crime, the distance from home at which it was practiced, and the relative requirements for speed and violence.

Compared to apartment burglaries and muggings in the youths' own neighborhood, chain snatching on the subways and commercial streets was in some ways less exposed, with far less likelihood that the victim would recognize the perpetrator during random later encounters. Lucky Giles, for example, turned to heavier involvement in chain snatching on the subways after he returned from his trip down south to escape irate neighbors.

Compared to purse snatching, chain snatching was much more lucrative. For Larry Jefferson and Ben Bivins, in fact, chain snatching was a direct outgrowth of the purse snatching that they had practiced when they were younger. But the profit from purse snatching was uncertain.

> *Johnny Singleton:* Some of 'em around the way, they like to be about snatching pocketbooks. I won't snatch pocketbooks myself. If a person press charges on you for that, you could go to jail. And half the time there ain't no money in the pocketbook anyway.

A gold chain, by contrast, brought a minimum of $30 and might bring several hundred.

Besides being more lucrative, chain snatching also tended to be more violent, since gold chains do not always break easily.

> *Larry Jefferson:* My aunt came over and she had a big gold chain and I told her, "Hide it, these people will snatch it and they be choking people." Especially those people that wear them big ones, they hard to pop. One day I saw this dude snatch this lady's chain in the train station. The chain didn't pop and he was dragging the lady down the steps. Her knees got all scraped up.

The amount of violence risked in chain snatching, however, was still less than that involved in armed robbery. Chain snatchers did not risk either an actual stabbing or shooting or a conviction for possessing a weapon. Chain snatching required a willingness to risk some violence and the ability to run fast. It tended to occur in an individual's career after such nonconfrontational crimes as burglary, picking pockets, and shoplifting and before armed robbery.

The risks changed during the summer of 1980, however, as the police took note of the new crime phenomenon and altered some of their procedures. In the early stages the police tended to treat chain snatching like purse snatching and to charge "larceny against the person"—a felony but a less serious crime than robbery. Then, as chain snatching became a more serious problem, the police concentrated on trying to bring robbery charges against the perpetrators. Lucky Giles learned of this procedural change through personal experience.

Lucky Giles: I had snatched a little chain once before. I got caught for that, but they let me go. That's when it was grand larceny. Now if you snatch a chain, it's robbery.

Like the knifepoint robberies of the youths from La Barriada, chronic chain snatching eventually led to apprehension, conviction, and substantial incarceration for these youths. Lucky Giles spent four months in jail for his first robbery conviction and came back to the neighborhood on three years' probation. He was convicted again a few weeks later along with Jerry Barnes in the incident described above, and both received prison terms. Ben Bivins spent two years in prison on a burglary charge, though his friends' assessment was that his prior arrests for shoplifting and chain snatching contributed to his receiving such a stiff sentence for burglary. Larry Jefferson was still only fifteen when his mother, after seeing him arrested on several occasions for chain snatching and finally discovering that he was stealing from her, filed a petition to have him placed under state supervision in a home for juveniles.

These outcomes show clearly the limits of confrontational street crimes as a source of income. One, two, even several crimes may be perpetrated with impunity, but continued involvement in such visible and violent crime does lead to serious sanctions. Some other data from Projectville confirm the suggestion in the *New York Times* article that the ones who really profited from the wave of chain snatchings were the dealers in stolen gold. Several of the small restaurants and shops that were the targets of a police campaign against buyers of stolen gold were located in the Projectville area, although such establishments were by no means the only receivers. Lucky Giles reported selling stolen gold right in Manhattan's major jewelry district:

Lucky Giles: I sold it right in midtown.
Interviewer: You mean in the big stores? Aren't they supposed to ask you for a certificate?
L.G.: Some do, some don't.

Int.: You just keep trying until you find one?
L.G.: I know where to go.

We also interviewed some older individuals hanging out on the commercial streets of Projectville who made a business of buying gold right on the street. A twenty-two-year-old professional drug dealer who had grown up in the projects told of a business offer he had received from some associates in the drug business who had branched out into stolen gold.

> *Sky Wilson:* I went to check out some people I know yesterday. They owed me some money. Now they have a new thing. They buy and sell gold. They stand in front of the jewelry store and catch people on the way in and say, "I'll give you top dollar." They have a kit with acid, a pennyweight scale, just like a jeweler. They check the prices everyday. Of course you got to have money to make money. He said you need about five, six hundred dollars a day to do this. But the other day he bought a bracelet for seven hundred and resold it for fifteen hundred. That's all profit.

Another individual working the street corner in Projectville explained his operation in more detail:

> *Field Notes:* He explained to me, "Since the price of gold went up, the kids and the pawnbrokers have kept right up with the changing economy." He said he buys gold from the hustlers in the neighborhood. He carries a mini-scale with him and buys it right on the corner. When he gets a certain amount, he takes it inside the store where his friend who works inside lets him store it. In return, he keeps an eye out for shoplifters from in front of the store. He says he has to worry about buying from young kids. Sometimes kids will steal from their mothers and the mothers come looking for the buyer, which is trouble. He also has to watch out for the cops. "If the cops see you on the same corner day after day, they figure you're buying gold." He claims the cops often pick up young kids and, if they have gold on them, the cops keep it for themselves. He himself sells the gold to a licensed pawnbroker who switches it for legitimate gold with certificates that people have pawned. When they come back for their gold, he gives them the stolen gold. The corner buyer told me he has been to court many times but nothing has ever happened to him.

In this wave of gold snatching, as in most youth crime, youths took the big risks while older people profited from their crimes with virtually no risk.

By their late teens, even the members of this clique who had been involved in regular predatory street crimes were decreasing their involvement because they perceived that the risks outweighed the benefits, as Ben Bivins did when he returned from prison at the age of nineteen.

Ben Bivins: I just decided I don't want to be doing that no more. You could be risking your life, robbing somebody's mother, and for what? Two dollars. That's all you get sometimes.

Drug Selling

Another pattern of economic crime that we documented among Projectville youths was selling drugs, primarily marijuana (our observations were made in the early 1980s, before the cocaine and crack epidemic of the later 1980s). Career patterns in drug selling contrasted sharply with patterns of predatory crime in involving direct recruitment of youths by older people, higher levels of organization, and the possibility of advancement to more lucrative and less exposed criminal roles with age and experience.

The earlier stages of this progression are illustrated in the career of Johnny Singleton. During the summer of 1980, when some of the youths he had grown up with were participating heavily in the wave of chain snatching precipitated by skyrocketing gold prices, Johnny discovered that he could make steady money without performing distasteful and risky violent acts, by selling marijuana in Central Park in Manhattan. His initial discovery occurred almost by accident.

Interviewer: Do your friends put pressure on you to commit crimes? I mean, if you're walking along the street and there's somebody you could rip off and they say "Let's do it," what do you do?
Johnny Singleton: They say, "Let's go get paid," you know, but it all depends on what they mean by "getting paid." If they talking about ripping off somebody, I don't even talk about it with 'em. I just go the other way. Most of the time, I be right in Central Park, sellin' reefer. That's what I call "getting paid," not tryin' to rip somebody off or snatch somebody's mother's pocketbook. That's messed up. That could be somebody, like you might know their son, or it could be their last money. My mother told me about that. She told it to all of us.

[163]

Int.: How often do you go to Central Park?

J.S.: Every day. If I wasn't here now, I'd be out there.

Int.: How much do you make on that a day?

J.S.: I spend fifteen dollars on the reefer and I make fifty to sixty-five dollars back.

Int.: That sounds like pretty good money.

J.S.: I know.

Int.: How long have you been doing this now?

J.S.: I just started recently, no more than a month ago, in May sometime. That's when I found out that's where the money's at, instead of . . . you know, going out and tryin' to kill somebody for a couple of dollars, for a fifty-fifty chance of no money.

Int.: How did you find out about it?

J.S.: We went out there one day, right, and we only had trey bags [three-dollar packages] of reefer. We sat down on a bench and started rollin' up skinny joints. This dude came up to me and said, "Y'all sellin' reefer? Ya'll sellin' joints?" So we said yeah and sold him ten joints for a dollar apiece. Then this lady saw us sellin' to him and came up and bought the last three. We was really happy cause we ain't have no money to get home. So then we went and bought some more and just kept rollin' it and sellin' it, rollin' it and sellin' it.

Int.: I've heard about guys getting ripped off doing that. Did that ever happen to you?

J.S.: Nah.

Int.: Do you go alone?

J.S.: My friend Jerry go with me, but he stands on one side and I'm on the other.

Int.: How do you get the reefer? Do you have someone you depend on for it?

J.S.: It's a reefer store, only a couple of blocks from my house, but I can't depend on him, unless I got money to buy it.

Int.: You mean you don't always pay for it when you get it?

J.S.: Right, sometime he trust us and we pay him when we get back.

Johnny Singleton's drug-selling career came to a halt at the end of the summer when his mother, after talking it over with him, had him placed in a residential institution out of the city, where he remained for the next year. By that time Johnny was no longer speaking to his partner Jerry Barnes, because Jerry had given Johnny's brother's name to the police.

Many of the elements of getting into the marijuana business that he described appear in the biographies of individuals from all three study neighborhoods. Consignments from older dealers to youths for street sales and work in the "reefer stores" or "smoke shops" provided occasional to steady sources of income for some individuals in each clique. We investigated the career progression and social context of such activity in the lives of three young men in their early twenties who lived or had lived in other sections of Projectville.

Like Johnny Singleton, these older respondents had learned from experience the limits of petty stealing as a source of regular income and had found it easy to enter into drug selling through the informally organized recruitment provided by the consignment system and the "reefer stores." Unlike Johnny, however, these older individuals had stayed at it long enough to encounter the constraints on the drug business posed by the police, by suppliers, by competition, and by predatory criminals who know that dealers carrying money and drugs are not protected by the police. Each of the three had developed different ways of handling these problems and had found different places in the web of vertical and horizontal relationships that organize drug distribution.

When we first contacted Juice Baker, he was twenty-three years old and living with his mother and one younger brother in Projectville's Simpson Houses. His mother had worked in a day-care center for many years. Juice had finished high school and also completed a year and a half of college. At that time, he was working for a maintenance company on a daily shape-up basis. He had already experienced several kinds of jobs and several kinds of crime, making a success of none of them. He had worked in gas stations, factories, and messenger agencies and had quit or been fired from all of the jobs, usually after disputes with supervisors over working conditions or attendance. When he was younger, he had engaged in larceny and also some armed robberies. He now considered himself too old for those crimes.

> *Juice Baker:* Yeah I used to boost. I call 'em "snatch dudes" . . . like go down to the garment district, grab a rack, and go. I've done stickups too, caught 'em comin' out of the bank . . . but you end up runnin' away from the police too much. I don't know . . . as you get older you get out of the runnin' part.

Baker's only arrest at that point had put an end to a short-lived career in auto theft. He had arranged to steal cars and deliver them to a receiver who would pay him $50 per car. The third time he did it, he ran a red light and was stopped in a stolen car with no license: "Dumb move. I didn't have a record so they threw it out, but that was the end of that." Baker had also tried various other hustles, including stealing checks from mailboxes and buying stolen goods from younger "snatch dudes" for resale at a profit. His main hustle, however, had been selling marijuana on the street. He started in his own neighborhood but then learned that he could make more money if he went into Manhattan and sold "loose joints" to office workers coming outside at lunch time. He had made regular money doing this off and on for a couple of years, but he had also run into various difficulties.

Juice Baker: You pick yourself a good spot, you stand out there for a couple of days, you get a steady customer, he spreads the word, and you start to get the clientele. Like they say, "Clientele will tell."
Interviewer: You have one regular spot?
J.B.: You got to drift. I had one good spot, I used to try to stay there, but it got too hot. Too many people around, other dealers start showing up, soon there's a crowd, people start askin' "What's going on over there?" and then the next person askin' that question is gonna be The Man.
Int.: I'm confused. First you said you have to pick one spot, then you said you have to drift.
J.B.: If you visit one spot regularly, you build up a clientele. In the beginning you gotta stay out there, but, once you known, you can just move, they'll look for you. You got to keep movin'.
Int.: Did you ever have trouble like that with the police?
J.B.: Well, yeah, out here in the city [Manhattan] they get kind of foul. Back home [Projectville] they'll pick you up, but out here basically you get ripped off. The cops take your product, they take your money . . .
Int.: You mean they take the money out of your pocket, and they don't arrest you?
J.B.: Yeah, they take everything, and then they say, "Tough luck, now you got to start all over again."
Int.: How many times has this happened to you?
J.B.: It happened to me twice. That's when I learned how to move around. It happened to me twice because they knew I'd be back: "Well, his clientele's here, he'll be back." That's when I learned that if I move around he can't get me like that. So I moved further downtown and then, when he comes, you know he goes through his little journeys and he sees I'm not there any more and then while he's looking at somebody else, I'll come back and be there for just that amount of time and then just get back out. I can't let him be takin' my stuff you know, 'cause sometimes I get things on consignment. You get somebody to throw you something like that, they don't want to hear about you gettin' busted. When they put you out of business . . . say you had a quarter of a pound that cost you a yard and a quarter [$125], right. Now they put

you out of business, you gotta pay the yard and a quarter to the man
who give it to you on consignment and you gotta take another yard and
a quarter for the next one . . .
Int.: Why, if you're paying him back?
J.B.: 'Cause you got popped for the first one, which means he'd be
takin' a risk.
Int.: But how does he know you got popped?
J.B.: Because you won't be bringing him the money that night. If you're
gonna be late, you better tell him too, because . . . well, anything
could happen.
Int.: Over marijuana?
J.B.: Come on, man. People get shot for coats out there.
Int.: Would you say this has been your main source of income for a
while?
J.B.: Yeah, basically, for about the last three years. I had to let go of the
cars, so yeah, a couple of little things, a few stickups, but basically herb.

By this point, however, Baker was beginning to suffer reverses in marijuana selling and was again trying legitimate work at the maintenance
agency.

A friend of his had been supporting himself by selling drugs for several
years. Sky Wilson had lived with his aunt in Projectville's Simpson
Houses between the ages of twelve and fifteen. Unlike Juice Baker,
Wilson had no history of teenage theft and had not held a job since he left
school in the eleventh grade, partly because he had grown up in a more
affluent family situation. Wilson said, "I never had to steal cause I had
money in my pocket." Another reason was that he had begun selling
marijuana in the streets soon after dropping out of high school, and he
had prospered. In a series of interviews over the next year he described
in some detail his methods of doing business and the reasons he had
done so much better than many of his associates, like Juice Baker.
During that same period of time, however, he also changed his business
considerably in response to a series of crises that eventually drove him
off the streets and away from the marijuana market into the cocaine
market.

Sky Wilson's first major connection with the drug business came
through a woman, an older woman with whom he lived for a year after he
left his aunt's house. When he was nineteen, he took his first consignment of marijuana from a male friend of this woman's sister. He had
previously bought and sold small amounts from time to time, working
with a friend his own age; he described that period of his life, in which he
had very little money, as "pure hell." But he had already become a

"connoisseur," he said, and his ability to recognize quality drugs had always helped him in the business. It was then that he was approached by the older dealer, who "knew I was into something," about taking consignments for more sustained selling. Unlike Juice Baker, Wilson was able to accrue in a few months enough working capital to protect himself against embarrassment in case of being robbed or having his merchandise confiscated by the police.

Wilson attributed much of his success to the fact that he sought out older hustlers from whom he learned good business values and who provided him with business opportunities. Many of these contacts occurred in after-hours social clubs throughout New York's inner-city neighborhoods.

Field Notes: Wilson began to describe the after-hours places: "When I say after-hours, I mean some of these places don't even open up until three o'clock in the morning." He said that a lot of what goes on in these places has to do with cocaine. People go there to buy, sell, and take cocaine, mostly to take it. Given the hours of these places, most of the clientele are hustlers. I asked, "What kind of hustles are we talking about: gambling, prostitution, organized theft, drugs?" He said, "Some of all of that, but mostly drugs." I asked, "What kind of drugs?" He said "All kinds of drugs. These places are like trade schools in the drug business."

When he first tried to get into such places, he was refused because he was too young. Many had rules limiting entrance to those over the age of twenty-five. But when he began to dress up in suits to make himself look older and got to know some of the older hustlers through taking consignments and working for them in the reefer stores, he began to gain admittance to the "spots." He continued to cultivate the older hustlers, and as he showed himself to be reliable and respectful, his opportunities expanded: "Once you get into hustling, there's a lot of things you can do. You go from one thing to the next."

Between the ages of nineteen and twenty-one, Wilson worked the streets in good weather and in smoke shops owned by older associates during the winter. Of the two forms of work, he preferred the streets.

Interviewer: How does working in a store compare to working for yourself?
Sky Wilson: Well, it gets cold in the winter, you might decide to move inside. But it's like that nine to five thing. It's a job in itself, just like in a numbers joint. Somebody's got to open up. Somebody's got to be there

when the people come. Somebody's got to sweep the place out. Reefer store's the same way. After a while, you decide to move on. I like the open air.

After alternating between the streets and the stores in this manner for about two years, he got the chance to open his own storefront operation. He fixed up an abandoned building and stayed there for about three months.

Sky Wilson: It was nice. We made money there. The city marshals chased us out finally. We had already stayed there too long.

He went back to selling in the streets, and by the time we met him, he had established several business procedures designed to maximize his clientele while minimizing his exposure to arrest and competition. He refused to sell around the Simpson Houses, because people there had known him since he was small. Instead, he traveled to the central business districts on weekdays to sell to office workers; and later in the day and on weekends he concentrated on the avenues of Brooklyn to sell to the working people of the inner city. During this period he was still dealing mainly in marijuana. He sold cocaine in the spots, mostly to pay for what he himself consumed, but he refused to sell cocaine on the street, considering that too risky.

He also specifically dissociated himself from the heroin traffic—although his connections provided him with opportunities to participate in it as well—partly on moral grounds.

Sky Wilson: Like an older hustler once told me, "Dope [heroin] kills," and I ain't about that. I provide a service. Go back to prohibition, people like the Kennedys made their money selling booze. Now they're respectable businessmen. I sell coke and smoke, and I wouldn't sell anything I wouldn't take myself.

His moral objections, however, were accompanied by perceptions of heroin traffic as involving much more money, competition, violence, and danger. One day he reported that Juice Baker had been arrested while transporting a large amount of heroin.

Sky Wilson: I heard they're going to put him away for a long time. He got in over his head. He just wasn't ready to get mixed up in something like that. Now I ain't sayin' nothin' against him, but that's the kind of guy he was and that's what happened to him.

[169]

Wilson's knowledge of similar cases had helped keep him away from the heroin business.

Sky Wilson: I knew another guy. They called him the Invader. He got big real young. He was only eighteen or nineteen. He had a crew of about thirty people working for him, coke and dope. He had three Mercedes. He was dead before he was twenty-one. I don't want to make it like that.

In contrast to Juice Baker and the Invader, Wilson stressed that he did not trade in heroin, worked at a level where hustlers cooperated with each other, had established himself as trustworthy with both customers and business associates, paid attention to older hustlers and learned from them, and avoided violence. He referred to being a reliable businessman as "diplomacy" and said that the lack of this quality rapidly thinned out the ranks of aspiring hustlers.

Sky Wilson: You know, everybody can't hustle. Some guys just don't make it. They may have money, good drugs to start with, but they still don't make it.
Interviewer: What do you need to make it as a hustler?
S.W.: Let me see, what's a good word? Just call it diplomacy: be trustworthy, consistent. You and I make a deal. We're both happy. Let's keep it that way. Do it the same way next time. A lot of people out there are knuckleheads. You would never do business with them the second time.

Wilson claimed that he made a practice of avoiding violence—again, both on moral grounds and as a matter of good business practice.

Sky Wilson: I'm a hustler, not a gangster.
Interviewer: How do you mean? What's a gangster?
S.W.: A gangster is like Al Capone, might makes right. But like an older brother told me, "You live by the sword, you die by the sword." There's a lot of shooting out there. A lot of people my age are caught up in something that's not real. They go too fast and they get killed. I don't want to make money like that. What they say is, "If the money is funny, so is the honey." I'm a hustler. I provide a service. That's why I can survive. Life ain't about getting killed, it's about being able to go to your brother and say, "Help me out." There's a lot of people out there who take care of me and I take care of them.

[170]

Some of our field observations confirmed the cooperative nature of Wilson's associations with other hustlers. One of his selling spots in the central business district of Manhattan was informally considered the territory of a small group of regular hustlers.

Field Notes: When I arrived today, Sky wasn't there yet, but the other regulars were all out there. A little altercation was just ending when I got there. The people who work in the same area as Sky were arguing with this guy, telling him he couldn't sell there. They referred to him as an "independent operator." The situation almost got violent before the independent succumbed to their demands and moved on. When Sky got there I asked him if he was in business with these guys. He said, "No, we just get together to protect ourselves because these guys only come in one or two days a week and steal our business. We're here everyday."

In a subsequent interview, Wilson described how such informal associations originate and are maintained.

Interviewer: How does a new man get established in one of these situations?
Sky Wilson: There's no room for a new man, now. I was the last one in and I closed the door. There's only a certain amount of money to go around.
Int.: How did you get in?
S.W.: Well, I heard about it, at first, in a joking kind of way. I didn't say nothing. I let them come to me. By that time, I already knew something about them. You'd be surprised. It's a very close-knit thing among hustlers. You meet someone you've never met before in a place you've never been before, you find out you know someone they know. They may even have heard of you.

Field observations around this time also revealed the relationship between this loose network of drug sellers and the police.

Field Notes: I met Sky today and he took me into the park over to the part where he and his friends work. Just as we got there, a white man in a business suit carrying an attaché case came over and asked Sky where he could buy a half ounce of reefer. Sky asked the man to sit down on the bench and wait. After a few minutes, Sky walked over and they made a transaction. Afterwards I asked him why he did that. He said,

[171]

"Because the police are always around here." Sure enough, there were two policemen stationed about eighty yards away from where all this was going on.

In interviews, Wilson told us more about his manner of dealing with police.

Sky Wilson: The thing is, you just have to give him respect when he's around. Wait till he turns the corner. Don't do it right in his face. You got to show him that respect.
Interviewer: Have you ever had your stuff confiscated?
S.W.: Just recently, as a matter of fact. I was having an argument with a guy who was selling T-shirts. I knew him, I was just arguing about the price, but we got loud and the cops came over. I told them it was all right because we were friends. But then he found my bag on the ground with the drugs in it and said, "This makes it different, doesn't it?" He said to his partner, "What can we do? It was on the ground so we can't arrest him." So they just confiscated it. I waited for a while and then I bumped into the guy about an hour and a half later outside the park. I tried to buy it back from him. The drugs in there were worth about seven or eight hundred dollars to me. I would have paid him a hundred and fifty to get it back, but he said, "Sorry, there were witnesses and besides it's been a slow night. But next time I'll make sure you don't take the fall."
Int.: I was wondering if you were feeling more heat out there with the [1980] Democratic Convention coming up?
S.W.: Yeah, I've been feeling it. That always happens, like if the Pope comes to town or Castro. It affects prostitutes, numbers, drug dealers, gamblers. But the black market never goes away. It's always there. It just gets a little harder for a while. I'll tell you something, they could clamp down on all this shit tomorrow if they wanted to. I know that. They could arrest everybody or make it impossible for us to operate.
Int.: Why do you think they don't?
S.W.: There's too much money involved. So it just goes in cycles. Right now the heat's on. There's been too many killings.

A few days after this interview, Sky became involved in a series of incidents that demonstrated the mobilization of the hustlers' network but also pointed up the limits of his ability to avoid violence and to coexist with the police. While dealing in the area just described, he was robbed at knifepoint by a customer who stole the bag containing his drugs as well as all his money and gold jewelry. The next day, when this same individual reappeared before Wilson arrived, Wilson's associates attacked him and beat him severely. The customer pressed charges against one of his assailants. Wilson then pressed charges against the customer for the original robbery. In court, the judge and prosecutors had little patience with the evasions and countercharges, and both cases were thrown out. As it turned out, however, Wilson's robber had several outstanding warrants and remained in custody.

That would have been the end of the whole affair had it not focused police attention on the dealing area. A week later, as Wilson and some of his associates were sitting on a bench waiting for business, the police appeared, found a weapon in a bag underneath the bench, and arrested Wilson and some others on a weapons charge. This was the first serious arrest of his life. Previously, he had been arrested only once, for smoking marijuana, a misdemeanor for which he paid a fine. Now he was involved in a major case, which dragged on for the next several months.

In interviews after these incidents, Wilson talked more about the role of violence in the drug business. He maintained that there was no basis for the charge against him, since he did not carry weapons. He had owned and carried weapons in his life, he said, but he had stopped carrying them in order to avoid just this sort of incident. He preferred to handle threats of violence in other ways. His previous countercomplaint to the police had been one way. Letting his associates retaliate was another. He explained that someone with experience in the underworld does not necessarily have to handle violence personally.

Sky Wilson: There's a lot of people who respect me. That knucklehead who ripped me off should have known better. It's like an unwritten law. I know people who would kill for me. I would do the same for them. I've known lots of gangsters, but I don't believe in all that shoot 'em up. When your brother needs you, though, you got to be there. It doesn't matter if it's money or trouble. I give people money, drugs, whatever. I don't expect them to pay me back. I know they probably will, but it doesn't matter if they don't. That's not why I do it. White people are always counting every penny, but it's not about that. It's about taking care of your brother, your woman, whoever, and you know they're going to take care of you when you need it.

Besides the fact that in the previous instance his associates had retaliated for him, he was taken care of in the weapons charge by one of his older associates from the after-hours spots, an owner of several reefer stores for whom he had often worked, who bailed him out and provided him with a private lawyer.

[173]

After these incidents Wilson gradually moved away from selling in the streets. At first he merely gave up his sales to office workers and concentrated on the avenues of Brooklyn, where he encountered less police presence. He also began to depend more on sales of cocaine in the spots for his income. In addition, he looked for a straight job as cover should he have to go to trial, but he was unwilling to take the low-level messenger jobs that were most readily available to him, and he eventually gave up seeking legitimate work.

He next tried to open his own smoke shop again, hoping to establish a source of income that would not expose him directly to robbery or arrest. He and four "junior partners" invested $3,000 and opened a shop in an area where there were already several similar establishments. They hired local handymen to install a heavy door and a plexiglass window in the interior through which marijuana could be exchanged for money. The junior partners staffed the place, along with extra help whom they paid on a daily basis. Wilson came by only occasionally to check on the operation.

The police raided the establishment on the third day and arrested two of the junior partners. Wilson himself was not arrested and lost little money, since the operation had barely broken even in two and a half days. He subsequently evaluated this operation, the factors that had led to its demise, and ways to do it differently next time.

> *Sky Wilson:* It was in a heavy drug area. I knew it might get raided, but then I knew there would be a lot of clientele. It got totally raided too. The police busted the door right out of the frame, a steel door. Probably we got busted because we were too busy. We had cars lined up in front of the place. That was a mistake. Next time I'll have somebody to steer the cars somewhere else to park. Either the cops noticed the cars, or somebody dropped a dime on me. Probably it was the tenants. That's why abandoned buildings are good, but then you could get burned out. Basements and storefronts are good because the clientele don't have to walk past the tenants. I anticipated a problem with the tenants, too, but I thought it would last longer than it did. Next time I won't do it in a high drug area. No senior citizens or long-time residents. I know people who have spots where the tenants look out for them. They don't call the cops and they keep the crowds out.

When this incident occurred, his court case had been dragging on with no progress for several months. Shortly after his store was raided he was arrested again, this time in one of the after-hours spots for possession of cocaine. At this point, he began to get seriously worried about going to jail. After his older partner again bailed him out, he did not go back to the streets at all. He no longer sold marijuana for income but relied solely on cocaine sales in the spots. Previously, he claimed, he had sold only casually in the spots, going there to hang out and making sales incidentally. Now he reversed the pattern, cutting down on the time he spent inside but maximizing his sales.

He was eventually convicted on both charges, but somewhat to his own surprise he received only probation on both convictions. One reason was that he had no prior felony convictions; he also got last-minute support in the form of letters from some prominent politicians, which the mother of one of his women friends arranged for him. At the age of twenty-three he found himself in a difficult situation. He was making a lot of money: estimates derived from regular interviews over a period of several months put his income at between $500 and $1,000 a week, untaxed, and not including the considerable quantities of his own expensive drugs that he consumed himself. Yet as his troubles with violence and the police multiplied, he talked more and more about getting out of New York and out of the drug business.

Sky Wilson: I'm a good businessman, no doubt about it. I know how to buy and sell. But I've been ripped off, cut, and arrested. Now I'm on probation and I won't get off so easy next time. But how am I gonna get a job now? I know I could run lots of kinds of businesses, but I can't go up to somebody and say, "Listen, I know how to buy and sell. I've been buying and selling drugs for years." And I sure don't want to be no messenger, not after the money I'm used to. What I'm trying to do now is get enough money together to start my own business, maybe a boutique or a penny arcade. Something that has nothing to do with drugs.

His only hope for raising a large amount of money, however, lay in the drug business—but he had become increasingly reluctant to take risks. He reported turning down offers from his older associates to do large cocaine deals or operate another reefer store. He referred to his current place in the drug hierarchy as the "middle shalons [echelons]" and was reluctant to move down or up.

Sky Wilson: It's getting bad out there. Too many power struggles, too many people getting killed, people shooting each other over territories.
Interviewer: What about territories?
S.W.: Well, that's for cocaine and heroin. With reefer it doesn't matter except for large operations. It doesn't really affect me because I have clout in a couple of places. Also, I don't do it that often and I move

around a lot, so I'm not a threat. I could be moving on into the higher shalons of things, but I'm staying away from it. When you get seriously involved in the drug business, there's thousands of dollars at stake. It's a lot more pressure, a lot more hassles. You have to worry about people making deals with the D.A. You could get bumped off. People think you're moving in on their territories. They rip off your workers, your spots. They be diming on you. I really don't have to worry about that at my level.

The third individual from Projectville who had worked on and off in the drug business for several years was Sly Landers, age twenty-three when we contacted him. He was living in a small section of Projectville still occupied by private houses. His was a wide-open block where gambling and street drug sales flourished, drawing many customers from the nearby housing projects.

When we met Landers, he was working a few days a week for a furniture store, loading the truck and making deliveries as needed. He had made his living from temporary work of this sort in combination with petty theft and a low-level place in the drug business since he was fifteen years old. Although he reported serving as a lookout for some armed robberies in his late teens, most of his thefts were work-related. He was generally nonviolent and avoided robberies after a few experiences.

Sly Landers: Most of the guys I did that with are dead or in jail now. I won't do that now. As you get older, the scenery changes.

His work in the drug business had included selling marijuana on the street and working as an attendant in heroin "shooting galleries." But none of his endeavors, legitimate or not, alone or in combination, had ever yielded him much income. Both his legal and illegal work had always been irregular and poorly paid. Though he had never been a heroin addict, he described himself as having been a borderline alcoholic and heavy user of marijuana and hallucinogens for several years.

During the period of several months when we were in touch with him, he continued the same pattern of seeking income. He first left the furniture store and worked steadily through a temporary agency for about four months, still supplementing his income with on-the-job theft when possible. After a quarrel with the agency, he began working for two local "stores." One establishment sold marijuana; the other took numbers bets and sold marijuana, food, and "bootleg" liquor (commercially produced but sold without a license and usually after hours). He obtained these jobs on the basis of being known as a neighborhood regular, even though he had lived in the area only a few months. His working shifts at these establishments were at night and paid about $40 for eight hours work, untaxed. This rate of pay was better than the minimum wage ($3.35 an hour, or $26.80 per day before taxes) paid by the temporary agency, although the availability of work varied from seven to only two nights a week, and he had to worry about being robbed, burned out, or arrested. Neither as careless a worker as Juice Baker nor as ambitious and upwardly mobile as Sky Wilson, Sly Landers treated both low-wage legitimate jobs and low-wage tasks in the drug business as interchangeable, short-term employment.

The experiences of these individuals in the drug business contrast sharply with the experiences of younger individuals engaged in predatory crimes. Both stealing and dealing are ways of gaining income, but dealing, unlike stealing—or at least unlike the relatively unorganized and spontaneous stealing typically committed by teenagers—can be sustained over time. Whereas youthful stealing relatively quickly saturates the environment and becomes less possible with increasing age and involvement, selling drugs can lead to sustained and expanding income opportunities. Though far more dangerous than legitimate jobs, the drug business offers inner-city youths the potential of earning more than they ever could for honest work.

[8]

Crime in Hamilton Park

Our field contacts in Hamilton Park were among a group of youths who had all grown up together and who represented a cross section of the several different ethnic sections—principally Irish, Italian, and Polish—which make up the neighborhood. Most of these youths lived in the geographical center of the neighborhood, where the more established and affluent residents lived and where there was no strong concentration of single ethnic groups, like the heavily Italian and Polish areas on the borders of the neighborhood.

Hamilton Park bore certain ecological similarities to La Barriada, particularly in the proximity of residential buildings and factories, which often coexisted within the same block. The Hamilton Park youths, however, did not live in an isolated section but very near the intact and busy major shopping streets. The primary type of housing consisted of wood-frame rowhouses, many of which predated even the old tenements in La Barriada.

In economic level and social organization, however, Hamilton Park differed greatly from both La Barriada and Projectville. Most of the households in which the Hamilton Park youths lived were supported by adult men who worked in relatively high-paying blue-collar jobs; additional income was brought in by working wives and children. Most families owned their own homes, though the houses were not expensive and often belonged to the eldest of three generations living in different apartments. The higher economic level of the neighborhood, the presence of adult men in most households, and the existence of well-organized church groups and block associations all contributed to a type of public order in this neighborhood quite different from that in the two poorer minority neighborhoods. Hamilton Park residents used both the police and informal social control methods to curtail the occurrence of street

[178]

crimes within the neighborhood. As a result, Hamilton Park appeared in official police statistics as a low-crime neighborhood and had a reputation as a place where the streets were relatively safe both day and night.

In many respects, however, our observations and interviews belied the neighborhood's reputation as a low-crime area. It is true that we found very few street robberies committed by local youths, but we did find a considerable number of other crimes among these youths: some types were similar to those found in the other two neighborhoods, and some—notably those connected to local organized crime—were distinctive to Hamilton Park.

As noted earlier, patterns of noneconomically motivated violence were basically similar among all three neighborhoods. The Hamilton Park youths fought over their turf during their mid-teens just as often and just as violently as the other youths, and as they reached their later teens, they continued to fight in bars and discos. They also participated in income-motivated burglary, larceny, and even some robbery in ways ostensibly similar to the adolescent theft patterns found in the other neighborhoods, at least in the exploratory stages. During their early and mid-teen years, the Hamilton Park youths did a certain amount of breaking into local factories and shoplifting from local stores. As they reached the ages of sixteen and seventeen, they also began to steal automobiles.

Closer examination of their theft patterns, however, shows that the Hamilton Park youths differed in both the motivation for and the intensity of their involvements in economic crime, particularly during the mid-teen years. None of them went on to become involved in systematic theft as a primary source of income. By their mid-teens most of them were already working, even if only part time and off-the-books, and earning better than minimum wage. Wages, not theft, provided their primary source of income during those years. The way they committed theft reflected their lack of dependence on stealing for income. Thrills rather than the pursuit of income often seemed to dominate their motives for breaking into factories, stealing cars, and occasionally mugging Polish immigrants.

Those who did steal for profit were more likely to do so from the workplace, which they were able to do because, unlike the minority youths, they were employed during the mid-teens. As they reached their later teens, some of them did in fact come to rely on illegal sources of income, often to supplement rather than substitute for wages, but these sources were drug selling and doing errands for local adult organized crime figures rather than the high-risk, low-return thefts so prevalent among the minority youths.

[179]

The initial experiences of Hamilton Park youths with factory burglary were quite similar to those of the youths from La Barriada. The Hamilton Park youths too lived quite near many factories, and their first exploratory break-ins were often carried out as much in a spirit of play as in pursuit of income. Most of the youths interviewed admitted breaking into factories occasionally at about thirteen to fifteen years of age.

Peter Murphy: When I was younger, I never used to, like, get into sports. I always used to climb roofs and hang out. Down right around my block there are factories. I used to climb roofs, go into some of them, sometimes, you know, rob some things.

Charlie Gaberewski: You go down the street from where I live and there's where the lots and factories are. I know the rules over there like a book. There's this one trucking company, we used to hang out in the trailers during the winter and outside during the summer, and we used to climb around on the roofs all smashed out of our minds, drinking and smoking or sometimes, you know, take a little mescaline or acid. One time we were running around and one of my friends fell through the skylight, and we got a rope to pull him out and he goes, "I don't want to leave. There's toys down here, bicycles, everything." So we tied up the rope and we were pullin' the stuff up through the roof.
Interviewer: What did you do with it?
C.G.: We sold most of it. Some of it, the big guys came and stole it from us. We sold some of it right on the street: "Hey, you want a bicycle frame, ten dollars."

These accounts reveal the same sort of mixture of expressive and economic motives found in the accounts of initial factory break-ins by the youths from La Barriada except that the expressive component seems, if anything, more pronounced in these cases. Comparison of later developments reveal even more pronounced differences between the two groups. Whereas the youths from La Barriada went on to commit systematic burglaries in pursuit of income and developed specialized criminal methods and skills, the Hamilton Park youths were deriving most of their income from wages during these same mid-teen years and did not develop into systematic burglars.

Besides having alternative sources of income, the Hamilton Park youths were constrained differently by the local social control environment. There was little of the social separation between local residents and factory owners and managers that characterized La Barriada. Many of these managers lived right in the neighborhood, knew the local youths, had access to local sources of information, and used it to invoke sanctions against local youths who had gone too far in their break-ins. Peter Murphy and his friends were identified by the owner of a factory that burned after they had left a lit candle behind them:

Peter Murphy: When I was about twelve, I almost got arrested for a fire. Me and Mike and Billy lit it. Billy ratted on us. The guy that owned the factory said, "I'll give you a hundred bucks if you tell me who did that." So Billy told him it was me.
Interviewer: The guy who owned the factory, he lived right there in the neighborhood?
P.M.: Yeah, right around the corner from me. The factory was right there too. So, Billy said it was me. I went to my uncle, he's a cop, not in the precinct here, but he knows everybody there. So my uncle said, "Ah, you did it," and I told him Billy did it too, and my uncle went to the guy and told him that. So Billy ended up getting blamed for it. I think Mike got away.

This incident reveals two kinds of differences between the social control environment in Hamilton Park and in the other two neighborhoods. Not only were Hamilton Park residents more willing and able to use the criminal justice system to control youth crime, but youths who were in trouble were also more able to influence the criminal justice system through personal ties. In this instance the confrontation between victim and offender ended in a stalemate. The very fact that the offender was identified and had to resist sanctions, however, demonstrates the greater effectiveness of the Hamilton Park social control.

Another incident following a factory burglary shows yet another side of the social control environment.

Field Notes: Brian Deutsch and his brother's girlfriend and I went out to the park. We were sitting on some benches when Brian's friend Kenny came up to us and told us about an incident that had happened a couple of weeks before. He said that he had been walking home from work when a couple of guys ran out of a factory and grabbed him. They accused him of robbing their factory and they forced him inside. He said one of them hit him in the face and another started beating him with a stick. He showed us a big bruise under his arm where he caught one of the blows from the stick. Finally, he managed to raise some doubt in their minds that it had really been him and they asked him if he knew another guy. He said he knew the guy but didn't hang out with him. They put him in a van and made him take them to where the other guy was hanging out, jumped out and grabbed him. Then they went back to the factory, tied this guy up and started hoisting him up by his feet. They told Brian's friend to get lost.

Once they had identified the offender through local information networks, Hamilton Park residents were as likely to exercise informal sanctions as they were to use the criminal justice system. A third incident we recorded concerns another would-be burglar who was hung by his heels, this time from a lamppost near the Italian section of the neighborhood.

> *Field Notes:* Charlie told me the guy was badly beaten and nearly unconscious when they found him. Charlie said that the mafia is quiet over there, but when someone tries them, to see if they're still around, they find out the hard way that they are.

Still other field notes record the $1,000 reward offered by a local social club after its premises were burglarized, together with the assurance that no police would be involved.

As a result of both effective social control, formal and informal, and safer alternative sources of income, legal and illegal, none of the Hamilton Park youths developed into systematic burglars. Most of their accounts of factory break-ins concerned only early to mid-teen experiences and were characterized by a predominance of expressive over economic motivations. After a few experiences with the ability of local factory owners to discover and punish such activities, most youths desisted.

Accounts of auto theft by the Hamilton Park youths followed this same general pattern. Several of them reported stealing cars, but they did so mainly for joyriding.

> *Charlie Gaberewski:* One year, we were about sixteen, seventeen, this guy Mark started stealing cars, and everybody else started stealing with him and shit like that, right, and finally he got caught and everybody else stopped. Like everybody learned his lesson.
> *Interviewer:* So what did you do when you stole cars?
> *C.G.:* Just cruise around. Some cars were nice, some were shitty. Most of the time you steal a shitty car because that's the one you can get into. We weren't professional or anything like that. Like we'd steal one car and take a ride out on Long Island, then steal another one there, leave the first one, and bring that one back and drive it around here for a while. Sometimes you'd make out on a deal, like, take the radio, the spare tire, sell them. That guy Mark did it for profit most of the time, until he got caught.

This pattern of auto theft differs from that described in La Barriada, in which initial experiences with joyriding quickly developed into systematic theft for profit, the development of specialized criminal skills, and connection to regular buyers of stolen cars and parts. There was only one reference to organized auto theft in the Hamilton Park neighborhood: Charlie Gaberewski said that he knew of such an operation but that it was very quiet, specialized in very expensive cars, and did not involve teenagers. He was unsure whether or not it had any connection to "the mafia."

Although their criminal activities did not generally include street robbery—again in striking contrast to the crime patterns in the other two neighborhoods—the Hamilton Park youths did engage in one specific kind of person-to-person predation. The neighborhood had a subpopulation of very recent and frequently undocumented immigrants from eastern Europe, mostly but not exclusively from Poland. Even though many of the youths we interviewed were themselves the grandchildren of earlier Polish immigrants, they referred to the newcomers as "refugees" and "polacks" and sometimes beat and robbed them, knowing that undocumented aliens are unlikely to go to the police. These attacks generally occurred on weekends when the immigrants, often men living several persons to a room in order to save money for their families in Europe, made themselves easy targets by getting very drunk and staggering down the streets with a week's pay in cash in their pockets. Local youths moving from bar to bar preyed upon them.

Pete Calderone: There's a lot of dumb polacks in my neighborhood, I mean dumb because they're just from Poland, they don't know any better about anything in America. They drink a lot. They become targets to get hit on Friday, Saturday night. You know, you see a drunken polack, always have a lot of money. Don't have to do much to them, just grab him from behind, grab his wallet . . . a lot of guys are into that.

Charlie Gaberewski: It's not like everybody gets ripped off, it's just these stupid polacks. They work all week and then they go out on the weekend with a full paycheck and they get smashed, out their mind, where they can't even walk no more. They're sitting there on the stoop, three or four kids walk by, say "Hey, you got a dollar?" He takes out a wad of bills, you gonna take them, you know. I did it a couple of times myself, like last year. Like I didn't even need the money. You get a little stoned and shit like that, just hanging out and this stupid polack walks by, just for being stupid he gets beat up. While you're there, you take his money.

[183]

Although this kind of behavior was characteristic of Hamilton Park youths in their late teens, the predominance of expressive over economic motivations recalls their factory burglaries in their early and mid-teens and again differs from the more systematic, income-motivated robberies reported by youths in the other two neighborhoods. It is otherwise similar, however, to the robbing of undocumented Hispanics reported by the youths from La Barriada during their later teens, when they had begun to get jobs and to deintensify and become more selective about their income-motivated crimes.

The patterns of burglary, auto theft, and robbery among Hamilton Park youths, then, all differed from ostensibly similar crimes in the other neighborhoods in that the Hamilton Park youths were less motivated by purely economic considerations and did not continue to engage in these crimes on a systematic basis as a substitute for employment. This does not mean that they did no more stealing after their mid-teens, only that they did not become involved in high-risk, low-return street crimes as a primary source of income. Some of them, including Pete Calderone and Charlie Gaberewski, did in fact claim that they no longer stole; others, such as Barney and Teddy Haskell, described themselves as unlikely to steal unless they just happened across a particularly good opportunity. Most members of this group who engaged in theft after the age of sixteen stole not on the street but from the workplace, a crime pattern discussed below.

One faction among them, however, did engage in a series of highly risky and also inept commercial burglaries when they were around the age of seventeen: Peter Murphy and Brian Grady broke into several jewelry stores in a clumsy and unplanned way that led quickly to their arrest. Their activities bear the closest resemblance to the patterns of systematic theft found in the other two neighborhoods, but even for them, expressive motivations played a large role. Whereas the burglary, larceny, and robbery patterns described for the other two neighborhoods involved a wide cross section of local youths, these commercial burglaries involved only two, who were among the most violent and also the heaviest users of drugs in the Hamilton Park neighborhood. Also unlike the minority youths, whose peak involvement in theft occurred before they had entered the labor market, these two burglars were active after they had had several legitimate jobs, although they were not employed at the time of the burglaries.

Their own accounts suggest considerable personal disorientation as a result of heavy drug use and also downplay the economic motive.

Peter Murphy: I got arrested five times that summer. That was the

[184]

worst year of my life. The last time I got busted was the worst. We went into Manhattan. I was high on Quaaludes, did two, then another one. I don't know why I went that time. I had a whole bunch of change in my pockets. I went to jail with fifty dollars in my pockets. I was so high I couldn't even find my way back to the car, so the other guys left without me.

Peter Murphy's and Brian Grady's willingness to take greater risks than the rest of their peers was evident not only in these daring and blundering commercial burglaries but also in other aspects of their behavior. Peter Murphy was the heaviest drug user of the entire group. He had been taken to the hospital several times after overdoses of barbiturates and had been in and out of drug programs since his mid-teens. Brian Grady came from a family with a criminal history. His father had spent several years in prison for an armored car robbery and had given his son a gun for his eighteenth birthday. That same day, Brian shot two people in a distant neighborhood, shootings with no connection to a robbery or other income-motivated crime. Both youths had acquired and enjoyed the reputation of being the wildest, most dangerous, and most unpredictable young men in the neighborhood.

The final pattern of youthful stealing encountered in Hamilton Park was that of work-related theft. Unlike the commercial burglaries just described but like the exploratory factory burglaries and weekend muggings of immigrants, this sort of crime was common behavior among most of the youths interviewed, as well as among many adults in the neighborhood.

Work-related theft differs substantially from most of the theft patterns described thus far for this and the other neighborhoods. Work-related theft in La Barriada, for example, was the crime pattern that those youths grew into as they grew out of the high-risk street crimes of their jobless mid-teens. Stealing on the job is generally much less risky than street crime, since it is frequently not discovered and, even when it is, may not involve the criminal justice system; employers have more immediate sanctions at their disposal in their ability to fire employees who steal. Despite the predominance of youths among those arrested for theft, it is likely that the bulk of theft is committed by adult workers rather than by jobless youths.

Since they had access to more employment at earlier ages, the Hamilton Park youths also had more opportunity to steal from their employers. Work-related theft began for most in their mid-teens. The earliest recorded instance in our notes concerned two brothers, Otto and Brian Deutsch, who kept all the proceeds from the paper route they had when

Otto was only ten years old, then told their boss they had been robbed and relinquished the job. Thereafter, they continued to evaluate their various jobs for potential theft opportunities.

> *Field Notes:* Otto told me he used to work in a factory which made fancy baby clothes. I asked if he ever had a chance to take anything while he was working there. He said that the security was too tight at that place. Then he told me that his brother was working in a clothing factory in Manhattan, one that made nice velours and other things. He said his brother had been cleaning up selling velours he brings home from work.

As this example shows, not all jobs offer the same opportunities for theft. Those held by both youths and older residents of Hamilton Park, however, were often the kinds of blue-collar jobs that involved handling merchandise and thus did present good opportunities for theft. During the research period Barney Haskell worked for a few weeks on a truck that delivered meat products; each evening he went around the neighborhood asking people he knew if they wanted to buy canned hams. Before he embarked on his commercial burglaries, Brian Grady worked in an auto shop, where he stole hubcaps and auto parts from his employer. The traffic in stolen goods in Hamilton Park was pervasive though not as flagrant as in La Barriada, where youths and older heroin addicts peddled their goods openly in the street.

Some of our data suggest that work-related theft was also common among older residents. Otto Deutsch's sister-in-law, a woman in her late twenties with a five-year-old daughter, came home from work one day lamenting the fact that the inventory procedures at her retail job had just been tightened up.

> *Field Notes:* She said that she could have fixed up the paperwork in such a way as to be able to ship large amounts of goods to her friends and relatives without the company finding out about it. She had been working there such a short time, however, that she was afraid to risk it. Now the company was starting to become more strict in their accounting.

Our field data from Hamilton Park confirm the conclusions of other researchers (Klockars 1974) that theft is endemic to many blue-collar work roles; work-related theft is thus properly seen as a crime more typical of adults than of teenagers. The Hamilton Park youths had more access to this type of theft than others simply because they had more access to employment.

[186]

The accounts of income-motivated crimes committed by the Hamilton Park youths demonstrate that although most of them did steal, few had ever depended on theft as a steady source of income; rather, they indulged in the less risky forms as opportunities arose. By far the major source of illegal income for these youths derived not from theft but from selling drugs. As in the other neighborhoods, drug selling in Hamilton Park was a form of illegal enterprise which, unlike most youthful theft, involved the recruitment of youthful workers by adult entrepreneurs.

The selling and consuming of illegal drugs were quite as pervasive in Hamilton Park as in the other two neighborhoods, although they took place in a very different social control environment. Like the other youths interviewed, the Hamilton Park youths themselves consumed mostly marijuana but also used a wide variety of other drugs that were less common in the other neighborhoods: cocaine, amphetamines, hallucinogens, barbiturates, and PCP ("angel dust"). As in the other neighborhoods a number of slightly older residents, men in their middle to late twenties, were heroin addicts, and by the end of the research period two of the youths interviewed were also beginning to use heroin, whereas the cliques in the minority neighborhoods included no heroin users.

Despite the pervasiveness and variety of drugs consumed in Hamilton Park, however, public drug use and drug sales were vigorously opposed by local residents acting both informally and through organized community groups and the local police. Observations and interviews in the neighborhood indicated an ongoing struggle of several years' duration between local youths and older residents over these issues.

Field Notes: While I was walking down the avenue Friday night, I ran into Teddy Haskell, Brian and Jake Deutsch [Brian and Otto's older brother]. They had been inside the bar there and come outside to smoke a joint as they usually do. It was raining slightly so they had to stand under an awning. They started telling me about the park across the street. Jake said that about ten years ago the park had been "very cool." All the kids used to hang out there with their radios all blaring the same station in unison, about fifty radios in all. At that time, the park was the biggest drug marketplace in the area. Some people they knew had made a lot of money there. Apparently, after a couple of years of this, the local community decided to crack down and the local police started to come down hard. One of the biggest dealers even had the FBI after him, quit dealing, and joined the Hare Krishnas in Manhattan.

Pete Calderone: Right now the cops are being real hardass. I guess it's because people in the neighborhood want to straighten things out. You could be hanging out on the corner now just drinking a beer and the cops'll come along and give you a summons, take you down to the station. You walk out, rip it up, it's a hassle.

Interviewer: Is this pressure from the police recent?

P.C.: It was always like that but now it's really heavy. Block associations, coalitions, civilian patrol, you know, you're hanging out on the corner, your neighbors make a complaint. So that's it, people getting on their backs, the cops get on our backs, they're just doing their jobs.

At the time of the field research the situation with regard to public drinking, drug sales, and drug use had reached something of a stalemate. The teenagers still used the parks for these activities, but they did not dominate the parks. David Henry, whose mother was actively involved in the block associations even though he and his brother had sold marijuana and amphetamines in the local parks, described the changes.

David Henry: They used to call it needle park over there, my own brother OD'd there a couple of times. My mother still calls it that, "needle park." She says, "What are you hanging out in needle park for?" I say, "It ain't needle park." When I was there, there was no needles—that was in the sixties. Now, forget about it, it's all baby carriages.

Our observations confirmed the absence of heroin addicts in the park and the presence of both mothers with small children and teenagers taking and exchanging soft drugs, each group keeping to its separate end of the park.

Not only did the teenagers not dominate the parks, but they continually shifted the location of their activities in order to avoid periodic police sweeps. The youths' special nemesis was one particular police officer by the name of O'Connor, who had embarked on a personal crusade against public drinking, drug use, and drug selling.

Charlie Gaberewski: You know, I've done a few things, but I never really got caught by the cops. I'm too sneaky. The only times have been this guy O'Connor. He's a real big guy, he's enormous, and he's a boxer so nobody wants to fuck with him. You could be hanging out and drinkin', you see the cop car, everybody throws their beers away. So one day I was sittin' by the checker tables, we didn't see him come up, he sneaks up behind us, and then, you can't throw the beer right in front of his face, he'll get you for littering too. He dumped the beer out on us that time and says, "I'm giving you a warning. My name's

O'Connor, and I'm telling you I'm cleaning up this park." Everybody
laughed at him when he got back in his car. But after that, if he caught
you just sittin' next to a beer, he'd take you all the way down to the
station, just to give you a summons. Nobody pays 'em. It's just to ruin
your night, that's what it is. I remember he brought down a paddy
wagon and loaded everybody into it. That's bad news.

Field Notes: As I was coming out of the hamburger place, I saw a police
car on the corner with three teenage boys crowded around it. The cops
were giving them a summons for drinking in public. It was a game to
them. They were all trying to hide their beers so they could salvage
them after the police left. One of them told me after he was trying to
hide his "cheeb" (as he called his marijuana) under a car. They were all
familiar with the game: the first summons is a $5 fine, the second time
it's $25. Two of them said they had over $200 in fines, which they had
never paid and had no intention of paying. I asked them if one of these
cops was O'Connor. They said no, it wasn't his time on duty (they knew
his schedule), but that he had started this aggressiveness by the cops
and the others had followed his lead.

Another sign of local efforts to limit public drug selling was the
absence of "reefer stores," storefronts selling marijuana. No such establishments existed within the neighborhood. One bar and a pizza stand
sold small amounts for a while, but both were rapidly closed down by the
police. Unlike the minority youths, who usually bought marijuana and
pills from storefronts (in La Barriada right on their block and in Projectville a few blocks away), the Hamilton Park youths made their pur-
chases either in the parks when the police were absent or privately
through personal networks. A few reefer stores did exist in an adjacent,
much poorer Latino neighborhood, but the Hamilton Park youths pa-
tronized these establishments only when their local sources went dry.
   The drug-selling involvements of the clique were shaped both by this
social control environment and by the context of their other economic
opportunities. Unlike the youths from Projectville and La Barriada who
worked in the reefer stores and traveled into Manhattan to sell "loose
joints" to office workers, the Hamilton Park youths did most of their selling within the neighborhood, either in the parks between police sweeps
or in their own homes—where they often encountered conflicts with
their parents. Some also sold at their jobs. During the summer, when
many residents went to their bungalows near the municipal beaches,
much of the traffic moved to the beaches as well. None of these youths
worked in reefer stores, and none of them sold full time on the streets of

Manhattan, though a couple of them did a little selling in Manhattan parks on their lunch breaks from work.

Although most of the Hamilton Park youths interviewed had sold marijuana and/or pills on more than an occasional basis, most of them did so while they also held legitimate jobs. Their profits from drug selling were considerably more regular than those from their occasional acts of theft, but the income still served to supplement rather than to substitute for wages. The consignment system evident in Projectville also existed, though it was not as prevalent; the Hamilton Park youths were more often expected to pay their wholesalers in advance. Since they depended on their wages for front money, their drug selling could suffer during times of unemployment, rather than expanding to fill the gap.

Otto Deutsch provided the most detailed illustration of this pattern of drug selling as a supplement to wages. He and his girlfriend Bonnie O'Brien were both working when we first contacted them. Together they bought from one-quarter to one-half pound of marijuana a week, which Otto resold in smaller quantities, making as much as $50 to $100 profit or perhaps only enough to support their own consumption. At this point, Otto was working only part time and devoting the rest of his time to selling. He and Bonnie were trying to save enough money to buy larger amounts and get a head start on their competitors by being the first ones in the park with plentiful supplies of good marijuana for the first warm days of spring. Shortly afterward Otto lost his job, and his marijuana selling suffered for a couple of weeks, during which he sold only when he could manage to get a quarter-pound on consignment.

When Otto found a good full-time job that summer, doing building maintenance work on the night shift, he not only had the front money to sell again but began going to the beach during the day, thus greatly increasing his sales. He had some trouble at his new job as a result of burning the candle at both ends, and he and his girlfriend had a falling-out during this period, but they continued to put their money together on marijuana deals. Several months later, however, after they had become reconciled, they quit both consuming and selling marijuana; Otto settled down to his job and girlfriend and left the street drug scene behind.

Many of the other youths interviewed reported similar patterns of low-volume sales—sometimes during periods of unemployment, more often while employed—as a secondary earning strategy. Most of them had engaged in selling marijuana or pills at some time. Charlie Gaberewski and John Gutski sold marijuana and amphetamines, respectively, on their lunch breaks from their jobs in Manhattan. David Henry had sold marijuana extensively while he stayed with a brother and worked in a supermarket in California for two years. He returned to Hamilton Park only when he got into a dangerous dispute over a drug deal. When interviewed, he was between jobs and selling fairly regularly in the local parks with Carl Pollini. (Neither Henry nor Pollini had had much experience with theft.) John Gutski claimed that he had occasionally made profits of over $1,000 selling angel dust. Despite his reputation for exaggeration, several other youths confirmed that angel dust was highly popular and only sporadically available, with the result that they could make a lot of money if they could get it. Although observations in the local bars revealed considerable use of heroin and cocaine in the neighborhood, these youths in their late teens confined their activities chiefly to marijuana and pills.

Members of our study group were all about nineteen years old during this period, but the field data indicate similar patterns of drug selling among slightly older people as well. In fact, the youths in their late teens made some of their best deals by connecting older, more stably employed neighborhood residents with suppliers. The youths had more experience with drugs and more connections; the older people had more money to invest.

Field Notes: I saw Austin today. He told me that yesterday he made an easy fifty bucks. He had set up Joe, the guy who runs the corner grocery, to buy five pounds of marijuana. I was surprised when I heard who the buyer was. Joe is a really clean-cut guy, about twenty-seven years old. Apparently he doesn't even smoke pot, because Austin said he brought along two sixteen-year-olds to test it for him.

Another individual who sometimes bought marijuana from the youths in their late teens was a twenty-six-year-old friend of Charlie Gaberewski, a postal employee who supported his wife and two small children. He sold as much as twenty pounds a week; he also consumed some but claimed that he sold in order to supplement his income.

Although selling regularly but at a relatively low volume and as a sideline to legitimate employment was the more common pattern among the Hamilton Park youths, Teddy Haskell and Brian Grady appeared to depend on drug sales as a major source of income. Both came from families with a history of criminal activity and were themselves involved in other aspects of professional and organized crime. Grady and Haskell controlled one section of a local park where most of the day in, day out drug traffic occurred, between police sweeps. Otto Deutsch's younger brother Brian, who sold drugs himself, was a close friend of these two but was not allowed to sell in their section of the park unless he was working for them. At various times Haskell and Grady, both nineteen years old, also had youths of about sixteen working for them.

During our field research Haskell was "employed" part time in a job that also involved other kinds of crime; Grady was unemployed, having been in and out of drug programs for several years. Both depended on drug sales as a major source of income and were involved in other illegal activities as well. Both also began using heroin toward the end of the research period.

Brian Grady's and Teddy Haskell's greater dependence on illegal income in comparison with their peers reflected their family backgrounds. Both youths came from families that mixed legal and illegal income to a greater extent than those of the other Hamilton Park youths. Grady's father had served several years in prison for armored car robbery and had sold cocaine, though in large quantities and not at the street level. It was he who had given his son a gun for his eighteenth birthday, which Brian promptly used to shoot two people. In this case, the son's involvement in drug dealing, drug abuse, and random violence seems to have grown out of his father's example more than his father's direct encouragement: his father did not approve of Brian's wildness and took back the gun after the shootings; nor did he approve of his son's street-level drug dealing.

Teddy Haskell's family tradition was one of organized rather than independent professional crime. Both Teddy and his brother Barney had sources of illegal income that were directly provided for them through family connections. These did not involve drugs; in fact, the Haskells' father strongly disapproved of drug use and did not like his son's selling in the park, even though some of the father's friends also did higher-level drug deals. The Haskell's father had been a construction worker for many years but had carried gambling slips when he was younger. He still retained many of his associations from those days, and the opportunities he passed along to his sons were those associated with such traditional activities of organized crime as gambling, loan-sharking, fraud, and violence for hire. Crime opportunities of this sort were not as visible in the other two study neighborhoods. The more organized forms of crime there were auto theft in La Barriada and drug selling in Projectville, both of which involved relatively loose and low levels of organization and constant shifts in location in response to constant pressure from the police. The Haskells' crime operations in Hamilton Park, in contrast, were associated with more established organizations of the sort known in the neighborhod and elsewhere as "the mafia." These activities were rarely even known to the police. Hamilton Park did not have a reputation as a major center for this sort of activity, and most of the youths we interviewed knew of it only indirectly.

Both Haskell brothers had had a weekly "job" carrying gambling slips, as their father had done when he was younger. Barney had also worked as a debt collector in the same gambling operation, a job for which he was qualified by virtue of his experience as a boxer.

> *Barney Haskell:* I used to run numbers and collect a little money.
> *Interviewer:* Was that for the Italians?
> *B.H.:* Yeah. I used to collect money for them. Me and this other guy. Like, if you owed fifty dollars and you didn't wanna pay, we'd have to talk to you.
> *Int.:* How did they pick you for these jobs?
> *B.H.:* See, I used to box a lot . . .
> *Int.:* So you were well known?
> *B.H.:* Yeah, but see, I'm not a troublemaker. I don't look for fights, but, if they come, fuck it . . .
> *Int.:* So how come you stopped running numbers and collecting?
> *B.H.:* I'm getting older now, not that I'm old, but when you go in front of a judge . . . if you get caught doing any thing, he's not gonna look at you if you're sixteen.

Barney was the older of the two brothers and had passed on the job of carrying gambling slips to his brother Teddy, two years his junior. This task involved only a few minutes each week and regularly paid $75.

Only one other youth interviewed reported involvements of this sort. John Gutski had been recruited for similar activities through his association with a social club operated by his brother-in-law. Unlike Barney Haskell, Gutski was very much a "troublemaker" who was involved during his mid-teens in peer-recruited theft, including armed robbery, and violent fights. At this point he was still in his mid-teens and still involved in occasional peer-recruited burglaries, but he reported also having been recruited for various assignments while hanging out at the social club.

> *John Gutski:* I used to rob cars too.
> *Interviewer:* What do you mean?
> *J.G.:* I did insurance jobs for a lot of rich people. I got paid good—two hundred, three hundred, five hundred dollars. Used to rob the cars, drive 'em to the river, dump 'em in the river.

Int.: How did you get hooked up with these people?
J.G.: I got connections, the mafia, dope dealers, people who are into anything that's illegal. I used to have a club, like a social club, it was my brother-in-law's but I used to have some money in it too, the money I made from angel dust. Anyway, most of the time, whenever they wanted me they used to come to me there. Like, most of the time I used to make my money with fighting. They used to tell me, "Here's fifty dollars. Go fuck up this guy." I used to say, all right, get the address, go right to the door with two or three guys, beat the shit out of him. Walk out. There's a lot of bookies I know, they take bets, numbers, this, that, sometimes people don't pay. . . . One time this lady gave me four hundred dollars to beat up this guy who had been bothering her. We went up to him, four of us and said, "Look, if you ever bother her again, you're dead." Then we beat him up.

Gutski had gotten into serious trouble at the age of sixteen, having been arrested on various charges of robbery, burglary, and assault. Put on probation, he left the country for a few months to visit relatives in Europe. After his return, he largely ceased participating in these violent, income-motivated crimes and confined his illegal activities to occasional and largely inept drug dealing.

Although Barney Haskell ceased to be involved in violence for hire before he was ever arrested and John Gutski did not stop until afterward, their places in the organization of these illegal enterprises were essentially similar. As in the auto theft operations in La Barriada and drug selling in Projectville, teenagers carried out the riskiest and most exposed jobs in enterprises organized by adults. When the youths became too vulnerable to the police and courts, either because of accumulating sanctions or simply because they had gotten too old to expect leniency, they were replaced with younger operatives.

Whether or not any of these youths with experience at the lower levels of organized crime were likely to advance to higher levels was difficult to assess. John Gutski's generally wild and unpredictable behavior did not make him a likely candidate; in fact, his crime opportunities appeared to be diminishing as his reputation for personal disorientation and untrustworthiness grew. The Haskells were more businesslike but also had more opportunities for legitimate employment. Barney Haskell was a full-time college student, and his brother Teddy had been promised an opening in the construction unions by their father. Teddy Haskell seemed the most likely of the three to continue into adult crime, depending on the progress of his heroin use. Besides his extensive involvement with drug dealing, he also sold guns and worked with his cousin in a business that involved considerable illegal activity.

Field Notes: Teddy told me that he is now working with his cousin. He said that the business they're in is a real scam. They service fire extinguishers for businesses, only they spend most of their time ripping people off. Customers pay them $60 to $80 to take care of each fire extinguisher, but sometimes all they do is take them outside to the truck, wipe them off and take them back in. Besides that, the cousin buys replacements that are hot from some people he knows. Then Teddy started telling me about all the times they have ripped off customers. He said the first thing they do when they go into an establishment is to check out the office. They go through purses, drawers, open safes. They look for hiding spots, pry open desks, closets, sealed boxes, drawers, and so on. Teddy describes his cousin as a great bullshitter. If someone disturbs them as they are casing a place, the cousin just starts trying to sell him fire extinguisher service. More often than not, they make more money stealing than from the actual work they do. Sometimes the places they go to service extinguishers are chosen more on the basis of opportunities for rip-offs than for the likelihood that they need their extinguishers serviced. He told me about one time they almost ripped off a butcher for $1,800 in cash. The butcher thought Teddy's cousin was the guy from the meat plant and handed him the receipt to sign for the cash just as the real guy walked in. Of course, they realized that this guy was trying to rip them off, but there was nothing they could do about it.

Even so, Teddy Haskell seemed dissatisfied with working for his cousin. Sometimes he made good money, but the work was irregular, and he disliked waiting by the phone each day to find out whether he would get work. If the Haskell brothers continue with adult crime, it seems more likely that their criminal activities will be a sideline to legitimate jobs, as had been the case with their father, rather than full-time membership in organized crime.

Despite these various criminal involvements, few of the Hamilton Park youths interviewed had ever spent more than a few days in jail. Their ability to escape serious consequences for their acts was in part the result of the types of crime in which they engaged. For the most part, they did not become involved in repeated high-risk street crimes, as did many of the youths in the poorer, minority neighborhoods. The minority youths were also able to escape serious consequences for their first few acts of theft but encountered arrest, conviction, and jail or probation when they continued to pursue theft as a major source of income. Since the Hamilton Park youths had more income available to them from employment, their income-motivated crimes tended toward safer enterprises like drug selling. If they did steal, they did so either in response to a good opportunity or on the job, where theft was less likely to be penalized through the criminal justice system.

In addition, they had resources for dealing with the criminal justice system that were not available to the youths in the other neighborhoods. When they did get caught, they sought to manipulate the system—and were often successful in doing so—by means of money and personal connections. Although Hamilton Park residents were not wealthy, they were considerably better off economically than the residents of La Barriada and Projectville. The families of the Hamilton Park youths frequently owned their own homes and had some money in the bank. As a result, their children were able to make bail and hire private attorneys, in contrast to the minority youths, who had to rely on public defenders and often pled guilty while incarcerated.

John Gutski and Brian Grady, for example, who had been most involved in theft and were most similar to the youths from the other two neighborhoods in their criminal activities, were both arrested for these crimes. Gutski, at sixteen, faced charges of burglary, robbery and assault. Grady, at seventeen, faced several charges of burglary. But neither ever received an incarcerative sentence, and one reason was that they were both able to make bail, thus escaping the pressure to plead guilty to serious charges which confronted the incarcerated defendants from the other neighborhoods. They also knew how to find experienced criminal lawyers and were able to pay for them.

> *John Gutski:* Yeah, I was in jail too, but I was only in there for a couple of weeks. Then I called up my sister and told her to bail me out 'cause I was going crazy. So she came and bailed me out.
> *Interviewer:* Did you have a private lawyer?
> *JG:* Yeah, about three thousand I paid for that lawyer. I still owe money on that, I got to pay my sister off for that too.

Gutski actually spent two years on probation, the only Hamilton Park youth to report a felony conviction. Brian Grady cited legal expenses, rather than fear of incarceration, as his reason for ceasing to break into jewelry stores.

> *Brian Grady:* That's why I stopped. Cost me too much money.

[196]

Interviewer: You needed to hire a lawyer and all that?

B.G.: Yeah. A lawyer that my mother's friend knows. He used to be a D.A., so he knew everybody in there. Still charged me a thousand dollars, you know, but if it was somebody else it woulda been two thousand.

Perhaps even more potent than their financial resources were their personal connections to criminal justice system personnel. When in trouble, many of them went immediately to relatives on the police force or in the courts for advice and aid. When he was suspected of having burned down a local factory, Peter Murphy went to his uncle, a police officer in another precinct, who managed to get the blame turned around against Peter Murphy's associate, who had accused Murphy. The most extensive family connections to the criminal justice system were reported by the Haskell brothers.

Barney Haskell: We got it all wrapped up. My cousin's a cop, right? His brother's a district attorney. My other cousin was a lawyer in the Navy, now he's a lawyer out here. He just married a lawyer and he's gonna be a judge in another two years. All wrapped up. If any of us ever gets in trouble, my old man goes down to the precinct and works it out. He knows the captain; shit, the captain eats over my house.

As another example, Otto Deutsch had an acquaintance who was something of a local legend for having stabbed a police officer and gotten away with it.

Field Notes: When we got into the park, Otto called for a friend of his to come over. I say friend, although Otto says he doesn't much like the guy. Anyway, the guy started telling us about the time he got busted a couple of months ago. He said the cops caught him with all kinds of drugs, including a big bag of mescaline. He got into a fight with them and slashed one of them with a knife. He started talking about his connections (Otto says "mafia" connections) and said that as a result he got all the drug charges thrown out and was only charged with assault. He felt very lucky.

Even six months later, whenever this individual went by, someone would comment about the fact that he was still walking down the street after having stabbed a cop.

Besides having direct family connections to the police and courts, some Hamilton Park youths were able to gain leniency through neighborhood politicians. When David Henry was caught joyriding in a stolen car, his mother, head of a local block association, was able to get him released on recognizance. Barney Haskell was arrested, mistakenly, for arson while he was doing odd jobs for a man who had run for local office.

> *Barney Haskell:* I was loadin' these cases when the cops came in and clapped handcuffs on me. My boss was a big man in politics, you know, and he starts yellin', "You take them cuffs off him unless you got a warrant to come in my place."

As a result of such resources, Hamilton Park residents did not react passively to the workings of the criminal justice system. They used the system both to control their environment and to resist when they were themselves the objects of control. Teddy Haskell, after being beaten by a police officer in the course of an arrest occasioned by a drunken car chase, instituted a lawsuit for $50,000, which he seemed well on his way to winning. Several youths who had been the victims of Officer O'Connor's campaign to clean up the parks went to court to charge him with harassment.

> *Pete Calderone:* A few of them have tried to bring him to court, like, say, "I got eighteen summonses in one month, this guy is hassling me," and a few times it's worked. The judge says, "You're hassling people."

Despite its reputation as a low-crime neighborhood, Hamilton Park did in fact accommodate a certain amount of criminality among its youthful and older residents. The types and amounts and sequences of criminal involvements among its youths, however, differed considerably from those found in the other neighborhoods, especially in the amount of local street crime.

[9]

Empirical Comparison
of Crime Patterns

As preparation for the discussion in Chapter 10 of the relevance of our research to the questions of social theory raised in the opening chapter, this chapter discusses the empirical patterns of youthful crime careers in three stages. First, it compares the crime patterns in the ethnographic data with neighborhood police statistics in order to determine the extent to which the youths we studied were representative of their local areas. Next, it compares and analyzes the qualitative patterns of youthful criminality in the ethnographic data. Finally, it summarizes the patterns of relationships between crime and employment in youthful careers.

Ethnographic Data and Police Statistics

The decile rankings of police precincts listed in Table 14 are based on index rankings of the seventy-three precincts in New York City according to reported crimes per 1,000 population for the year 1977, two years before the beginning of our study: "1" represents the highest rate of reported crimes for an area; "10" represents the lowest.

The patterns in police statistics generally show the same qualitative and quantitative differences between the neighborhoods as those found in the ethnographic data. The patterns are similar even though police precincts are relatively large areas, much larger than the few blocks that we studied. Police precincts comprise many census tracts and are thus even larger than the areas for which census data on demography, schooling, and employment patterns were presented earlier. These police statistics are also based on reported crimes in the area, which cannot be easily classified by residence of the perpetrators. It is therefore all the more remarkable that the ethnographic data are so congruent with these official statistics.

Table 14. Index rankings of reported crimes in police precincts incorporating the neighborhoods (deciles)

	La Barriada	Projectville	Hamilton Park
Violent, non-income crimes			
Murder	5	3	9
Rape	10	3	10
Aggravated assault	4	2	9
Income crimes			
Robbery	7	2	10
Burglary	4	6	10
Larceny	9	8	10
Motor vehicle theft	4	9	9

Source: New York City Planning Commission 1978. Rankings of reported crimes per 1,000 population have been converted to deciles in order not to identify neighborhoods.

In fact, however, there are a number of reasons why these factors should not be expected to produce more difference between the patterns in the two data sources. As noted throughout this study, youth crime tends to be localized. Moving beyond their familiar, residential turf to commit crimes occurs more often as young criminals become older and more sophisticated in their criminal enterprises. It is likely that reported crimes in an area more accurately reflect the patterns of crime commission by younger than by older residents of the area.

The ethnographic data also suggest that two of these precincts do cover fairly homogeneous areas, though this is not always so either generally or in the case of the third precinct. For both Hamilton Park and Projectville, the precinct boundaries coincide with ecologically distinct, named neighborhoods that are relatively homogeneous in terms of income and ethnicity. The precinct that includes La Barriada covers a much more mixed area, including sections not only of very poor Latinos but also of working-class whites and Latinos.

The police statistics show the rates of reported crimes in Hamilton Park to be among the lowest in the entire city. This neighborhood rates in the lowest or next to lowest decile for reported crimes in all categories. As the ethnographic data reveal, however, this does not mean that local youths are not involved in crimes, only that the rate at which their crimes take place locally and are officially recorded by the police is low.

Consistent with the ethnographic data, the rates of reported crimes in La Barriada and Projectville are much higher than in Hamilton Park. The police statistics also show Projectville's crime rate to be higher than

La Barriada's for most crime types, especially for crimes of personal violence. This pattern contrasts somewhat with the ethnographic data but may reflect the more mixed nature of the precinct that includes La Barriada, in which there are significant areas of stable, working-class households. The ethnographic data show substantial amounts of both economically and noneconomically motivated violence in the small area of the precinct that we studied.

The comparison of different categories of economic crime in La Barriada and Projectville, however, shows the same qualitative differences in crime patterns as do the ethnographic data. For example, both neighborhoods are ranked relatively low in reported larcenies (probably reflecting the fact that both are primarily residential neighborhoods; most larceny arrests are for shoplifting, which is concentrated in commercial districts), whereas the crimes of robbery, burglary, and motor vehicle theft are distributed quite differently in the two neighborhoods. Robbery rates are much higher in Projectville; burglary and especially motor vehicle theft rates are higher in La Barriada. These patterns are repeated in the ethnographic data.

With minor exceptions, then, there is remarkable congruence between the ethnographic data and police statistics, a congruence that holds both for amounts and types of crime. This similarity suggests that even though our samples were small and intentionally recruited among the criminally active in each area, the criminal activity we documented was representative of the criminal activity in each area. The striking contrasts in local crime patterns suggests in turn that environmental influences and not just individual, psychologically driven deviance played an important role in the development of these youthful crime careers.

Patterns of Youth Crime in the Study Neighborhoods

Continuities. Comparing sequences of motivations and opportunities for illegal income in the three different environments reveals several features of the resulting crime patterns that are essentially similar across all three neighborhoods.

The underlying similarity in the prevalence of adolescent street fighting establishes a baseline for comparing the extent to which youths from different neighborhoods then went on to apply violence to the pursuit of income. It appears that all these youths had an equal capacity for violence and that street fighting was equally common in all three neighborhoods but peaked well before the age of peak involvement in income-motivated crime. The fact that the youths from the two minority neigh-

[201]

borhoods went on to participate in much more violent street crime must then be explained in the context of their alternative legal and illegal opportunities for gaining income.

There were common patterns of peer-recruited, exploratory theft during the early and middle teens. Most of the youths in all three neighborhoods had done some stealing between the ages of thirteen and sixteen. These exploratory acts of theft were generally conceived and carried out within the context of the adolescent peer group and not as a result of recruitment or direction by adults. They usually occurred within a mile of the youths' residences and tended to involve two or more persons. The motivations for these early thefts included some element of thrill-seeking in addition to the pursuit of income.

Each neighborhood offered ready markets for stolen goods. The youths engaging in exploratory acts of theft all found that some local adults were willing to buy stolen goods. This indirect yet essential support provided one element of reinforcement for their stealing, without which these youths could not have progressed with age from exploratory stealing for thrills to systematic stealing for profit.

Although the proportion of local youths who became involved in each of the various crime types varied considerably among the neighborhoods, the progression in participation from one type to the next followed a uniform sequence from "sneaky" forms of theft (burglary and larceny) in the early teens to robbery in the middle and late teens to drug dealing, work-related theft, and participation in adult-recruited and -directed criminal operations in the later teens and thereafter. This progression was influenced by differing opportunities, motivations, and capacities associated with age and forms a bell-shaped curve with respect to the application of violence to the pursuit of income. Younger teenagers were reluctant to engage in violent crimes for money, because they had not yet developed sufficient capacity for violence. Older and more professional criminals, who had developed considerable capacity for employing violence, nevertheless applied it as sparingly as possible in order not to interrupt "business." Peak participation in street robbery and other crimes involving the regular use or threat of violence, for relatively uncertain and low monetary returns, generally occurred in the middle to late teens.

The three study neighborhoods differed considerably in the types and amounts of crime they would and could tolerate, but none of the neighborhoods easily tolerated youthful thefts occurring within a few blocks of the offender's residence. Such acts were universally feared, condemned, and penalized, with the result that even those youths who continued to pursue income from illegal enterprise as they reached their twenties shifted the types of crime they committed away from localized predation.

Variations. Beyond their common characteristics, the neighborhoods varied considerably in the amounts, types, and sequences of opportunities for local youths to gain illegal income. The single most striking difference was the concentration in the two poor, minority neighborhoods of sustained involvement in high-risk, low-return theft as a primary source of income during the middle teens. This pattern not only was more prevalent in La Barriada and Projectville than in Hamilton Park but was in fact the common experience of most of the youths we interviewed from those two neighborhoods. The primary causes for their greater willingness to engage in desperate, highly exposed crimes for uncertain and meager monetary returns were the greater poverty of their households, the specific and severe lack of employment opportunities during these same mid-teen years, and the weakened local social control environment, itself a product of general poverty and joblessness among neighborhood residents. Although the Hamilton Park youths engaged in similar amounts of noneconomic violence and similar amounts of exploratory theft during the early teens, most of them did not go on to commit regular acts of burglary, larceny, and robbery as a substitute for employment. For the youths from Projectville and La Barriada, theft amounted to a short-term occupation that was their major source of income for a few months or years until their criminal activities eventually saturated their environment.

Other neighborhood differences may be summarized in terms of the comparative characteristics introduced in Chapter 5.

A major difference in neighborhood *ecology* was the physical isolation of Projectville from factories, stores, and easily entered housing; this was related to a relative lack of burglary by local youths, despite generally high levels of involvement in other forms of theft. The role of social organization in modifying the opportunities presented by the physical environment is evident in the different intensity of involvement in factory burglary between cliques from La Barriada and Hamilton Park. Both of these neighborhoods were characterized by a proximity of residential and industrial buildings, and youths from both neighborhoods engaged in exploratory factory break-ins during their early teens. The Hamilton Park youths, however, did not pursue these break-ins to the same extent as those from La Barriada, both because they had more alternative sources of income and because the Hamilton Park factory owners and managers were more integrated into the neighborhood and thus better able to control local youth crime.

Local markets for illegal goods and services existed in all the neighborhoods, but there was considerable variation in the particular combinations of diffuse and specialized markets and in how openly the buying and selling took place. La Barriada contained by far the most open and diverse of these markets. Heroin was sold only behind closed doors, but other drugs and stolen goods were peddled on the sidewalks and in the middle of the street to all sorts of customers, including some of the block's more respectable residents. Even the local reefer store was located right on the block. Such transactions could not be carried out as openly within the public housing projects of Projectville because of the presence of housing authorities, housing police, and a group of tenants who complained to the authorities if such activities became too visible. In Projectville the reefer stores were located in the neighborhood's few remaining tenement houses, several blocks away from the projects. The buyers of stolen gold chains worked the nearby, rapidly deteriorating commercial avenues. No reefer stores could maintain operations within the boundaries of Hamilton Park, and stolen goods were sold there behind closed doors and through personal networks.

Some aspects of the *social organization of criminal operations* have already been noted: the adolescent peer group as the primary recruiting ground for youthful theft as a common feature of all three neighborhoods; the greater intensity of involvement in peer-recruited youthful theft, particularly robbery, of the youths from the two minority neighborhoods. The neighborhoods also differed in the local youths' opportunities to participate in adult-recruited criminal enterprise. Such opportunities were available in all three, although they involved only a few youths from each clique.

Drug selling, common to all three neighborhoods, was by far the most prevalent kind of opportunity for involvement in adult-recruited crime. The members of the clique from La Barriada had the least involvement in drug selling, although some of them, like the Projectville youths, did work in the reefer stores. Projectville youths showed the greatest involvement in drug selling, and some went on with age to participate in drug markets that extended far beyond their local neighborhood. Many of the Hamilton Park youths sold drugs but generally did so as a sideline to legitimate employment and confined most of their selling to their own neighborhood.

Other types of adult-recruited youth crime were highly neighborhood-specific. La Barriada's auto theft industry was closely intertwined with its legitimate auto repair industry and provided diverse opportunities for illegal income to both youths and adults. The auto theft operations were loosely organized and shifted continually in location and organization in response to police pressure. The organized crime operations in Hamilton Park, though not extensive, were of a more established and sheltered kind, involving gambling and loan-sharking activities that rarely came to the attention of the police.

In adult-recruited youth crime in all three neighborhoods, youths were assigned the most risky and least remunerative tasks, while adults reaped most of the profits.

Each of the three neighborhoods had a distinctive *social control environment*. La Barriada residents had the fewest resources for controlling their criminally involved youths. The thefts committed by their youths also were the most redistributive in terms of channeling a flow of cheap goods into the neighborhood from outside, and the openness with which stolen goods were sold in the streets partially reflected the fact that these goods were coming from factory and car owners who had little connection to the immediate neighborhood. When local youths struck too close to home, La Barriada residents did respond, although they were the least likely to resort to the criminal justice system for redress. Some Projectville residents attempted to control the criminal activity of their local youths by bureaucratic means, but they were largely unsuccessful, given the concentration of so many poor and jobless youths in such a heavily populated and anonymous environment. Hamilton Park residents made the most extensive use of both the criminal justice system and informal methods of control, with the result that their local youths were much more quickly deterred from localized predation. The ability of Hamilton Park residents to control local youth crime, however, was accompanied by the sheltering of local organized crime elements and also by the ability of local residents to manipulate the criminal justice system when they were accused or arrested.

Relationships between Employment and Economic Crime in the Study Neighborhoods

This book differs from many previous *ethnographic* studies of delinquency and youth crime in its comparative framework and in its explicit focus on economic opportunities and strategies. It also differs from many previous *economic* studies in that the perceived social and psychological factors such as the thrills and/or "noxiousness" of crime, the perceived returns from legal and illegal forms of labor, and local structures of legal and illegal opportunity are all described and compared with reference to the same individuals and cliques. The comparison of career patterns within and across cliques allows consideration of both structural and individual factors, as has not been possible within the theoretical and methodological limits of most previous studies.

The analysis here focuses specifically on the career-patterning of the various possible types of relationship between employment and crime indicated by the Vera project's review of existing literature (Thompson, Sviridoff, et al. 1981) and pilot interviews with inmates in New York City jails (Sviridoff and Thompson 1983). Whereas both early economic studies and existing popular stereotypes envision the relationship between employment and crime as a series of trade-offs between competing, mutually exclusive, and equally available sources of income, both the indeterminacy of more sophisticated economic models and the Vera project's pilot studies point to a number of additional ways in which employment and crime can be related. They may be mutually exclusive economic pursuits for some; others combine the two with either alternating or overlapping involvement. Some people engage in neither and allocate their time to leisure or to investment in human capital. Research on youth employment and on segmented labor markets suggests that employment may not be a competing option for many inner-city youths because it is simply not available.

The following analyses examine variations by age, neighborhood, and individual in patterns of schooling, work, and crime. These patterns are summarized with respect to both correlations of various activities at any given time and the way in which employment and crime involvements develop over time as career patterns. This chapter examines the interrelationships of schooling, employment, and crime, and the sequences and combinations of these activities. The holistic ethnographic data are also used to examine the functional compatibility or incompatibility of various employment and crime activities: for example, whether or not they compete for time allocation and whether or not they are compatible in terms of social identity.

The analyses presented in this chapter, like those preceding, pay a great deal of attention not only to the mere presence but also to the types of employment and crime. Many of the patterned relationships described are between a particular type of employment and a particular type of crime. If the data were presented without consideration of these qualitative factors, many relationships would disappear, and the results of the comparative analysis would be much more indeterminate (as they are in many existing economic and survey studies).

Continuities. Most of the continuities apparent both within and between the three neighborhood groups in patterns of relationships between employment and crime were related to changes with age.

[206]

First, crime preceded work. Most respondents from all three neighborhoods reported gaining income from theft before they entered legitimate employment. Their thefts ranged from petty acts in childhood,
such as stealing fruit from local groceries or coins from parents, to more
serious acts of burglary and pickpocketing between the ages of ten and
thirteen.

Second, occasional crime for economic gain overlapped with early
employment. Early jobs were generally irregular and thus easily combined with exploratory crimes, which also occurred irregularly. Even at
this stage, however, employment appeared to produce some moderating
effects: within each group there were youths who stopped committing
crimes for money during their early employment and others who reported one or two crimes. Differences between groups in the development of systematic crimes for money during the mid-teens were considerable, however; they are outlined below.

Third, most members in each local group moderated their economic
crime involvement as they grew older and began to work more steadily.
More often than not, they were in the labor market and working by their
late teens. Some ceased engaging in economic crime altogether at this
point; others shifted to less severe, risky, and frequent crime, though
this process was much slower in the two poorer neighborhoods.

Fourth, a small minority of each group became involved in full-time
crime to the exclusion of work during the late teens. One or two individuals from each group did not fit the foregoing pattern, increasing rather
than moderating their dependence on crime for income as they aged.
These individuals, however, also shifted from early acts of unskilled theft
to ongoing criminal enterprises that were safer, more lucrative, and
more capable of providing a steady source of income in lieu of wages
from legitimate employment.

Variations. The single most striking difference between neighborhoods was the greater amount of employment and lesser amount of
systematic economic crime during the middle teen years among the
Hamilton Park clique than among the two poorer, minority cliques. As a
comparison at the group level, this contrast was pervasive. Most of the
youths we interviewed from La Barriada and Projectville reported systematic involvement in criminal activity—generally unskilled theft—
and very little work during their middle teens; they fit West's (1974)
classification of "serious thieves" involved in "short-term careers."
Crime, not wages, accounted for most of their income during the middle
teens. Though most entered the labor force and had some employment
during these years, the difficulties in finding jobs were such that they

spent most of this period in their lives either unemployed or out of the labor force. In contrast, most of the respondents from Hamilton Park reported considerable employment during their middle teens, usually part time and off-the-books, and their criminal involvements tended to be more infrequent and more expressive in motivation. Violent street crimes for money, in particular, were much less prominent in the mid-teen careers of the Hamilton Park youths than among their peers from the other two neighborhoods.

This difference suggests an influence of employment on crime that is much stronger over time than at any particular moment of individual decision making. As noted before, early employment experiences did not necessarily lead every individual to cease crime altogether; even some of the Hamilton Park youths engaged in occasional "drunk-rolling" on weekends when they were employed. Nevertheless, the difference suggests that the greater amount of mid-teen employment in Hamilton Park did serve to limit the development of involvement in systematic economic crime as a primary source of income.

Neighborhood differences in youthful career patterns cannot be solely ascribed to individual employment experiences, however. The youths from the minority neighborhoods also lived in much poorer households in which adults too suffered significant employment problems; severe youth unemployment was embedded in much higher levels of general poverty, unemployment, and underemployment. Neighborhood-wide differences in levels of poverty and employment contributed to differences in local social control environments, which in turn contributed to differences in patterns of delinquency and youth crime. The intensive criminal involvements during the middle teens of the youths from La Barriada and Projectville were the result not only of their severe individual employment problems but also of their greater and earlier need to procure income as well as the inability of their parents and neighbors to control their crimes, even though the local community was generally the locus of their youthful predations.

As the age of the members increased, the crime patterns of the three groups converged somewhat. The minority youths greatly reduced their reliance on criminal income as they found more work and faced mounting sanctions from the criminal justice system, and most of those in each group who continued to engage in economic crime restricted themselves to relatively low-risk activities that entailed much less chance of confrontation with the criminal justice system. The main crimes reported during the later teens in each of the three groups were theft from the workplace and drug selling as part-time supplements to wages. The groups differed primarily in that the Hamilton Park youths began to develop these patterns earlier and to maintain them more securely, while the minority youths still faced much more unemployment and the attendant possibility of continuing or reverting to their reliance on criminal income.

In addition to these major differences between the Hamilton Park group and the two minority groups, there were other more subtle and qualitative differences between La Barriada and Projectville in types and sequencing of school, work, and crime experiences. The youths from La Barriada showed a preference for both work and crime that involved manual labor. They engaged in more burglary and auto theft than did their peers in the other neighborhoods, and many of their early and subsequent experiences of legitimate work were in building maintenance, factories, and auto shops. Some displayed considerable manual skill, partially obtained in school shop classes but more often acquired informally through work, crime, and contact with older males in the neighborhood.

This qualitative dimension of their careers, cross-cutting schooling, work, and crime, also affected the sequence of their involvements. The unskilled manual jobs that were so prominent in the careers of these youths and their older relatives and neighbors were among the most poorly paid in this regional labor market, did not require much formal education or even necessarily a knowledge of English, and employed many women and immigrants (documented and undocumented) on a seasonal basis. As a result of these conditions within their community, these youths were the earliest among the three groups to leave school and to enter the job market in earnest. They were out of school and seeking work earlier than the Projectville group, though their entry into the job market resulted primarily in unemployment at first. Their short-term careers in serious theft also lasted longer than those of the Projectville clique, partially because their proportionately greater involvement in nonconfrontational manual crimes entailed less risk of arrest or incarceration.

Careers in youthful theft in La Barriada were prolonged also by the fact that their neighborhood was the most isolated from police and other official agencies. Many of their early predatory crimes, though committed close to home, brought goods and money into their community, and local residents felt little threatened by the losses of factory and car owners. As these youths grew older, began to work more, and no longer had the time to plan and execute these manual crimes, they began to go farther afield to commit street robberies. At this point, they encountered much more serious sanctions and were forced to moderate their criminal activity.

The Projectville youths, in contrast, showed comparatively little interest in either manual work or manual crime. Their crimes were more often those involving personal contact, either violent predation or selling drugs. They frequently described or fantasized about con games, though they maintained that cons usually required an older person because youths could not gain the necessary trust. The legitimate jobs they desired and began to acquire were clerical and service sector jobs, which also involve more personal contact than manual skill. These qualitative patterns affected the sequence of work and crime involvements by prolonging the period of schooling and hastening the end of systematic predation, relative to the careers of their counterparts in La Barriada.

Clerical and service sector jobs require more formal education than does low-level manual work. Most desired among the Projectville clique were government jobs, which require at least a high school diploma. Formal education also appeared to be highly valued for its own sake in this neighborhood, as part of the heritage of the civil rights and black pride movements and because of the kinds of jobs that employed neighborhood residents actually held.

Prolonged involvement with schooling and training kept these youths out of the labor market longer than the youths in La Barriada, and community factors contributed to the process: ecologically because the neighborhood's physical isolation exacerbated youth joblessness; demographically because Projectville had some moderate-income families better able to support children attending school. Its residents were also native speakers of English, and education levels among adults were higher than in La Barriada. Even the Projectville families who were primarily dependent on welfare maintained more stable residences than the families in La Barriada, somewhat facilitating continuity in schooling; most of them had been in the projects for years. Families from La Barriada were much more transient; indeed, their residences had almost all burned down by the end of the study period.

The Projectville youths' briefer careers in systematic predatory crime were related to their proportionately greater participation in crimes involving personal confrontation, particularly chain snatching. They also committed their early crimes close to home, where at first the anonymity of the massive projects provided some measure of protection. But although the residents were more separated from police and other official agencies than Hamilton Park residents, Projectville was a more bureaucratically controlled environment than La Barriada. Hence, the Projectville youths preying on their own neighbors encountered localized sanctions—often involving the housing authority and the housing police as well as informal retaliation and the city police—more quickly than La

Barriada youths, whose early victims were also physically proximate but more socially distant. Like La Barriada youths, but sooner, Projectville youths went farther from home to commit violent crimes for money and began to encounter serious sanctions as they did so. Several were incarcerated or institutionalized for substantial periods of time, further delaying their participation in the job market. Those who managed to stay out of prison and/or acquire diplomas, however, found somewhat broader labor market prospects than those in La Barriada, who were generally confined to low-level manual jobs.

Individual Variations within the Cliques

In addition to variations between cliques, there was variation within each clique, individuals whose career patterns differed from those of their immediate peers. For example, the orientation toward manual work was not uniform among the youths from La Barriada; those of their group who had gone furthest in school and had the best language skills tended to seek and find clerical and service sector jobs. Some within-group variations were related to economic and social differentations within the communities and others to more individual, psychological differences rooted in the quality of family relationships.

Two individuals among the group from La Barriada reported never having engaged in any serious crimes for money. Both described themselves and were described by the others as different from their peers, though in opposite ways. Julian Acosta (whose younger brother Sonny was extremely active in crime) had fathered a child when he was sixteen and three more by the time he was twenty-one; he was content to live on a welfare budget and openly tried to avoid work, though at his wife's prodding he did take factory jobs for short periods; he was an object of ridicule for his extreme passivity. Carlos Hernandez, whose older siblings had all been involved in crime, took advantage of his family's eventual business success to stay in school and complete a master's degree. Yet even this upwardly mobile youth reflected his peer group's occupational orientation: his degree was in construction management.

One member of the clique from La Barriada did manage to obtain a high-paying, skilled, unionized construction job. Mario Valdez, who was involved in systematic theft in his mid-teens, followed the pattern of reducing criminal activity in his later teens, during which he looked continually for work. A government-sponsored program trained him in construction skills, then failed to place him in a private job, but he eventually found his construction job through his former supervisor in

[211]

the program. Valdez attributed his high regard for work to his father, even though there was considerable friction between them. His father, though always poor, had always supported their household.

Within the Projectville group, the major variation concerned the extent of involvement in repeated acts of violent predation. Chapter 6 noted a split within the group as several became involved in regular chain snatching while others either terminated their criminal activity or began to sell marijuana rather than steal. Family factors could only partially account for these individual differences.

One individual from Projectville reversed the work and crime patterns of his peers. By his early twenties Sky Wilson had been making a lucrative living selling drugs for about three years; he was the only person in this group who reported several part-time jobs and no theft in his mid-teens. Wilson attributed these differences to his family's better financial status: "I always had money in my pocket. I didn't have to steal, and when I got older, I had money to buy drugs to sell."

Family background in fact appeared to make some difference within each clique, although family factors alone could not be said to account for all the broad-based involvement in crime in La Barriada and Projectville. Even youths from the more nurturing, honest, and cohesive families in these two neighborhoods participated in systematic crime. In La Barriada, however, Arturo Morales and Mario Valdez reported moving away from crime primarily in response to their families' support and emotional pressure; in Projectville, Johnny Singleton and Larry Jefferson, after discussions with their mothers, both voluntarily entered youth homes in order to "get out of the neighborhood and stay out of trouble." But there were youths within all three groups who came from particularly stressful family situations or had criminal traditions within their families and who developed into the more intensive and seemingly irrational criminals within their cliques.

In the Hamilton Park group, John Gutski was the only individual who reported systematic and violent theft during his middle teens and a felony conviction, though he also reported a great deal of work during the same period. His more intensive criminal involvements were perhaps related to the fact that his family had recently immigrated from Europe, was poorer than the families of the other youths in the clique, and lived in a more rundown section of the neighborhood.

The Hamilton Park group included one individual who reported never having committed any crimes for money. Pete Calderone compared his own job networks unfavorably with those of his friends; he was working in a low-level factory job when contacted, and he expressed frustration at not knowing how to get a better job. But he had spent his late teen years neither working nor committing crime, preferring leisure to both, as did La Barriada's Julian Acosta.

With these exceptions, the careers of the members of each group generally fit the patterns of continuity and variation described above. The difficulty of comparing individual and social causes, given the theoretical problem of defining the dividing line between society and individual psychology, is discussed further in the following chapter.

[10]

Youth Crime and
Social Theory

Our empirical findings have implications for recent theoretical questions concerning the relative influences of individual, economic, and sociocultural factors in the etiology of crime and delinquency. As the opening chapter pointed out, both theoretical problems with the once dominant concept of subculture and the results of recent research have led to a renewal of interest in individual rather than social characteristics as the source of delinquency and criminality. Such characteristics as age, gender, intelligence, and personality have been shown to correlate with differential rates of participation in illegal activities. This renewed emphasis on individual characteristics has led some to deemphasize social and economic inequality as the source of high rates of crime among young, minority, inner-city, low-income males such as those portrayed here.

This book has acknowledged and described a range of variation among individuals within each of three local cliques. There is no suggestion of a monolithic subculture within each neighborhood, impelling all its youth to uniform patterns of participation in schooling, employment, and crime. Yet the overall effect of our research is to reaffirm the importance of social rather than individual factors in accounting for the distinct differences among youthful career patterns in the three neighborhoods. Individual differences, some of them rooted in personality and family background, do appear to account for variations within the cliques, but the most striking differences revealed by our research are those between cliques. I have analyzed these group differences in terms of systemic differences in the social ecology of the neighborhoods.

Despite our small ethnographic samples, census and police statistics show that the detailed qualitative differences described by the ethnographic data are also characteristic of the larger populations of these neighborhoods. It is difficult to say exactly how representative the young men we studied are of the rest of the youths in their communities. We did in fact make an effort to contact the more criminally involved youths in each community. Yet the career patterns of involvement in schooling, employment, and crime that we identified in the life histories of these young men differ between these neighborhoods in ways very similar to the ways in which the official statistics on these neighborhoods differ. The congruence of the ethnographic data and the official statistics strongly suggests that differences between these cliques in the quality and quantity of criminality must be understood in social rather than individual terms.

Individuals and Groups

Beyond reaffirming the importance of social sources of delinquency, our data do describe individual variations, some sources of which are discussed below. First, however, it is necessary to consider the theoretical basis on which individual attributes can legitimately be distinguished from factors affecting groups.

The manner in which some recent writings have contrasted individual and social factors as alternative sources of criminal behavior is highly questionable. In some widely read studies the causal significance of social factors has been questioned by pointing to individual characteristics of offenders which, it is claimed, "explain" their behavior without recourse to social explanations. Individual and society are counterposed in these arguments as mutually exclusive entities.

Age, sex, intelligence, and personality have been cited as individual attributes that independently correlate with crime and delinquency to such an extent that they obviate the need for social explanations. Hirschi and Gottfredson (1983) and Gove (1985) have advanced this argument with respect to age. Wilson and Herrnstein's (1985) comprehensive theory stresses all these supposedly individual attributes and systematically debunks most social explanations.

The problem with these arguments is that the source of individual variations in psychology and even in biology can often be traced to society. The only individual variations that might be said to be completely independent of the effects of social differentiation are those based in genetics. To the extent that prenatal nutrition and health care are unequally distributed in society, for example, even biological differences among individuals are concentrated in distinct social groups as a result of social inequality. The effects of poverty and inequality then continue throughout early childhood, adolescence, and beyond.

This is not to deny the existence of individual differences, including

[215]

both those that are strongly related to social differentiation and those that derive from genetics or the interaction of genes and environment. There is no reason, however, to deny social causes of crime on the basis of such allegedly individual-level explanations as have been advanced to date. Data can be mustered for arguments that propose to replace social with individual explanations only by a methodological blindness to the existence of human groups and communities of interaction. Social surveys study individuals, not groups. Not surprisingly, a method that ignores group behavior leads to conclusions that discount the importance of economy, society, and culture (Schwendinger and Schwendinger 1985).

It is important to search for individual as well as social causes and also to be very careful in considering the relationships between the two (Reinarman and Fagan 1988). The overdeterminism of previous subcultural studies of delinquency represents one avenue of error, as in the contention that delinquency is a generic consequence of lower-class culture (Miller 1958). From this perspective, individual variations and the development of individuals over time, such as those portrayed in the present study, disappear from view, along with the real ambivalence toward crime within poor communities.

Serious problems arise in the other direction when methodological individualists systematically ignore group effects and then reinvent them out of supposedly individual differences. Hirschi and Gottfredson (1983) have proposed that high rates of criminality among young males in different societies prove that social effects are not relevant to the understanding of the age distribution of criminality; they imply that biology may be the source. Gove (1985) is more explicit in asserting direct biological causality. Yet young males are also at a status disadvantage in all kinds of societies and thus may have socially derived motivations for deviance. At the same time, the amounts of crime committed by young males differ a great deal according to social circumstances. Biology can tell us little about that (Greenberg 1985). Wilson and Herrnstein (1985) have proposed that the labor market circumstances of blacks have little to do with their high rates of criminality but that low intelligence probably does, yet they also refuse to support the view that group differences in measured intelligence between blacks and whites are inherited.

These confused appeals to biology in an attempt to repudiate social causation ignore the very facts that they try to explain: namely, the concentration of serious delinquency and criminality among young, poor, minority, inner-city males. What is more, no direct biological evidence has been offered. There may conceivably be a biological basis for the aggression of young men, but it has not been demonstrated and

[216]

would not in any event be very helpful in explaining why this aggression is channeled into football in some communities and robbery in others. Many experts also believe there may be a genetic component to intelligence, as measured for individuals within groups (Gould 1981). Few, however, with the exceptions of Jensen (1979) and Herrnstein (1971) at an earlier point in his career, believe that biological inheritance accounts for average differences between groups. Without evidence of group inheritability, the facts that blacks as a group score lower on intelligence tests than whites and also have higher crime rates have nothing to do with each other, except inasmuch as both lower measured intelligence and higher crime rates result from the socially disadvantaged conditions suffered by blacks—perhaps including biased intelligence tests and certainly including the social phenomena of substandard nutrition and health care.

Appeals to biology and psychology as in some sense separate from and prior to society simply have not provided us with any new evidence or understanding of the glaring discrepancies in crime rates between the inner cities and the rest of society. Meanwhile, considerable evidence on the accumulating social and economic disadvantages of the inner cities does exist. Before examining the structural transformation of the inner cities in more detail, however, let us look more closely at some dimensions of individual variation within our samples and ask in what sense these individual differences can be considered as separate from social circumstances.

This book has described a range of variation within each of the three neighborhood-based cliques of young men in their involvements in schooling, employment, and crime. Most of those we studied had participated in criminal activities, but the degree of involvement within each clique ranged from exploratory to extensive. Similarly, members of each clique varied considerably in their individual attainments in school and the labor market. Yet despite individual variations, the similarity in career patterns within each group has a qualitative wholeness. Individuals within each group are more or less successful, but they are strikingly similar in the kinds of endeavors at which they are more or less successful. The members of the three cliques experience not just different *amounts* of involvement in schooling, employment, and crime but also different *kinds* of experience within each realm of activity. This qualitative dimension testifies to the importance of structural rather than individual factors in accounting for differences between groups.

Individual differences within each clique, however, cannot as easily be accounted for in structural terms. Within-group differences are more appropriately explained in terms of such factors as family background

[217]

and intelligence. Even with small samples of about a dozen in each neighborhood, it is worth taking a closer look at within-group variation in family background, intelligence, and age in an effort to assess the effects of these factors on levels of involvement in crime. The discussion of such variations also probes more deeply into the question of how we may properly think about the relationship between individual and social causation.

Family Factors. Family background influences a youth's career in at least two important ways, through socialization and through the resources provided by the family. The family is the crucible of personality; therefore, the origins of violent and antisocial behavior are frequently traceable to childhood experiences (Patterson and Dishion 1985; Loeber and Stouthmer-Loeber 1986). At the same time, the resources provided by the family make a tremendous difference in a child's ability to be successful in school, to make a favorable entry into the labor market, and to survive the experiments with risk taking that are common in adolescence. A poor family may be nurturing and yet unable to provide the advantages necessary for launching a career that will allow a child to escape poverty. A middle-class family may possess such resources and still produce violent and antisocial children.

It is easier in theory than in practice to separate the effects of nurture from those of resources. The fact that poverty, joblessness, and the structure of the welfare system often separate adult men from households in poor neighborhoods has enormous implications for the way children are raised and neighborhoods are maintained (Edelman 1987). Even with respect to family background, then, it is difficult to separate individual from structural factors. Our data, however, do provide some material to work with.

Some effects of family background on differences in involvement in criminality are indeed apparent in our data. These effects are of several types. Some are clearly related to structural factors; others are less so, especially in regard to within-group differences. The Hamilton Park families had higher levels of resources that allowed their sons to move more quickly out of exploratory criminal involvements and into employment. They had higher incomes than those in the two minority neighborhoods, and they were more likely to be two-parent households. They also had much more extensive labor market networks, which enhanced the employment prospects of their children both during the mid-teens and into adulthood. These effects are clearly structural and explain differences between groups.

Within the groups, however, there were other kinds of family differences that did appear to be related to the sons' different levels of involvement in delinquency and crime. The most striking of these within-group patterns was the presence in some families of older males who themselves had had criminal careers. In La Barriada, Mike Concepcion's father and uncle had been involved in organized auto theft. In Hamilton Park, the fathers of both Peter Murphy and Brian Grady had been involved in professional criminal activities. The sons of these men were among the most criminally active within each of their cliques. The type of criminal activity varied, however. Mike Concepcion was a very cool-headed auto thief who stayed clear of drug use and arrest. Brian Grady and Peter Murphy, in contrast, became heavily involved in drug use and were arrested frequently for a very inept series of crimes.

The association between father's and son's criminality has been documented in surveys (Farrington 1979), but the mechanism of transmission appears different in the cases described above. Mike Concepcion's father and uncle seem to have provided role models for professional criminal activity. Brian Grady's and Peter Murphy's fathers' criminality seems to have produced in them a generalized anomie leading to expressive rather than instrumental antisocial behavior.

As a counterexample, it should be noted that only one of the youths from Projectville reported a criminally active father. Reggie Hawkins's father had spent many years in prison for crimes related to heroin addiction, yet Reggie himself reported very minimal criminal involvement; he completed high school and moved quickly into fairly steady employment afterward. Reggie was raised almost entirely by his grandparents. He maintained a warm relationship with his father whenever the elder Hawkins was not incarcerated, but he reported that his father's career—indeed, his father's direct advice—had served as a warning to him to stay clear of heroin and heavy crime.

Some within-group differences also appeared to be related to family neglect and abuse. Chucho Rivera of La Barriada had been separated from both parents by the time he reached his early teens. He lived with an older sister who was preoccupied with her own small children and had little time for or control over him. Gaspar Cruz of La Barriada had left his mother's house after fighting with his stepfather over the stepfather's sexual abuse of his sister. Lucky Giles was described by others in his Projectville clique as neglected; they said that his mother was often away from home for days at a time. Jerry Barnes of Projectville moved back and forth between his parents. He was one of the few whose father was employed at a good city job. His father was extremely strict, however, and his mother drank heavily, with the result that their son was angry and rebellious as he moved between them. All these individuals were among the most criminally active of their cliques; they engaged in the riskiest types of crimes and were eventually arrested for robbery.

With the exception of Cruz, an unusually canny thief, they took few measures to avoid arrest. Their friends, even those who participated in some of the same types of crimes, tended to describe them as "crazy" and more irrational than themselves.

One aspect of family structure which did not appear to contribute to within-group differences in criminal involvement was the presence or absence of the father in the household. In La Barriada and Projectville a majority of youths in each clique had not grown up with their fathers continuously present, but the few who had became just as involved in crime as the others. At the neighborhood level, however, the lack of adult men officially attached to households did make a difference by contributing to a weakened social control environment. Part of Hamilton Park's higher level of public safety derived from the direct social control provided by adult men outside the context of the criminal justice system. The absence of adult men in the households of Projectville and Hamilton Park was in turn closely related to the lower levels of employment opportunity in those neighborhoods. The link between high proportions of female-headed households and high crime rates appears here to result as much from patterns of social control within the neighborhood as from patterns of socialization within the household. Other studies, including many surveys, have also found that the lack of a father in the household contributes far less to delinquency than do family abuse and neglect (Wilkinson 1974; Loeber and Stouthmer-Loeber 1986).

Ascertaining the separate effects of employment, neighborhood social control, and family socialization is difficult, even with rich ethnographic data. Since employment conditions have such a strong effect on both family structure and local-level social control, it is certainly invalid to cite family factors as more important than employment conditions in explaining high rates of crime, and then to claim that individual explanations have replaced structural ones. Inner-city neighborhoods where employment conditions are poor and proportions of female-headed households are high are the neighborhoods in this society in which crime rates are high (Sampson 1987). Because of the link between poverty and female-headed households and because young men's criminal activities are generated and controlled not just within their own families but, crucially, within the context of their neighborhood environments, it is more valid to analyze the contributing effects of family background within rather than between neighborhood environments.

Intelligence. The effects of different levels of intelligence on levels of criminality and labor market success are also difficult to assess. We did not administer formal intelligence tests, but we did ascertain levels of schooling and found no clear relationship between school success and labor market success at the group level. We found lower levels of schooling among the youths from La Barriada than among those in the other two cliques. The approximately equal levels of schooling among the youths from Projectville and those from Hamilton Park did not correlate well with the differences between these two cliques in their success in the labor market or their involvement in crime and the criminal justice system: with no more schooling than their Projectville counterparts, the Hamilton Park youths fared much better in the labor market and became much less involved in street crime. Differences in levels of schooling did make a difference in labor market success within the groups, however, especially in Projectville. With respect to the contributions of school success to labor market success, individual differences account for within-group variation more than for across-group variation. Differences at the group level were clearly related to structural factors, such as the structure of the labor market and the articulation of each neighborhood's population with different sectors of the labor market.

Even without formal intelligence tests, it was possible, given our extensive contact with these youths, to make some assessment of differing levels of intelligence, based on verbal ability and quickness (disregarding formal grammar and other marks of schooling) and on their reports of problem solving in various contexts. In these terms, it is not clear that the apparently more intelligent members of each group became less involved in crime; indeed, some of the more intelligent individuals became deeply involved, in a coolly calculating and rational way and with more success than some of their peers. It might be said that some of the smarter individuals engaged in smarter crime. Mike Concepcion from La Barriada and Sky Wilson from Projectville both fit this description. Both appeared to be highly intelligent, and both had progressed rather quickly from high-risk, low-return street crime to more organized, lucrative, and protected forms of criminal enterprise.

These findings about the ambiguous connection of school success to labor market success and avoidance of criminality are seemingly at odds with the results of many other studies (e.g., Crowley 1984; Elliott and Voss 1974). The contradiction probably arises from the restriction of this study to a small segment of the class structure. In relation to the middle class, the youths from all these neighborhoods have low school and occupational attainment and high criminality. The detailed comparisons of these local cliques, however, suggest that community conditions have a powerful effect on the ways in which native intelligence is channeled into school attainment. To the extent that this is so, school attainment appears to be a poor proxy for intelligence.

Age. This study has certainly confirmed the influence of age on criminality, yet it is not at all clear that these age effects can be understood as
rooted in individual biology and psychology rather in the society. Aging
clearly has both an individual and a social aspect. The fighting reported
in all three neighborhoods among males in early adolescence is common
in many societies and also among primates. There may well be a biological dimension to such aggression (though it has not been demonstrated
directly in biomedical research on human beings; in fact, the contribution of biological studies to the understanding of crime and delinquency
has been minimal), yet this aggression is also channeled quite differently
in different environments, as demonstrated in a vast amount of social
research. Families, schools, the labor market, and the criminal justice
system all construct social definitions of age-appropriate behavior, and it
is these social aspects of aging which are most amenable to research and
to practical intervention.

In sum, this study found that individual differences did contribute to
differences in criminality but that these differences were more apparent
within the cliques than useful in accounting for differences at the group
level. Individual age, family background, and school experience are
certainly important correlates of delinquency and youth crime, but
these factors cannot be neatly separated from social factors.

Economic Process: Entrepreneurs and Structure

Although individual-level explanations of youth crime cannot super-
sede social explanations, real problems have arisen in understanding the
ways in which sociocultural and economic factors influence crime and
delinquency. The problem with much existing research is that sociocultural and economic factors have been considered separately, obscur-
ing the fact that sociocultural and economic processes are intricately
interwoven, both generally and especially in economic crime. Serious
misunderstandings arise when delinquency and youth crime are seen
exclusively either as the product of individual cost-benefit calculations
or as behavior dictated by the values of a subculture of unexamined
origins. It is only within social context that the economic motivations and
calculations of delinquents or their cultural understanding of crime and
delinquency can be understood adequately (Cornish and Clarke 1986).
The comparative nature of this study highlights the interpenetration of
the social and the economic by showing the different ways in which
youthful careers develop in different neighborhoods.

Youth Crime as Individual Enterprise. Economic theories of crime have ignored its social context by assuming that individuals decide to commit or not commit crimes merely on the basis of the projected risks and returns relative to other possible investments of time and energy and resources (G. Becker 1968). Such microeconomic analysis begins from the heuristic assumption of open markets in which firms and individuals compete for the highest rate of return from investment of resources. The economic model of crime derives explicitly from a theory of labor markets in which individual careers are seen as the results of investments in "human capital." In human capital theory differential investments in education and training, combined with native abilities, are seen as leading to differential degrees of success in the labor market. Decisions to commit crime for gain are treated as equivalent to other career decisions.

Microeconomic theories are extremely individualistic. They see the structure of the labor market as no more than the aggregation of individual choices. The application of microeconomic theory to the analysis of crime patterns thus represents one extreme in the tendency to explain crime in terms that are either purely individual or purely structural. This tension between structural and individual levels of explanation has led to a state of confusion in the study and explanation of crime. The failure of empirical studies based on the economic model of crime to produce coherent or expected results is one aspect of this confusion. Despite the demonstrable concentration of high levels of crime among poor inner-city residents, particularly young males, the ambiguous and conflicting results of economic studies have contributed to an atmosphere in which economic causation of criminality has been repudiated in favor of explanations based either on individual biology and psychology or on culture. It is extremely curious that the new emphasis on individuals assigns no importance to the notion of the individual as economic entrepreneur.

Three distinct types of studies have contributed to the disillusionment with efforts to understand crime in economic terms. First, aggregate studies of the relationship between crime rates and employment rates have not always shown a significant positive correlation between high levels of unemployment and high levels of crime. Of particular concern is the fact that employment and crime were both at very high levels in the late 1960s. Second, self-report survey studies since the 1960s have shown very ambiguous relationships between the labor force status of youths and their involvement in crime and delinquency (Tittle, Villmez, and Smith 1978). The broader issue of the relation between social class and delinquency has also been controversial in the interpretation of these surveys. Third, most efforts to prevent crime directly through job

[223]

creation and training have not been demonstrably successful. Nevertheless, the concentration of serious criminality among young males in poor inner-city neighborhoods with high rates of joblessness is undeniable.

Some of these apparent contradictions and controversies are resolvable on the basis of more careful semantic distinctions and empirical research. The question of the relationship between social class and delinquency, in particular, is not so muddy if one specifies what kinds and amounts of delinquency are related to social class. Self-report surveys have shown that there is an age effect on criminality which is independent of class: young men are more likely than others to commit criminal acts in all types of communities (Hirschi and Gottfredson 1983; Greenberg 1977, 1985). At the same time, young men in poor inner-city communities commit greater amounts of more serious crime than young men in other communities (Elliott and Huizinga 1983; Elliott and Ageton 1980).

Similarly, recent research has suggested that conclusions about the lack of relationship between aggregate rates of crime and unemployment may have been premature. If the global relationship between crime and unemployment is broken down into more specific relationships between particular *types* of crimes and *patterns* of unemployment, a more consistent pattern of significant, positive relationships begins to appear. Rising unemployment has more effect on property crimes than on violent crimes. The relationship between unemployment and crime also appears to have been stronger during the 1970s than previously and stronger for subnational than for national levels of aggregation (Chiricos 1987; Allan and Steffensmeier 1989).

Ultimately, however, understanding the patterns of relationships between employment conditions and levels of crime requires an investigation of structural economic factors that are ignored in most microeconomic and survey studies. The theoretical bias of these studies toward the assumption that individuals are decision makers with equal opportunities for schooling and labor market success has led to the many attempts to disclaim economic causation of crime, even in the face of the increasing concentration of crime among residents of economically deprived inner-city neighborhoods.

In order to reconcile these conflicting findings, one must look at economic processes from a perspective that integrates individual decisions and structural factors. Two such perspectives are employed here. The first is that of segmented labor markets, in which attention is directed to structural factors that produce noncompeting groups in the labor market. The second perspective, drawn from economic anthropology, views market competition as only one possible mode of economic organization, existing along with nonmarket processes of reciprocity and redistribution which allocate goods and services by other means than market competition. The application of these perspectives to the findings of this study helps to reconcile the conflicting findings of previous economic studies of crime by analyzing the interpenetration of social and economic factors in the generation and control of youth crime.

Youth Crime and Segmented Labor Markets. Inner-city residents do not compete as equals in the existing labor market. Their access has been blocked by the organization of the labor market itself, as well as by institutional arrangements in the education and welfare systems which perpetuate the isolation of inner-city residents from sufficient access to decent jobs. As a result, the economies of the inner cities, isolated from the mainstream economy, rely heavily on the nonmarket economic processes of reciprocity and redistribution.

Segmented labor market theories acknowledge market competition but also take account of the structure of the labor market along with the choices and achievements of individuals. The careers of individuals are seen as the result of their choices and investments in a market that is not completely open, a market that is structured and segmented into a series of partially noncompeting groups (Cain 1976). Market competition always operates within the context of institutional arrangements that structure the labor market. Segmentation of labor markets in recent history has served to divide jobs and workers on the basis of race, ethnicity, citizenship, age, and sex. Despite legal and social challenges, the current labor market still reflects the powerful influence of such divisions (Gordon, Edwards, and Reich 1982), which contradict the meritocratic assumptions of human capital theory.

The effects of labor market segmentation are particularly severe for minority youths. All school-age youths are legally and socially barred from many jobs by long-standing conventions, traditionally justified by the assumption that parents will provide support for young people while the schools prepare them for future work. This assumption is doubly contradicted by the situation of inner-city, minority youths. Their parents are too poor and suffer too much joblessness themselves to support their children adequately. In addition, the schools that serve them are in disarray and cannot in any event make up for the area's lack of decent employment opportunities accessible to those with a high school education.

These effects of community and life cycle are left out of research that examines aggregate relationships between employment rates and crime rates. Youths, and minority youths especially, account for a significantly

[225]

disproportionate share of all crime, yet they are often not even in the labor force and are thus not included in unemployment figures, for reasons that are deeply rooted in a societal consensus about the importance of schooling for persons under the age of eighteen. Not surprisingly, one of the positive findings of research on aggregate relationships between crime and employment rates is that of a significant inverse relationship between youth labor force participation rates and crime rates (Phillips, Votey, and Maxwell 1972). The expectation that young people should go to school rather than work is also reflected in findings that nonparticipation in school is a stronger predictor of delinquency than is unemployment. School-age males who are not in school are more likely both to work and to become involved in crime than are those who attend school (Crowley 1984; Elliott and Voss 1974).

The segmentation of labor markets is evident in our data. The labor market advantages of the Hamilton Park youths over their peers in the two minority neighborhoods derive not from their greater investment in human capital but rather from their personal networks. These networks afford them entry into more desirable sectors of the labor market which recruit not on the basis of education but on the basis of personal connections. The structure of the labor market, rather than the investments of individuals, thus accounts for much of the difference between groups in labor market success. The greater involvement of La Barriada and Projectville youths in street crime as a short-term occupation derives not just from their failure as individuals to invest in human capital but from the structure of opportunities created by a segmented labor market.

Labor market segmentation affects the career patterns described in this study not only by providing competitive labor market advantages to one group but also by weakening social controls in the other two. The unionized workers of Hamilton Park enjoy relatively greater job security and pay, which allow them to maintain more two-parent households and a more stable neighborhood environment. Youth joblessness in the minority communities makes economic crime more attractive, while adult un- and underemployment contribute to a weakened social control environment. These community-specific patterns are precisely those that have been obscured by the individualistic bias of the survey approach and by economic studies that correlate crime and employment rates for national samples of individuals without regard to community context.

Labor Market Segmentation and the World Economy. The segmentation of labor markets apparent in the comparative study of these three neighborhoods is not a purely local or even regional phenomenon. The regional labor market and the demographic makeup of these neighborhoods are themselves the products of structural economic transformations on a world scale (Wallerstein 1974; Amin 1974). Both the labor market and the population in the New York City region have changed profoundly as a result of the shift from an industrial to a postindustrial system of production. This shift has resulted both in a degradation of employment conditions for much of the population and the disruption and impoverishment of inner-city neighborhoods. The routinization and deskilling of work have produced a new supply of low-wage jobs that offer little security and cannot support families (Braverman 1974). The disappearance of manufacturing jobs providing a decent living has produced structural un- and underemployment and poverty for many, who must then subsist on welfare and low-wage employment.

The effects of deindustrialization are concentrated in the inner cities (Bluestone and Harrison 1982). The communal organization of the industrial cities of an earlier era was based on the location of residential neighborhoods in proximity to centers of manufacturing and distribution concentrated in large cities near major routes of water and rail transportation (Kasarda 1985). In the postindustrial city this congruence of residential and economic organization remains only vestigially; it has been replaced by new forms of production and residential organization. In New York City even more than elsewhere, information and service industries have replaced manufacturing in importance (Tobier 1984). Residential neighborhoods now house either the more highly educated workers in these newer industries or, paradoxically, those who have been displaced by the decline of employment in both manufacturing and agriculture.

Such structural transformations are particularly striking in New York City, the center of a world economic system in which capital and labor are pushed and pulled across regional boundaries in increasingly complex ways (Sassen-Koob 1981). Manufacturing jobs that provided entry-level employment for the minimally educated immigrants of previous generations have been leaving the city for generations, first to other areas of the United States and, more recently, to the Third World. At the same time, many of the residents of these far-flung areas have been displaced and have come into the city, where they are warehoused as a pool of marginal and surplus labor. The presence of poor and underemployed people in inner-city neighborhoods is thus the result of economic processes of international scope.

Not only have worldwide circuits of capital and labor produced a concentration of low-wage and surplus labor in the inner cities; segmentation in the internal organization of the regional labor market has also hardened. From 1978 to 1982 in New York City, for example, the predominance of white males in high-paying crafts jobs, which recruit through apprenticeships rather than schooling credentials, actually increased (Stafford 1985). Of course, the number of these high-paying blue-collar jobs continues to diminish, threatening the way of life of communities such as Hamilton Park. The disappearance of high-paying blue-collar jobs also puts additional pressure on minority employment, as whites who are displaced from their traditional jobs begin to compete with minorities for the lower-paying service jobs.

Minority members who are natives and citizens are also pressured by the presence of large numbers of immigrants within the regional economy. Recent immigrants, both legal and undocumented, predominate in the remaining low-wage manufacturing sector in New York City (Dutka and Freedman 1980). Their lack of education and inability to speak English make them a source of cheap labor for marginally profitable small manufacturers, who often prefer them to native-born minority workers because they are more easily controlled (Sassen-Koob 1979; Piore 1979).

Segmented Markets and Divided Communities. Institutional arrangements in human services and education perpetuate the concentration of un- and underemployed people in inner-city communities. The welfare system itself is an integral part of the postindustrial economy. The growing concentration of jobless people in the inner cities during the 1960s culminated in riots that led to the opening of the welfare rolls (Piven and Cloward 1971). The economies of the inner cities since that time have been based on a combination of low-wage jobs, transfer payments, and underground economic activities, including both off-the-books employment and crime (Harrison 1972a). Many employers who pay low wages depend on a pool of cheap labor provided by households that combine or alternate welfare and work. Over time, welfare dependency further isolates young people in these households from the family- and neighborhood-based job networks through which many entry-level jobs not dependent on high levels of education are allocated. Welfare takes the explosive edge off the existence of a concentrated pool of surplus and marginal labor in the inner cities. At the same time, the isolating effects of locally concentrated welfare dependency contribute to the reproduction of a segmented labor force.

The educational system also contributes to the reproduction of a segmented labor force. The new service and information-processing jobs require more education, even though they pay less, than the manufacturing jobs they are often said to be replacing. At the same time, New

[228]

York City's public schools suffer from inadequate resources and a rigid bureaucracy (Rogers 1968). In the aftermath of the city's fiscal crisis in 1975, just as the youths we studied were moving beyond elementary school, 19,000 public school teachers were laid off (Tabb 1982: 42). Good education has become increasingly privatized, with the result that advancement through education has come to be more dependent on parental resources.

The failure of the schools is deeply implicated in the concentration of street crime among school-age youths, even though desperately needed improvements in the school system would hardly be sufficient to alleviate crime. Schools serve both as direct agents of social control and as the agencies that mediate between families and the labor market. Most inner-city schools are inadequate for both these functions. They suffer many problems of management and morale, but ultimately they suffer because of the political withdrawal of resources and the economic transformations that have led to an exodus from their areas of decent employment that can be entered with high school credentials.

In this context of community and life cycle, the exploratory thefts committed by young people in all sorts of communities develop into short-term careers of serious theft in communities such as those portrayed in this study. These ethnographic findings conform better to economic theories of crime than do studies based on aggregate correlations of crime and unemployment rates. The youths we studied, like the delinquents that have been studied for generations (Tannenbaum 1938), began their criminal activities not out of rational economic choice but as play, but over time their involvement in these activities developed according to their entrepreneurial calculations of the relative worth of engaging in school, work, or crime vis-à-vis their actual opportunities for these activities. Their individual cost-benefit calculations are much more evident as they developed over time than at any given moment during their volatile youthful explorations.

The hardships of minority residents of the inner cities result not just from their material wants as individuals or within households but from their concentration within the inner cities. One must bear in mind these concentration effects (W. Wilson 1987) in interpreting research findings that purport to demonstrate an effect of race on crime separate from that of class (Wolfgang, Figlio, and Sellin 1972; Tittle, Villmez, and Smith 1978; Laub 1983). Because they are so geographically concentrated, poor minority individuals and households tend to be more deprived than nonminority individuals and households with similar income levels. A report from the New York Community Service Society found that "70 percent of the city's poor Blacks and Hispanics live in neighborhoods

[229]

where 30 percent or *more* of the residents are poor. On the other hand, 70 percent of the city's poor whites live in neighborhoods where *less than* 30 percent of the residents are poor" (Tobier 1984: 57). Under these conditions, the structural effect of a local concentration of poverty harshens the conditions of individual and household poverty.

The structural effects of the concentration of poverty and joblessness in inner-city minority communities help to account for the failure of economic studies to establish historical correlations between crime and employment rates. Although national employment rates were indeed high during the 1960s when urban crime rates were also soaring, the economic conditions of the inner cities were deteriorating. The concentration of poverty increased during the 1970s, along with persisting high crime rates (W. Wilson 1987). These structural economic conditions also help to explain the perceived failure of many employment programs designed to prevent crime by upgrading employment. These programs did not achieve the first goal, that of improving employment (Thompson, Sviridoff, et al. 1981). William Julius Wilson (1986: 8) has pointed to the relationship between employment programs and the economy: "If gainful employment is problematic because of a stagnant economy, as was frequently the case during the 1970s, participants in these programs understandably lose interest. Indeed, it would be surprising if program participants took training seriously when there is little or no chance for placement."

The connection of crime to employment occurs at the level of community as much as at the level of individuals and households. The link between employment conditions and crime is not universal: not all joblessness leads to criminality, and not all criminality is motivated by joblessness. Full-time students, retired persons, and highly educated middle-class wage earners who are between jobs are all likely to be out of work and yet not commit crimes. Conversely, most illegal gain goes to employed persons, in terms of both the absolute number of crimes and the absolute worth of everything that is stolen. Street crime accounts for less of the total of illegally transferred property than do inside trading, government corruption, tax fraud, and job-related theft among workers in all strata (Simon and Witte 1982).

Nonetheless, the link between un- and underemployment and high rates of street crime in inner-city neighborhoods is pervasive. This link is a matter not merely of the joblessness of individual youths leading them to commit crimes but rather of the concentrated joblessness and poverty in the community as a whole leading to both greater levels of stress and weakened social controls, and thus to high levels of crime. Attention to this link between social ecology and crime, once central to criminology,

[230]

virtually disappeared following the advent of self-report research in the 1960s and has only recently been revived (Reiss and Tonry 1986; Byrne and Sampson 1986).

The three neighborhoods portrayed here represent different aspects of these structural economic changes. Hamilton Park's residents monopolize many of the remaining desirable, high-paying, non-exportable blue-collar jobs. The stability of their employment allows them to maintain households of nuclear and extended families in which adult males are officially present. The stability of their communal institutions and the comparative safety of their streets stem from this stability of employment. La Barriada's residents, the most recent immigrants, must depend on welfare and low-wage factory work. They are advantaged in this local economy only by their citizenship, which positions them just above the undocumented, more easily exploited immigrant workers. Projectville's residents also depend heavily on welfare but are much more involved in the institutions of the larger society than La Barriada's residents through their access to some public jobs, their residence in public housing, their political organization, and their commitment to education as a means of advancement.

Redistribution: Youth Crime as a Nonmarket Economic Process

Thus far, I have argued that youth crime for gain must be understood in economic terms in at least two senses: that of the individual youth as an economic entrepreneur, and that of the inner-city neighborhood as an economic environment shaped by structural economic transformations of worldwide scope. If a young male's actions are not seen within this structural context, they appear irrational, and it becomes easier to conclude that street crime is only the product of low intelligence and defective personality and not a response to existing economic incentives.

Important as it is to look at both individual and structure, however, a shifting focus on individuals and the historical development of the labor force still misses the interplay between the two. Conceptually, one is left with an unsatisfactory choice between two sorts of determinism, individual and structural. The active, creative, and diverse responses of individuals to the structure of opportunities are lost, along with any possibility of understanding how these human responses can take a collective form and themselves lead to further transformation of the existing structure (Ortner 1984; Bourdieu 1978).

What remains unaccounted for is the social life of the community.

Individuals do not respond only individually to societal constraints. They respond also as members of distinct communities that mediate between them and the larger structures of economic and political organization. The social life of communities is powerfully constrained yet not completely determined by these structures. Within local communities people devise collective ways of coping with the demands imposed by the larger structures.[1]

This study has examined the development of youth crime patterns in the context both of the internal social organization of local communities and of the relationship of these local communities to larger, encapsulating political and economic structures. It has already noted that the social control of youth crime varies according to the extent to which particular crime patterns are redistributing extra resources into a community or simply recirculating resources within the community. The more redistributive a crime, the less likely it is to elicit social control responses from within the community.

Looking more closely at youth crime as redistribution makes it necessary to ask questions about crime as an economic process which are obscured in attempts to model crime solely in terms of the cost-benefit calculations of potential offenders. Attention to the redistributive aspects of crime reveals the ways in which local communities mediate between young criminal entrepreneurs and the political and economic structures that create such strong incentives for them to become involved in economic crime.

The concept of redistribution as a nonmarket process developed out of attempts by economic anthropologists to analyze the economic life of small-scale and ancient societies and to compare their economic systems with modern systems organized on the basis of market competition (Polanyi, Arensberg, and Pearson 1957; Dalton 1969). Though market competition is the primary means by which goods and services are allocated in modern Western societies, it is not the only way these economic functions have been or are accomplished. Alternative economic processes grow out of patterns of interaction fundamentally different from that of market competition. Grounding economic process in interaction makes it possible to understand a great deal more about economic processes in modern as well as ancient and small-scale societies than does restricting the concepts of economic analysis to the principles of market competition.

[1]For recent anthropological critiques of the overdeterminism of world-system theories such as those of Wallerstein (1974) and Amin (1974), see the counterarguments of Wolf (1982) and Roseberry (1983). For a more abstract argument in terms of systems theory concerning the possibility for internal autonomy at lower levels of hierarchical systems, see H. Simon 1973.

Nonmarket economic processes play a significant, if subsidiary, role in modern economic systems, particularly in the economic life of areas such as the inner cities, which are cut off from full participation in the mainstream market economy. An understanding of these processes may be applied to the problem of understanding how youth crime functions within the local economies of the inner cities. Since the analysis of interactions involved in comparing market and nonmarket economic processes also provides a means for connecting social action and culture, it is then possible to proceed to a consideration of the vexing problems of the cultural meaning of crime within these communities and the manner in which consciousness of crime is related to class consciousness. Interactionist analysis provides conceptual bridges between structure and the individual and between social action and culture (Arensberg 1972).

Market Competition, Reciprocity, and Redistribution. The interactional pattern of market competition is that of equal buyers and sellers entering into transactions from which each side hopes to profit. An important variation of this pattern is monopoly, in which the parties to the transaction are not equal and the monopolistic side controls the market to its advantage. In both cases, however, the transaction itself is purely instrumental; both buyer and seller are interested only in profit and have no intrinsic social relationship outside the economic sphere. The interactions involved in the market allocation of goods and services have no intrinsic relationship to other aspects of social life.

In other modes of economic organization, however, economic activity is intrinsically bound up with other social relationships. These forms of economic organization have been called "reciprocity" and "redistribution" (Polanyi 1957).

Reciprocity involves exchange based on ongoing social relationships that are not primarily motivated by profit. In the Trobriand Islands, for example, a man gives the better part of his yam harvest to his wife's brother and himself receives most of the harvest of his sister's husband (Malinowski 1929). The distribution and allocation of goods in this system is motivated not by personal profit but by ideologies of religion and kinship which organize all other aspects of social life as well. The economic life of many small-scale societies is based on reciprocity in this way.

Redistribution involves the flow of goods and services to a center and back out. The prototype is the system recorded in the Bible in which Joseph persuaded the Egyptian Pharaoh to collect great storehouses of grain as a hedge against recurrent famine. Individual producers took their surplus grain to the center in times of plenty and went back to the center to collect grain in times of famine. The kingdoms of West Africa and other parts of the world were organized in this way before they became incorporated into the world market. This form of exchange grows out of and maintains relationships of inequality, but unlike a monopolistic system, it is embedded in ideologies of kinship, religion, and politics which also regulate the rest of social life.

Market and nonmarket processes grow out of different patterns of interaction and are conceptually distinct. In practice, however, they can and do coexist. In some ancient and small-scale societies, market activities have been subsidiary processes within dominant reciprocal or redistributive systems. In the modern world, reciprocity and redistribution exist as subsidiary processes within the dominant market systems of economic organization. The reciprocal trading of favors among business people and politicians, for example, is frequently undertaken not for the purpose of immediate gain but for the purpose of building up enduring social solidarity that will allow both parties to escape the pressures of market competition.

To the extent that nonmarket processes are embedded in social relationships lying outside the instrumentalities of market exchange, they are patterned by, and themselves pattern, the realms of meaning and culture. Hence, analysis of interaction provides a bridge between the individual and structure in our thinking about both economic activity and culture itself. The products of patterned interaction include the allocation of goods and services along with definitions of self and other, solidarity and opposition, own group and outsiders. Nonmarket economic transactions are deeply intertwined with the total life of the community. Economic transactions based on reciprocity and redistribution grow out of, create, and maintain social relationships apart from the market. Reciprocal sharing is a nonmarket process embedded in a relationship of equality. Redistribution is a nonmarket process embedded in a relationship of inequality.

Reciprocity and Redistribution in the Inner Cities. These abstractions are exemplified in the relationship of poor people to crime in their own communities. Much of the economic life of the inner cities has been cut off from the labor market. Although inner-city residents constitute an important pool of low-wage labor, they also represent labor that has been defined as surplus within the world economic system. At any given time, many residents of the inner cities are cut off from the labor market. Unable to survive on the basis of the labor market, they rely on reciprocal sharing and redistribution for survival. Welfare and crime are both forms of redistribution that provide for the survival of inner-city residents but also exacerbate their isolation from the mainstream of society and ultimately reproduce inequality.

Stack (1974) has documented the importance of reciprocity in urban black communities where there is insufficient access to the labor market. In Stack's analysis, poverty breeds generosity out of necessity because "what goes around comes around." She describes circulation patterns that carry children, money, and goods through domestic networks of female kin. Though not described in detail here, such arrangements also characterize Projectville and La Barriada, whose residents have severely insufficient access to the labor market. Another kind of reciprocity is more evident in this study, the reciprocity that binds cliques of male adolescents. During periods when they are out of school and not working, they spend most of their time together. They seek thrills, jobs, and criminal opportunities together. They share money, drugs, alcohol, clothing, and possessions as long as—as in all sharing relationships— what goes around keeps coming around.

Reciprocity among poor urban people allows them to adapt to unstable and insufficient sources of income by circulating resources. Yet reciprocity merely circulates insufficient resources, evening the effects of uncertain income without augmenting it. Another set of nonmarket processes, those of redistribution, actually increases resources. Some types of crime create patterns of redistribution which, along with welfare, serve as adaptations to structural unemployment and underemployment, albeit adaptations that create and maintain the inner city as an economic periphery within the geographical core area of the world economy (Sassen-Koob 1981; Wolf 1982).

The analysis of crime patterns throughout this study has to some extent treated crime as just another form of enterprise. From this point of view, given the local structure of opportunities, these youthful criminal entrepreneurs were behaving rationally. Theft, however, is a form of direct appropriation, one that existed long before modern market economies became the prevalent modes of production and distribution, which does not produce value in the capitalist sense (Hobsbawn 1955). As such, theft is not easily understood in terms of market competition in quite the same way as are other forms of economic activity. Economists attempting to operationalize an "economic model of crime" discovered that the worth of crime as a source of income relative to other sources of income is difficult to determine because of the inherent "noxiousness" of crime and the wide variation in individual "tastes" (Block and Heineke 1975). The normative component in an individual's or a community's ability to tolerate crime has proved difficult to quantify.

Part of the difficulty in producing an economic analysis of crime derives from the fact that theft as an economic strategy is inextricably embedded in social relationships. The calculation by the potential thief of the worth of a contemplated crime depends not only on his potential take but also on his chances of getting caught. The chances of his getting caught are largely dependent on the place of both the thief and the victim in the community. The market value of the goods stolen and the efforts required to steal them must somehow be calculated along with the extent to which the personal networks of thief and victim are likely to result in the thief's protection or prosecution. In this as in other cases of nonmarket processes, both the rationality of the act and the socially constructed meaning of the act emerge from patterned interaction.

A closer examination of the redistributive aspects of various crimes will reveal the manner in which the perceived noxiousness of particular types of crime in particular communities is grounded in ongoing patterns of interaction. First, however, it is necessary to point out that redistribution processes move resources both into and out of the inner cities.

Both crime and welfare, as processes of redistribution which create and maintain the inner cities as pools of marginal and surplus labor, are brought into being by other aspects of redistribution, those that have led to the systematic transfer of jobs, housing, and quality public services away from the inner cities (Tabb 1982; Harvey 1975). The transfer of resources back to the inner cities through government welfare, housing, and social services has been largely a government attempt to compensate for the effects on the inner cities of suburbanization, privatization, and the international export of capital. These redistributive patterns at the regional and world level are the preconditions for the development of the crime patterns analyzed here. The creation of poverty in the midst of plenty and of structural un- and underemployment in the center of world capital has brought about a situation in which resources can be transferred illegally with relative technical ease.

Youth Crime as Redistribution. The extent to which youth crime redistributes resources into a community from outside has profound implications for local-level social control. Most of the analyses in this book, though acknowledging both structural constraints and individual variations in responses to these constraints, have in fact concentrated on local-level patterns of social organization as these affect not only the generation but the control of delinquency and youth crime.

The portrayal of local-level social control has been conspicuously lacking in much of the recent theorizing about crime and delinquency.[2]

---

[2]One prominent school of thought is called "social control theory" even though it pays scant attention to the actual processes of social control, such as those portrayed here (Hirschi 1969). Concentrating as it does on the psychological effects of attachment or lack of attachment to family, school, and peers, this theory could be more aptly labeled "attachment theory."

To the extent that the question has been dealt with at all, it has been called "social disorganization." Communities have been classified as more or less socially disorganized, as if social organization could be quantified on a linear scale. In contrast, I have attempted to show that social organization can be qualitatively quite different, even from one poor neighborhood to another. As in previous ethnographic studies of the inner cities (Suttles 1968; Whyte 1943), what one begins to see is not disorganization so much as a different form of organization. Many deviant activities, on close examination, turn out to be socially patterned behavior, not just the acting out of individual pathologies.

The question of the extent to which youth crime redistributes resources into the community from outside raises in turn the difficult question of whether and to what extent lower-class criminality is a class-conscious enterprise. Marx himself explicitly excluded criminals and other *lumpenproletariat* from the revolutionary classes (Wenger and Bonomo 1981), even though more recent radical criminologists have not always been so cautious (Quinney 1977). Even liberal observers who are at great pains to acknowledge the origins of poverty in exploitation and discrimination are perplexed by the fact that poor people both suffer most often from crime and yet refuse so often to use and cooperate with police (Silberman 1978). The high tolerance of inner-city residents for various kinds of deviance is explained as a gap between their tastes and resources: normatively, they display "value stretch" (Rodman 1963); practically, they just are not able to choose their neighbors (Suttles 1968). Even juvenile delinquents themselves are said not really to believe that what they are doing is justifiable; they simply "neutralize" norms that are widely accepted even in their own communities in such a way that the norms do not apply to what they are doing at the moment (Sykes and Matza 1957; Matza 1964).

One important reason for the reluctance of inner-city residents to call the police is that they are afraid of retaliation—with good reason: Mike Concepcion, for example, vandalized the car of the person who had "ratted out" his friend. Still, fear and intimidation aside, some crimes are tolerated more than others, and some are tolerated more in some poor neighborhoods than in others. An analysis of the crime patterns described in our field data helps to specify the ways in which inner-city neighborhoods both generate and control youthful crime for gain. It shows that even though most residents of an area may disapprove of various crimes normatively, the "value stretch" they exercise in ignoring what they see around them is quite responsive to the extent to which the particular crime is actually redistributing wealth.

The crime patterns described here represent different interaction

[237]

patterns that produce different patterns of circulation of goods, services, and money within inner-city neighborhoods and between these neighborhoods and the outside. By comparing these interaction patterns, we can see the processes out of which emerge both ongoing crime patterns and the specific consciousness of crime among inner-city residents, both criminals and noncriminals.

Consider first the incident in which Projectville's Zap Andrews and another youth robbed an adult woman of her purse in the elevator of a housing project building near his own. Abstracting from this incident, we can say that the sequence of interactions within the neighborhood for this type of crime is as follows:

1. Local youth A robs local youth B's mother.
2. Local youth B robs local youth A's mother.

This type of predation, completely internal to the neighborhood, could be termed reciprocal predation or negative reciprocity. The concentration of vulnerable poor women and their children in neighborhoods such as Projectville and La Barriada defines a structure of criminal opportunity. Many youths take advantage of this opportunity, but neither other members of their community nor indeed they themselves are able to neutralize the noxiousness of their crimes very effectively.

Everyone understands the threat that such crimes pose to their daily lives. Projectville's Ben Bivins returned from a jail sentence served for just this sort of robbery and expressed his desire to abstain from further crimes of this type: "You could be risking your life, robbin' somebody's mother, and for what? Two dollars. That's all you get sometimes." The circulation of money and goods produced by such a crime is completely internal to the neighborhood and does not bring in extra resources from outside. Moreover, because robbery is the most direct form of appropriation, it creates few new social networks. At most, the stolen goods may be sold to an individual customer or a fence, adding one further link to the chain of interactions.

At the other extreme from this pattern of reciprocal predation, consider the pattern of factory burglaries by the youths in La Barriada. Both the fact that the crime was burglary rather than robbery and the fact that the factories were not owned or managed by local people produced a set of interactions with much different implications. The sequence of interactions in the incident in which La Barriada's Mario Valdez and others burglarized a local coat factory is as follows:

1. Local youths burglarize factory owned and managed by nonresidents of the neighborhood.

2. Local youths sell coats at cheap prices to other residents of neighborhood.

In this case the activities of the youthful thieves brought a flow of cheap goods into the neighborhood that would not otherwise have existed. There occurred a genuine redistribution into the community from outside, producing interactions within the community which created a measure of tolerance for the activities of the youthful thieves. At the conscious level many La Barriada residents did not approve of burglary, but in fact they tolerated these factory burglaries quite easily. When the youths from La Barriada began to engage in street robberies, however, they sacrificed the shelter they had previously enjoyed in their burglaries. They were forced to go further from their familiar territory and were much more quickly apprehended.

Other types of criminal enterprise engendered much more complex chains of interaction which also producing ramifying social relationships resulting in local toleration and shelter for the illegal activities. Mike Concepcion's car theft operation in La Barriada involved many different steps and roles:

1. Local youth steals a car and brings it back to the neighborhood.
2. Others assist in stripping the car and marketing the parts.
3. The thieves pay little children small fees to watch for the police.
4. The mothers of the children, knowing of these payments, also watch for the police and call out a warning in time for the thieves and car strippers to disappear into abandoned buildings.

The whole community effectively became involved in protecting a criminal operation that brought money into the neighborhood from outside. Yet generalized normative disapproval of theft had not disappeared. The day following these observations, one of these mothers would not allow her child to go to a ball game with Mike's friend Arturo because Arturo was a convicted thief.

Drug-selling operations resemble legitimate enterprise more than does theft. Except for the fact that it is illegal, selling drugs is an activity much like selling anything else. It does not necessarily involve the noxiousness of predation. The illegality of drug traffic, however, embeds it in a web of personal relations. The interactions involved are not as neutral with respect to the rest of the life of the community as are legitimate business transactions. Illegal business activity is frequently embedded in personal relations more than legitimate business activity is: because of the need for protective social networks to shelter the enterprise from the authorities (Ianni with Reuss-Ianni 1972), people

[239]

prefer to buy from and sell to others with whom they maintain a personal relationship outside the context of the market transaction. When drugs are marketed more openly, outside the context of existing personal relationships, the risk is much greater. The drug seller becomes vulnerable both to the police and to thieves who know that the seller is not protected by the police. Personal violence, not the monopolized violence of the state, becomes the sanction underlying market agreements. Under these conditions, the reactions of the local community to a drug-selling operation depend on the extent to which the operation brings money and/or violence into the neighborhood.

Incidents from the field notes indicate a wide diversity in such activities and the consequent degree of shelter provided by local people. In La Barriada, for example, two different drug-selling operations involved much different patterns of interaction between drug traffickers and other local residents. The first was a marijuana "store" that was also an operating candy store and a center of communal life for old and young, marijuana smokers and nonsmokers. School children bought candy in the afternoon; young people, both working and nonworking, predominated in the evening. In good weather older men set up their domino tables just outside. The store housed the nearest public telephone, an invaluable resource to local residents (as well as field researchers). The store was staffed by local youths who had abandoned serious theft in order to be semilegal clerks. The store was part of a small complex of legal and illegal businesses, all operated by an unlicensed South American dentist who fixed teeth upstairs. Downstairs, in addition to the marijuana/candy store, his enterprises included a laundromat and a restaurant.

This drug-selling operation was well integrated into the economic life of the local community—until it was displaced by another that led to the community's destruction. A heroin-selling operation in the next building began to draw into the neighborhood large numbers of heroin users who supported themselves almost exclusively by theft and lived outside of family households. One day, the heroin sellers put a gun to the head of the underground dentist, and he and his businesses departed. The heroin users increased in number as building after building on the block burned.

Many other drug-selling operations were documented during our fieldwork, particularly those involving marijuana, the drug of choice at this time among the youths studied in all three neighborhoods. Since none of these operations lasted more than a few months in a given location, and all eventually succumbed to police raids, their stability and their acceptance among all local people should not be exaggerated. Nevertheless, this type of enterprise was considerably more stable than serious theft, primarily because it involved many local people both as customers and as workers, including older business people with capital and legitimate enterprises.

Drug traffic also constitutes a process of redistribution but not in the same way as theft. The selling of illegal drugs functions much as did the selling of illegal alcoholic beverages during Prohibition. Inner-city residents supply criminalized goods and services first to the local population and then to the wider community, as Projectville's Sky Wilson and Juice Baker sold drugs first to peers and then to office workers in the central business district. Inner-city entrepreneurs risk violence and stigmatization in their personal careers in return for a flow of money back to them and into their neighborhoods. Respectability flows out and money flows back in.

In the process, one sees clearly a pattern of structure and emergence. Organized crime is the structure that emerges and, over time, becomes progressively more entangled with legitimate enterprise as illegal profits are laundered and invested. This pattern of structure and emergence has characterized the economic life of United States cities for some time (Bell 1953; Ianni with Reuss-Ianni 1972; Ianni 1974a, 1974b). Drug trafficking may ultimately take more money out of the community than it brings in, taking some wealthy entrepreneurs out along with their money. Local attitudes toward drug enterprises are deeply divided. Violent flare-ups bring forth periodic calls for suppression and control. At other times, however, the drug business generates income and employment in areas that are otherwise deficient in both (Preble and Casey 1969; Johnson et al. 1985).

Processes of redistribution are ultimately political processes. As resources flow to the political center and then back to the periphery, redistribution embodies and creates inequality. Though they bring sorely needed additional resources into the inner city, both welfare and youth crime create and maintain the inner city as periphery. Welfare-dependent households are not only poor at a given time; they also cut their young members off from the labor market networks that account for most jobs. Youth crime provides otherwise unavailable funds for a short period but further separates inner-city youths from the labor market and stigmatizes them in their later careers.

Youth Crime and Culture

I have largely avoided the term "culture" until this point in the discussion because of the distortions that have arisen from its overly vague application in past studies of delinquency. For a long period,

[241]

delinquency was described primarily as the product of culture, with the unfortunate result that both the economic basis of much delinquency and the agency of individual delinquents were obscured. In their extreme forms, cultural deviance theories could be read as another form of structural determinism in which culture, rather than society or the economy, drove individual behavior without much input from the individual (Miller 1958; Lewis 1966; Banfield 1970).

Cultural deviance theories of delinquency actually vary in the extent to which they admit the influence of economic conditions on culture. The classic subculture writings all made some sort of connection between economic disadvantage and the formation of delinquent subcultures. Social and economic inequality figured prominently in all these theories, in contrast to later "control" theories based on survey research, which deemphasized social class and emphasized individual, psychological causation (Hirschi 1969). Nonetheless, the mechanisms connecting disadvantage to delinquency were often vaguely specified. As a result, the extent to which delinquency can be an economic strategy tended to disappear from view.

I felt it necessary to avoid speaking directly of culture until the economic aspects of the development of careers in delinquency and youth crime had been fully examined. That avoidance does not mean that I think there is no cultural element to be considered, as some propose (Kornhauser 1978) but rather that we can address cultural questions now, in the context of data already presented, without assuming that culture and economy are completely separate entities competing as explanatory principles.

Both culture and economy are the emergent products of social interaction. From this point of view, neither entity can be explained either as a mere aggregation from individual behavior or as a mysterious force existing outside of individuals and driving their behavior. Both the production and allocation of goods and services and the construction of symbols and beliefs are things that people do together. The development of all personal careers involves both a practical and a symbolic aspect. Both the practical and the symbolic are developed in social interaction (Becker and Carper 1970; Hughes 1971).

Because the culture concept has been more central in anthropology than in any other field, it is useful to turn to anthropological theory in an attempt to clarify the problems that have attended the checkered career of the term "subculture" in studies of crime and delinquency. Although anthropologists differ a great deal in their definitions of culture (Kroeber and Kluckhohn 1952), most have done research in community settings in which they have had to record interactions and deal in a concrete way

[242]

with the relationship between shared meanings and shared behavior. The mystifications that have often surrounded the use of the culture concept in sociology and other fields outside anthropology arise in part from this lack of a field research tradition in which attention to social interaction is central.

Although current opinion diverges as to how to define, study, and think about culture, there is some consensus as to how *not* to proceed. The notion that culture is a package of beliefs and customs handed down unthinkingly from one generation to the next with no modification of content or function is now largely discredited. In that form, culture appears as a mysterious, exogenous force that drives human behavior inexorably and inalterably, and its contents as a mere list of traits that have accumulated accidentally, a random collection of "shreds and patches" (Lowie 1920). That concept is flawed for many reasons. A mere listing of the elements within the package gives no sense of their interconnections. It is not possible to determine how culture comes to exist, how it changes, or how it varies among individuals or subgroups. Culture is reduced to an impenetrable black box of recalcitrant attitudes, values, and cognitions that serves as a residual nonexplanation for those aspects of human behavior that cannot be explained in other ways.

This black box conception of culture as a package of immutable traits was at the heart of the mistaken theories of the "culture of poverty" (Miller 1958; Lewis 1966; Banfield 1970). These theories attributed the existence of poverty neither to the constitutional inabilities of poor individuals nor to social causes but to the culture of people in poor communities. An enduring stream of American thought has maintained that poor people are poor because they share and transmit to their children a set of defective values, including the unwillingness to defer gratification, a sense of fatalism about their condition, and an inability to submit to authority. Culture has thus served as the only important third alternative to individual and social explanations of social inequality.[3]

In part as a reaction to such misuse of the culture concept and also as part of the ongoing development of their own disciplines, anthropologists and sociologists have sought in recent years to be more precise in defining and using the term. Anthropologists in particular are often in sharp disagreement over these definitions, but they at least know what they are disagreeing about, and they all avoid the notion of the unstudiable black box of immutable traits. Some prefer to concentrate on the internal connections among elements in a cultural system, the logic or structure of culture itself. Others concentrate on the functional relation-

[3]For critiques of the culture-of-poverty theories, see Valentine 1968; Leacock 1971; and Eames and Goode 1973.

ships of the cultural system to the environment, the adaptive aspects of culture.[4]

My own definition of culture is "the shared understandings of those in like circumstances." This definition gives equal weight to the content of culture and to the environment. Further, my view is interactionist (Fine and Kleinman 1979). I see both culture and economy as the products of patterned interaction. Both are structures that emerge from patterned interactions among individuals and in turn set the beginning conditions for subsequent interactions. Logically, then, culture neither determines nor is determined by individual behavior. It arises out of and is continually transformed in the process of social interaction. Rather than opposing individual and culture, the interactionist view sees culture as emergent from behavior and behavior as structured by culture (Arensberg 1972).

The discussion above of youth crime as a process of redistribution has shown the utility of the interactionist approach in analyzing the ways in which destructive behavior, and its control, crystallize in certain patterns. Both the structure of social opportunities and the entrepreneurial zeal of individuals contribute to these patterns, but the patterns take on concrete form as the result of specific localized patterns of interaction.

Both behavior and meaning emerge from these patterned interactions. Most of this book has concentrated on behavior and on the functional, adaptive aspects of the ways in which youth crime is both generated and controlled through collective responses to an environment in which access to the labor market is blocked. The discussion of youth crime as redistribution began to show the ways in which interaction produces not just behavior but also specific forms of consciousness and structures of meaning.

The finding that crimes are more or less tolerated at the local level according to the extent to which they redistribute scarce resources into a neighborhood, however, still does not address directly the question of the meaning of these crimes to local people. The youthful thieves who bring money into the neighborhood are not in fact Robin Hoods, stealing as an act of conscious political resistance on behalf of their oppressed communities. Whether their crimes are internally predatory or redistributive, they are not engaging in them for anyone's gratification but their own. Similarly, others in their neighborhood who may offer youthful thieves a measure of shelter from the police in return for a source of cheap or illegal goods and services do not thereby completely condone

[4]See Keesing 1974 and Ortner 1984 for reviews of these different approaches to defining and using the culture concept.

their crimes, as suggested in extreme forms of cultural deviance theory. Inner-city residents are profoundly ambivalent about crime, benefiting from it sometimes but suffering because of it at other times.

The notion that crime is culturally accepted in lower-class neighborhoods is an example of the fallacious tendency to conceive of culture as a list of traits. The cultural element in criminality is not to be isolated by constructing a hierarchical list of the extent to which different social groups disapprove of crime. Rather, the cultural element in criminality is found in the definitions of self and other and of own group and outsiders which determine what acts are considered crimes and the degree of seriousness attributed to different crimes.

Some previous theories have acknowledged the ambiguity of attitudes toward youth crime among both delinquents themselves and other residents of their neighborhoods. Notions of "value stretch" (Rodman 1963) and "neutralization" (Sykes and Matza 1957), however, merely designate ambiguous attitudes without tracing them with any specificity to the contradictions out of which they arise. My analysis has insisted on the economic rationality of certain forms of youth crime, yet there remains also an expressive element, a set of cultural meanings that have not yet been addressed.

For a short time in their lives, crime provides some youths not only with money and goods but also with a social and occupational identity that has meaning beyond its monetary returns. They call success in crime "getting paid" and "getting over," terms that convey a sense of triumph and of irony which is not accounted for in the grim depiction of their acts as the economic strategies of the disadvantaged. When they talk of "getting paid," they are not equating crime and work with utter seriousness, as if they do not know the difference. Rather, they are inverting mainstream values with conscious, albeit savage, irony. "Getting over" is a more general term that refers to success at any endeavor in which it seems that one is not expected to succeed. It is equivalent to "beating the system" and contains the notion of a place other than where they are, a place they are not allowed to cross into. What they "get over on" is the system, a series of odds rigged against people like themselves. Both phrases are spoken in a tone of defiant pride. They are phrases in the shared language of youths who are out of school, out of work, and seriously involved in crime.

The concept of "subculture" was originally introduced into sociology for the express purpose of portraying the delinquent as a member of a disadvantaged group that is attempting, as a group, to create an alternative to its structurally disadvantaged position. Both the notion of collectivity and the notion of the creativity of the collectivity's response to its situation are fundamental to Albert Cohen's (1955) formulation of the "delinquent subculture."

The very success of Cohen's subculture concept, however, obscured the economic rationality of much delinquency and youth crime. Subsequent writers adopted a distressing tendency to speak of subcultures as reified things, apart from the communities of interaction from which they arose. Cohen's use of the concept also addressed working-class culture as a whole by situating the genesis of delinquency in the encounter of the child of manual workers with a school culture that denigrated physical in favor of mental work and that insisted more on orderliness and punctuality than on effort and accomplishment. Many elements of this analysis remain valid, but it is impossible within such a formulation to approach the kinds of variations in working-class life that our data describe. The culture concept was shorn of the connection to specific community context that has distinguished its use in anthropology, whether in the hands of "materialist" or "mentalist" practitioners.

Cloward and Ohlin's (1960) work brought community-specific analysis to delinquency studies, but its abstractly theoretical approach forced a set of stylized predictions onto fragmentary ethnographic data. Following Merton's (1938) application of the theory of anomie (Durkheim 1893) to the United States, Cloward and Ohlin theorized that different local structures of opportunity would yield distinctive types of adolescent youth gangs. Depending on the presence or absence of both legal and illegal opportunities, local youth gangs would be conformists, fighters, thieves, or drug users. The present study and others (Short and Strodtbeck 1965; Moore 1978; Spergel 1964) have shown the distribution of these behaviors to be quite different from what that idealized model predicted. We found that each neighborhood we studied contained examples of each type of behavior. The neighborhoods differed not in the presence or absence of specific forms of anomie but rather in the amounts, sequences, and types of economic crime and in the patterning of economic crime in youthful careers and neighborhood economies.

In recent years the use of the subculture concept in delinquency studies has fallen into disfavor. It was unsatisfactory theoretically because subcultural causation was found overly deterministic and unable to account for decline in offense rates with age as well as the fear of crime in poor neighborhoods (Matza 1964). If cultural causation were as powerful as extreme forms of cultural deviance theory suggest, delinquents would not decrease their deviant activities so sharply as they get older, and inner-city residents would support crime far more than they do.

Nevertheless, the subculture concept has enjoyed a revival among

British sociologists, although it has been applied to phenomena that are more identifiably expressive and "cultural": namely, the progression of post–World War II youth cultures, including Teddy-boys, skinheads, mods, rockers, and punks. Writers have analyzed these cultural movements primarily as "magical" responses to structural situations of economic disadvantage (Hebdige 1979; Hall and Jefferson 1976). Yet as one critic has noted, "mundane day-to-day delinquency has always been petty theft" (S. Cohen 1980).

This book has grounded localized patterns of social action in neighborhood-specific structures of opportunity in much the way that Cloward and Ohlin intended. Systematically collected and compared data from three neighborhoods have permitted a more concrete analysis of neighborhood variations. Yet the comparison still remains at the level of social action. To discover the cultural meanings of crime within these neighborhoods, we must trace the connections between the social ecology of each community and the specific local meanings of crime in relation to other aspects of community organization.

The elements of creativity and collectivity posited by A. Cohen (1955) as well as the element of localized variation posited by Cloward and Ohlin (1960) are necessary for the cultural analysis of our comparative data. Such an analysis is posed here in the terms employed by Paul Willis (1977) in order to explain "how working-class kids get working-class jobs." Willis shows that they "choose" their jobs, avidly, in a joyful transition away from schooling. In a similar way, our data reveal that many of the youths portrayed here have "chosen" unemployment, crime, prosecution, and incarceration. The choices are not those of equal competitors in an open market with equal opportunities to invest in human capital and advance in the labor market. Neither are they the choices of deranged, isolated individuals. Rather, they are the collective choices of those in similar structural situations who refuse to accept the impossible contradictions of these situations.

The form of this analysis is similar to and compatible with the interactionist theory of structure and emergence established earlier. Although a somewhat different terminology is used, that of the "penetrations" and "limitations" of consciousness, the object remains that of describing the emergence of consciousness from specific forms of patterned interactions.

Willis begins with Cohen's thesis of the cultural opposition of school and the blue-collar workplace but carries the analysis much further into the ways that labor organization, household organization, gender, age, social race, and ethnicity come to constitute an interrelated set of cultural categories. The English vocational students he studied, living in one of the world's oldest manufacturing communities, manage barely to finish secondary school and then move directly into the same kinds of stable blue-collar jobs that have supported their families for generations. He traces their evolution from the counterschool culture to the workplace. Their opposition to the school order and their relentless teasing of those students who take school seriously and aspire to clerical jobs lead to their feelings of relief, joy, and the ascension of manhood as they move into the factories. Getting drunk on the last day of school is the annual rite marking this transition.

From the standpoint of meritocratic ideology, both these youths' opposition to the school and their acceptance of manual work would appear as failure. From the youths' own standpoint, however, they have chosen men's work and rejected the emasculating norms of the school and the office. They have preserved both the workplace as men's domain and home as women's domain. At the same time, they have set themselves off from newer, poorer, immigrant populations who may not be able even to expect to work. Thus, occupational identity is valorized in terms of gender, race, and ethnicity. The particular form of their transition from school to work is grounded in ideological constructions encompassing the existing social relationships in their community.

Willis maintains that the counterschool culture represents a temporary "penetration" of their structural circumstances. They see schooling as irrelevant to their future work. They find in their earlier sexual experience the validation of a masculinity superior to that of the less sexually experienced students who accept the rules and order of the school. They are correct in these perceptions and have temporarily penetrated the social structure with both clarity and precision. These penetrations, however, are not ultimately revolutionary; with time, they became "limitations" binding the young men back into the structure. Initially, they find the workplace far superior to school, a place where the masculine norms of their fathers are completely accepted. They also have more money at first than their upwardly mobile schoolmates who continue their education. Eventually, however, they find themselves locked into the jobs, making less money than those who did not participate in the counterschool culture, and having no place to go.

A similar analysis of our data begins with a consideration of the ways in which age, labor and household organization, gender, and race/ethnicity come to be represented in a set of mutually valorizing cultural symbols in each of our three neighborhoods. In each community the adolescent male peer group serves as a domain of interaction in a limbo separated from household, school, and workplace. The cultural meaning of crime is constructed in this bounded milieu of interaction out of materials supplied from two sources: the local area in which they spend their time almost totally unsupervised and undirected by adults, and the consumerist youth culture promoted in the mass media. Lacking the legitimate employment that would allow them to participate in this youth culture, they transform their local environment through criminal activities into sources of funds.

Although they sometimes suffer actual biological deprivation, these youths do not generally invest the proceeds of their criminal activities in groceries, better housing, or burglar alarms. In some cases they may respond to immediate pressing household need, but the first consumption priority for most of them most of the time is clothing. Next comes recreation, including the purchase of drugs and alcohol as well as more innocent teenage consumption activities such as participating in sports and going to movies and dances. The point of their participation in crime is not to lift themselves and/or their families out of the ghetto but to share in the youth culture that is advertised in the mass media and subsidized for middle-class teenagers who attend school by their parents.

The cultural meanings of crime and work within these adolescent cliques are also constructed out of materials specific to each local community, including locally specific ways in which gender, work, labor and household organization, and race/ethnicity constitute interrelated categories. Hamilton Park most nearly resembles the community of Willis's "lads." Most households contain an adult male who is also the principal wage earner. Good work to the neighborhood's residents means high-paying, unionized, blue-collar jobs passed down through male networks. The relation of schooling to such work is seen as tenuous. Racism is virulent and pervasive among these men, who see themselves as protecting both their jobs and their neighborhood from newer immigrants who are of minority racial and ethnic status. At the same time, they set themselves off from the "rich people" for whom they work and who are beginning to see their neighborhood as a likely candidate for gentrification.

In both Projectville and La Barriada, the connection between men's work and men's place in the household has been broken by structural un- and underemployment. An employed man is still expected to support his family, and some such households do exist. More than half of all households in each area, however, are officially headed by females. Whether or not a male child grows up with an adult male present in such areas, he cannot assume that he will grow up to find a stable job and be part of a stable household. Minority status in both neighborhoods also becomes an idiom of resistance and striving. Ethnic identity is constituted with reference to the wider society, not simply internally as a set of shared tastes and customs.

Profound differences also exist between the two poorer, minority neighborhoods in their local configurations of gender, ethnicity, household, and work as mutually valorizing symbols. La Barriada youths still cling to the notion of manual work as men's work, even though the manual work to which they have access pays far less and is much less stable than that pursued in Hamilton Park and consequently less likely to allow them to establish stable households. Projectville's youths have incorporated society's deprecation of manual work (Sennet and Cobb 1972) without ever having had much access to it. Their image of good work is office work following successful schooling. Some of the younger ones among them are beginning to learn to type and to use computers. The symbolization of male and female has been disengaged from the symbolization of work and household.

The cultural construction of crime for youths from Projectville and La Barriada begins from the longer, structurally induced period of enforced leisure which most of them go through. Crime is likely to become a short-term occupation for them, rather than the lark or occasional opportunity to make extra money that it becomes for their peers in Hamilton Park. This development of crime as an occupation takes place not just in social action but also in the development of personal identities and shared symbols. Their economic crimes are, for a period, penetrations of their condition. They are not resisting magically. They are not engaging in revolution. Their perception of their situation is transparent, not simply neutralization but a real, if temporary, alteration of their circumstances. Over time, this penetration becomes a limitation, binding them back into structure as they age out of youth crime and accept the low-wage, unstable jobs to which they did not have access during the period of their involvement in serious theft. Alternatively, some will die; others will spend much of their lives in prisons or mental hospitals. Few will graduate to lucrative criminal careers, and few will continue in the patterns of street crime of their youth.

[11]

Youth Crime and
Social Policy

Research on social problems does not always produce clear implications for detailed social policies to deal with those problems. The problem of youth crime is so serious and severe that even the best-informed experts cannot claim to know easy or certain solutions. Both a base of knowledge and a considerable amount of focused political action will certainly be needed to make any progress against the high rates of street crime that have made the large cities of the United States notorious throughout the world. Many different approaches have been attempted, but high rates of crime persist, and a pessimistic, cynical mood seems to prevail among scholars, practitioners, and the general public. Under these circumstances I would not venture, on the basis of this work, to endorse a set of detailed policy measures and to claim certain success if they are followed. Nevertheless, I do believe that research itself has contributed to the current state of confusion over how to deal with youth crime and that this book can at least help to dispel some of that confusion. Accordingly, I address here in very general terms some of the implications of our research for past and future policies.

This book challenges the notion that efforts to improve social control and efforts to enhance economic opportunity are alternative and opposed strategies for reducing youth crime. Rather, they must be seen as complementary. Our research has revealed in some detail the relationships between social control and economic conditions at the community level. High rates of youth crime in the inner cities are caused not just by the specific lack of employment opportunities for youths but, even more fundamentally, by poor employment conditions throughout these neighborhoods which produce both the stresses of poverty and weakened social control.

Programs to strengthen social control and programs to enhance employment opportunities have long been counterposed as alternative crime control strategies. The preference for one or the other has often been linked with an emphasis on either individual or social causation of criminality. In public debates about crime a focus on individual or social elements separates conservatives from liberals in the assignment of causality and blame (Jencks 1987). Is street crime the fault of the youth who snatches the gold chain and thereby injures himself as well as his victim, or of the bankers, employers, developers, and politicians who have gotten rich creating an environment in which it is possible and attractive for him to do the snatching? Surely both sides must be held accountable. Yet it is difficult to think about both kinds of accountability at the same time.

The focus on neighborhoods here helps to break down some of the dichotomies between individual and social causation and between social control and opportunity enhancement strategies which currently plague our thinking about crime control. By showing the connections between local-level structures of opportunity, local-level social control processes, and youthful careers in crime, this book has sought to show that social control itself grows out of economic conditions. Policies to improve social control cannot be separated from policies to improve economic conditions. The creation of a just society and the call for stricter standards of justice for individuals must be seen as parts of the same endeavor.

Besides calling attention to the ways in which social control and employment opportunity reinforce each other, the focus on local communities also suggests new ways in which each of these aspects of crime control policy can be enhanced. Both employment programs and social control programs affect communities as well as individuals, but the design, implementation, and evaluation of these programs are too often conceived solely in terms of their effects on individuals. The effects of programs and policies at the community level need to be given higher priority. This reordering of priorities needs to take place from the top down, as planners and change agents design, implement, and evaluate programs. In addition, effective change will depend on pressure from local communities upward, as community organizations and leaders demand and participate in new efforts for economic development and crime control.

Efforts to increase the amount and quality of employment among inner-city residents will not succeed or fail simply as they affect individuals. Rather, the amount and quality of employment throughout a neighborhood will affect the ability of individuals within the neighborhood to benefit from education and employment and training programs. Attitudes toward work, socialization into work habits, personal networks leading to employment opportunities, and political savvy about what workers can do to exercise some control over the workplace and the political processes affecting job creation and protection all grow out of employment conditions throughout the community. Improving employment conditions depends on community development and the political economy as well as on individual investments in human capital.

Similarly, efforts to improve crime control depend on relationships between the criminal justice system and local communities, not just on tinkering with the formal standards for individuals within the criminal justice system. This is not to imply that individuals from disadvantaged communities should be held to a different standard of accountability than others are. Such a view is at odds with the very idea of justice. Law and order campaigns, however, rarely stress the political participation of the poor and disadvantaged in efforts to make their own neighborhoods safer. This is exactly what must happen in any serious efforts to improve crime control.

Appendix

Procedures for Notifying Research Participants in the Neighborhood Study

[The following document is the official policy adopted by the Vera Institute of Justice to guide the conduct of the field research reported in this book. The standards described are not necessarily the same as those of the author: for example, I do not think it imperative to change the names of neighborhoods (as long as individual anonymity can be maintained); and I would not personally divulge confidential information to the authorities, even under threat of court action, unless I considered it necessary to do so in order to prevent future harm to someone I could protect. Nevertheless, agreement to the policy set forth below was required in order for me to conduct this study under Vera's auspices, and it was duly observed.]

During the past few months, Project staff have given a lot of thought to the kinds of protection we owe our research informants. Similar discussions have been conducted by staff and Vera management and members of Vera's Board of Trustees. While we regret not having written guidelines for field researchers sooner, the delay has been useful to all of us in exploring and clarifying precisely what obligations we incur with our research informants, and how we may best fulfill them. These obligations are as follows:

Research informants should have full knowledge of the objectives, procedures, potential risks, and conditions of participation in our study. This obligation arises from the respect we have for the dignity of each and every respondent. The person's participation in our research is voluntary, and therefore, it is necessary that each informant have all the information about the project he needs to make a self-interested choice about whether or not to participate.

[255]

It is clear that a research participant runs potential risks by his decision to participate in the study. While actual damage from these risks is unlikely, its remoteness must be balanced against its seriousness; namely, the risk of arrest and conviction if information about their past crimes— or even their present whereabouts—falls into the hands of prosecution or police authorities, or if information about their future crimes is divulged to us by the informant and by us to the authorities. We are obliged to point out these risks of participation, and to think seriously about how to minimize them in our daily research activities. "The Notification to Subjects" below spells out why these risks are real, though unlikely, and how we intend to make sure that they are not realized.

Earliest disclosure of the objectives and risks of the study makes good methodological sense. The fewer surprises about the study the informant encounters in the course of the research relationship, the more willing he might be to trust field researchers. Furthermore, early conversations about the objectives and risks of the study may be used as an opportunity for training participants, alerting them to the fact that we are looking for detailed but not personally identifiable information. Just as we hope that some research informants will identify with the study and in effect become agents of the Project, we also hope that they become sensitive to questions of disclosure and risk in their presentation of the Project to other research informants.

To fulfill these obligations, we will continue the practice of frequent discussions between the supervising ethnographer and field researchers of events in the field and problems that have come up. It is important that the field researchers reveal their observations fully in these discussions. If there are problems in the field, or if a researcher has become aware of impending crimes, it is very important that the supervising ethnographer be made aware of them. It is only through the supervising ethnographer that Project management and Vera management can be brought in on the problems. When that happens, the best interests of everyone involved will be considered in resolving the problems. As we have indicated in conversations, if a serious problem arises, Project staff will meet immediately with Vera management and, if necessary, with members of the Board to consider how to resolve it.

In addition, two procedures are given below for fulfilling these obligations to research informants. The first one is a draft "Notification to Subjects" listing the items of information about the study that we need to communicate to all research informants. This notification should be communicated orally and in language comfortable to you and the research informant, but it should be as faithful to the written notification as possible.

The second procedure details the manner and timing of communicating project information to research informants. The procedure recognizes that a field situation may prevent complete disclosure of all items of information at one time and on first contact. We should review the implementation of these procedures to make sure that they correspond to the reality of field contacts. But their intent should be clear: field researchers should take the aim of full and immediate disclosure as a serious responsibility of their job. As a corollary of this responsibility, be assured that a subject's refusal to participate after this disclosure will not be viewed as a failure on the part of the researcher.

Notification to Subjects

Before I ask you any questions, it's important for both of us that I go over with you a few things about the kinds of questions I want to ask you and about the confidentiality of your answers.

I work for a place called the Vera Institute. We are currently doing research in this neighborhood on crime and unemployment to see what problems young people have finding jobs and why some of them do crimes. We also want to know what kinds of jobs and education you and your family have had. In general, we want to know about your life and about what goes on in this neighborhood. We get funded by the Federal government to do this research. In the future, it is possible that the Federal government could create new job programs or educational programs which could help the neighborhood as a result of our findings.

My job is only to do research. I am not a cop or a social worker. I am only trying to get information. Any questions that I ask you that you think are too personal, you don't have to answer. You have the right to stop giving me information any time you want. In order to keep your identity confidential, we will make up a name for you (or you can tell us what you want to be called). We will also change the names of streets and of the neighborhood in our reports. All this is done to keep things confidential. Federal law says that any information you give me can only be used for research. It is possible that a law enforcement agency might still try to get some of that information. If that happens, we will fight it in court. Of course, there is always a chance we could lose, but we think that is unlikely.

I would also like to tell you that if you plan to commit a crime in the future or if you know of someone else who is, I do not want to know about it, because the federal law I just mentioned does not protect future crimes.

I realize that the things I have just told you may sound a little complicated, but I'll be glad to answer any questions about what I've just said or go over it again in the future if you want me to.

Procedures for Timing of Notification to Subjects

The Project's general aim is to give the potential informant all information contained in the "notification" upon first contact. Recognizing that such an aim might not be practicable in some field situations, the guidelines below try to specify the appropriate forms of Project information that may be revealed on first and subsequent contacts:

During initial and extremely casual contacts, researchers may refrain from mentioning that they are researchers or that they are studying crime under sponsorship of LEAA if, in the judgment of the individual field researcher, such identification would immediately preclude any further contact. It is desirable, however, for the researcher to identify himself at least in general terms as a researcher as early in the relationship as possible. The researcher should always avoid deceiving research subjects. It is expected that many of the subjects we seek may not be particularly knowledgeable about social research. Under these circumstances, a general presentation such as "I'm helping to write a book" may constitute the most understandable answer.

If the researcher has not made his general research identity known during the initial contact, he should do so as soon as possible. Initial self-presentation as a researcher should include informing the subject that his cooperation is voluntary and terminable at any time, and that information will be used only for research or statistical purposes.

By the point at which an initial contact seems to be turning into a continuing relationship, the researcher should explain aims, sponsorship, and anticipated results of the research to the subject. This turning point may vary, but by the time the second substantial, perhaps even the first, conversation is underway, the researcher should let the person know that he is being considered as a subject of the research.

The researcher should respond honestly to subjects' expressed need to know about the purposes and procedures of the research. At this point, all specific assurances and cautions should be offered, as are indicated in the "Notification to Subjects," above. You should understand that, from Vera's perspective, it is better for potential subjects to terminate relationships with you than for them to be misled about your purposes, and ours, in trying to establish this relationship.

Bibliography

Adams, Arvil V., and Garth L. Mangum. 1978. *The Lingering Crisis of Youth Unemployment.* Kalamazoo, Mich.: W. E. Upjohn Institute for Employment Research.

Akers, Ronald L. 1973. *Deviant Behavior: A Social Learning Approach.* Belmont, Calif.: Wadsworth.

Allan, Emilie Anderson, and Darrell J. Steffensmeier. 1989. "Youth, Underemployment, and Property Crime: Differential Effects of Job Availability and Job Quality on Juvenile and Young Adult Arrest Rates," *American Sociological Review,* 54:107–23.

Amin, Samir. 1974. *Accumulation on a World Scale: A Critique of the Theory of Underdevelopment.* 2 vols. New York: Monthly Review Press.

Anderson, Elijah. 1978. *A Place on the Corner.* Chicago: University of Chicago Press.

Arensberg, Conrad M. 1972. "Culture as Behavior: Structure and Emergence." In *Annual Reviews in Anthropology.* Pleasantville, N.Y.: Redgrave.

Banfield, Edward. 1970. *The Unheavenly City.* Boston: Little, Brown.

Beck, E. M., and Patrick M. Horan. 1978. "Stratification in a Dual Economy: A Sectoral Model of Earnings Determination." *American Sociological Review,* 43:704–20.

Becker, Gary. 1968. "Crime and Punishment: An Economic Approach." *Journal of Political Economy,* 76:169–217.

———. 1975. *Human Capital.* New York: Columbia University Press.

Becker, Howard S., and J. Carper. 1970. "The Elements of Identification with an Occupation." In Howard S. Becker, *Sociological Work.* Chicago: Aldine.

Bell, Daniel. 1953. "Crime as an American Way of Life." *Antioch Review,* 13:131–54.

Block, Michael K., and J. M. Heineke. 1975. "A Labor Theoretic Analysis of the Criminal Choice." *American Economic Review,* 65:314–25.

Bluestone, Barry, and Bennett Harrison. 1982. *The Deindustrialization of America: Plant Closings, Community Abandonment, and the Dismantling of Basic Industry.* New York: Basic Books.

Blumer, Herbert. 1969. *Symbolic Interactionism: Perspective and Method.* Englewood Cliffs, N.J.: Prentice-Hall.

Blumstein, Alfred, Jacqueline Cohen, and Daniel Nagin, eds. 1978. *Deterrence and Incapacitation: Estimating the Effects of Criminal Sanctions on Crime Rates.* Washington, D.C.: National Academy of Sciences.

Boissevain, Jeremy. 1974. *Friends of Friends: Networks, Manipulators, and Coalitions.* New York: St. Martin's Press.

Bourdieu, Pierre. 1978. *Outline of a Theory of Practice.* Trans. Richard Nice. Cambridge: Cambridge University Press.

Bowles, Samuel, and Herbert Gintis. 1976. *Schooling in Capitalist America.* New York: Basic Books.

Braverman, Harry. 1974. *Labor and Monopoly Capital.* New York: Monthly Review Press.

Bullock, Paul. 1973. *Aspiration vs. Opportunity: Careers in the Inner City.* Ann Arbor: Institute of Labor and Industrial Relations, University of Michigan.

Bureau of Justice Statistics. 1987. "Prisoners in 1986." *Bulletin, U.S. Department of Justice,* 1.

Byrne, J. M., and R. J. Sampson. 1986. *The Social Ecology of Crime.* New York: Springer-Verlag.

Cain, Glen G. 1976. "The Challenge of Segmented Labor Market Theories to Orthodox Theory: A Survey." *Journal of Economic Literature,* 14 (no. 4): 1215–57.

Chambliss, William J. 1973. *Functional and Conflict Theories of Crime.* New York: MSS Modular Publications.

Chiricos, Theodore C. 1987. "Rates of Crime and Unemployment: An Analysis of Aggregate Research Evidence." *Social Problems,* 34 (no. 4): 187–212.

Clark, John P., and Eugene P. Wenninger. 1962. "Socioeconomic Class and Area, as Correlates of Illegal Behavior among Juveniles." *American Sociological Review,* 27:826–34.

Clark, Kim B., and Lawrence H. Summers. 1979. *The Dynamics of Youth Unemployment.* Working Paper No. 393. Cambridge, Mass.: National Bureau of Economic Research.

Cloward, Richard A., and Lloyd Ohlin. 1960. *Delinquency and Opportunity: A Theory of Delinquent Gangs.* New York: Free Press.

Cohen, Albert K. 1955. *Delinquent Boys.* New York: Free Press.

Cohen, Stan. 1980. "Symbols of Trouble." Introduction to *Folk Devils and Moral Panics: The Creation of the Mods and Rockers,* rev. ed. London: Martin Robertson.

Cornish, Derek B., and Ronald V. Clarke. 1986. *The Reasoning Criminal: Rational Choice Perspectives on Offending.* New York: Springer-Verlag.

Crowley, Joan. 1984. "Delinquency and Employment." In *Youth and the Labor Market: Analyses of the National Longitudinal Survey.* Kalamazoo, Mich.: W. E. Upjohn Institute for Employment Research.

Currie, Elliott. 1985. *Confronting Crime: An American Challenge.* New York: Pantheon Books.

Dalton, George. 1969. "Theoretical Issues in Economic Anthropology." *Current Anthropology,* 10 (no. 1): 63–102.

Doeringer, Peter B., and Michael J. Piore. 1971. *Internal Labor Markets and Manpower Analysis.* Lexington, Mass.: Heath.

Durkheim, Emile. 1893. *On the Division of Labor in Society.* New York: Free Press, 1964.

Dutka, Ann B., and Marcia Freedman. 1980. "Where the Jobs Are." *New York Affairs*, 6 (no. 2): 3–19.

Eames, E., and J. Goode. 1973. *Urban Poverty in Cross-Cultural Context*. New York: Free Press.

Edelman, Marion Wright. 1987. *Families in Peril*. Cambridge, Mass.: Harvard University Press.

Elliott, Delbert S., and Suzanne S. Ageton. 1980. "Reconciling Race and Class Differences in Self-Reported and Official Estimates of Delinquency." *American Sociological Review*, 45:95–110.

Elliott, Delbert S., and David Huizinga. 1983. "Social Class and Delinquent Behavior in a National Youth Panel." *Criminology*, 21 (no. 2): 149–77.

Elliott, Delbert S., David Huizinga, and Suzanne S. Ageton. 1982. *Explaining Delinquency and Drug Use*. National Youth Survey Project Report No. 21. Boulder, Colo.: Behavioral Research Institute.

———. 1985. *Explaining Delinquency and Drug Use*. Beverly Hills, Calif.: Sage.

Elliott, Delbert S., and Harwin L. Voss. 1974. *Delinquency and Dropout*. Lexington, Mass.: Heath.

Empey, Lamar T. 1982. *American Delinquency: Its Construction and Meaning*. Homewood, Ill.: Dorsey Press.

Erickson, Maynard L., and Gary F. Jensen. 1977. "Delinquency Is Still Group Behavior: Toward Revitalizing the Group Premise in the Sociology of Deviance." *Journal of Criminal Law and Criminology*, 68:262–73.

Farrington, David P. 1979. "Longitudinal Research on Crime and Delinquency." In Norval Morris and Michael Tonry, eds., *Crime and Justice: An Annual Review of Research*, vol. 1. Chicago: University of Chicago Press.

Feldstein, Martin, and David Ellwood. 1957. *Teenage Unemployment: What Is the Problem?* Working Paper No. 274. Cambridge, Mass.: National Bureau of Economic Research.

Fine, Gary Alan, and Sheryl Kleinman. 1979. "Rethinking Subculture: An Interactionist Analysis." *American Journal of Sociology*, 85 (no. 1): 1–20.

Freedman, Marcia K. 1969. *The Process of Work Establishment*. New York: Columbia University Press.

Freeman, Richard B. 1980. "Why Is There a Youth Labor Market Problem?" In Bernard E. Anderson and Isabel V. Sawhill, eds., *Youth Employment and Public Policy*. Englewood Cliffs, N.J.: Prentice-Hall.

Gillespie, Robert W. 1975. "Economic Factors in Crime and Delinquency: A Critical Review of the Empirical Evidence." Report to the National Institute of Law Enforcement and Criminal Justice, Washington, D.C. (mimeo).

"Gold Chain Snatchers Slay 2nd Victim in Wave of Thefts." 1980. *New York Times*, September 22, p. B1.

Gordon, David M., Richard Edwards, and Michael Reich. 1982. *Segmented Work, Divided Workers: The Historical Transformation of Labor in the United States*. Cambridge: Cambridge University Press.

Gould, Steven Jay. 1981. *The Mismeasure of Man*. New York: Norton.

Gove, Walter R. 1985. "The Effects of Age and Gender on Deviant Behavior: A Biopsychological Perspective." In Alice S. Rossi, ed., *Gender and the Life Course*. Chicago: Aldine.

Greenberg, David F. 1977. "Delinquency and the Age Structure of Society." *Contemporary Crises*, 1 (April): 189–223.

———. 1985. "Age, Crime, and Social Explanation." *American Journal of Sociology*, 91 (no. 1): 1–21.

Hainer, Peter, Catherine Hines, Elizabeth Martin, and Gary Shapiro. 1988. "Research on Improving Coverage in Household Surveys." Paper presented to Bureau of the Census, Fourth Annual Research Conference, Arlington, Va., March 20–23.

Hall, Stuart, and Tony Jefferson, eds. 1976. *Resistance through Rituals*. London: Hutchinson.

Harrison, Bennett. 1972a. *Education, Training, and the Urban Ghetto*. Baltimore, Md.: Johns Hopkins University Press.

———. 1972b. "Employment, Unemployment, and Structure of the Urban Ghetto Market." *Wharton Quarterly*, Spring, pp. 4–30.

Harvey, David. 1975. *Social Justice and the City*. Baltimore, Md.: Johns Hopkins University Press.

Hebdige, Dick. 1979. *Subculture: The Meaning of Style*. New York: Methuen.

Herrnstein, Richard. 1971. "IQ." *Atlantic*, September, pp. 43–64.

Hindelang, Michael J., Travis Hirschi, and Joseph G. Weis. 1979. "Correlates of Delinquency: The Illusion of Discrepancy between Self-Report and Official Measures." *American Sociological Review*, 44:995–1014.

Hirschi, Travis. 1969. *Causes of Delinquency*. Berkeley: University of California Press.

Hirschi, Travis, and Michael Gottfredson. 1983. "Age and the Exploration of Crime." *American Journal of Sociology*, 89 (no. 3): 552–84.

Hobsbawn, Eric. 1955. *Primitive Rebels*. New York: Norton.

Hughes, E. C. 1971. *The Sociological Eye*. Chicago: Aldine.

Ianni, Francis A. J. 1974a. *Black Mafia: Ethnic Succession in Organized Crime*. New York: Simon & Schuster.

———. 1974b. "The Mafia Becomes an Equal Opportunity Employer: The Rise of the New Black Mafia." *New York Magazine*, 7 (no. 4): 36–46.

Ianni, Francis A. J., with Elizabeth Reuss-Ianni. 1972. *A Family Business: Kinship and Social Control in Organized Crime*. New York: Russell Sage Foundation.

Jencks, Christopher. 1987. "Genes and Crime." *New York Review of Books*, February 12, pp. 33–41.

Jensen, A. R. 1979. *Bias in Mental Testing*. New York: Free Press.

Johnson, Bruce D., et al. 1985. *Taking Care of Business: The Economics of Crime by Heroin Abusers*. Lexington, Mass.: Lexington Books, Heath.

Kalachek, Edward. 1969. *The Youth Labor Market*. Washington, D.C.: Institute of Labor and Industrial Relations, University of Michigan, Wayne State University, and National Manpower Task Force.

Kasarda, John D. 1985. "Urban Change and Minority Opportunities." In Paul E. Petersen, ed. *The New Urban Reality*. Washington, D.C.: Brookings Institution.

Keesing, Roger M. 1974. "Theories of Culture." In *Annual Reviews in Anthropology*. Pleasantville, N.Y.: Redgrave.

Klockars, Carl. 1974. *The Professional Fence*. New York: Free Press.

Kornhauser, Ruth Rosner. 1978. *Social Sources of Delinquency: An Appraisal of Analytic Models*. Chicago: University of Chicago Press.

Kroeber, A. L., and Clyde Kluckholn. 1952. "Culture: A Critical Review of Concepts and Definitions. *Papers of the Peabody Museum of Archaeology and Ethnology*, 47 (no. 1).

Laub, John H. 1983. "Urbanism, Race, and Crime." *Journal of Research in Crime and Delinquency,* 20:183–98.

Leacock, Eleanor, ed. 1971. *The Culture of Poverty; A Critique.* New York: Simon & Schuster.

Leveson, Irving. 1976. *The Growth of Crime.* Croton-on-Hudson, N.Y.: Hudson Institute.

Lewis, Oscar. 1966. *La Vida: A Puerto Rican Family in the Culture of Poverty.* New York: Random House.

Liebow, Elliot. 1967. *Tally's Corner: A Study of Negro Street Corner Men.* Boston: Little, Brown.

Lipton, Douglas, Robert Martinson, and Judith Wilks. 1975. *The Effectiveness of Correctional Treatment: A Survey of Treatment Evaluation Studies.* New York: Praeger.

Loeber, Rolf, and Magda Stouthmer-Loeber. 1986. "Family Factors as Correlates and Predictors of Juvenile Conduct Problems and Delinquency." In Michael Tonry and Norval Morris, eds., *Crime and Justice: An Annual Review of Research.* Chicago: University of Chicago Press.

Lombroso, Cesare. 1911. *Crime: Its Causes and Remedies.* Boston: Little, Brown.

Long, Sharon K., and Ann D. Witte. 1981. "Current Economic Trends: Implications for Crime and Criminal Justice." In Kevin N. Wright, ed., *Crime and Criminal Justice in a Declining Economy.* Cambridge, Mass.: Oelgeschlager, Gunn and Hain.

Lowie, Robert H. 1920. *Primitive Society.* New York: Boni & Liveright.

McGahey, Richard. 1982. "Labor Market Segmentation, Human Capital, and the Economics of Crime. Ph.D. diss., New School for Social Research, New York.

Malinowski, Bronislaw. 1929. *The Sexual Life of Savages.* New York: Harcourt, Brace & World.

Mallar, Charles, S. Kerachsky, C. Thornton, M. Donihue, C. Jones, D. Long, E. Noggoh, and J. Schore. 1980. *Evaluation of the Economic Impact of the Job Corps Program: Second Follow-up Report.* Princeton, N.J.: Mathematica Policy Research.

Manpower Demonstration Research Corporation. 1982. *Summary and Findings of the National Supported Work Demonstration.* Cambridge, Mass.: Ballinger.

Massey, Douglas S. 1979. "Residential Segregation of Spanish Americans in United States Urbanized Areas." *Demography,* 16 (no. 4): 553–63.

Matza, David. *Delinquency and Drift.* 1964. New York: Wiley.

Merton, Robert K. 1938. "Social Structure and Anomie." *American Sociological Review,* 3:672–82.

Miller, Walter B. 1958. "Lower Class Culture as a Generating Milieu of Gang Delinquency." *Journal of Social Issues,* 14 (no. 3): 5–19.

Moore, Joan. 1978. *Homeboys.* Philadelphia: Temple University Press.

New York City Planning Commission. 1978. *Neighborhood Profiles.* New York: City Planning Commission.

Orsagh, Thomas, and Ann Dryden Witte. 1981. "Economic Status and Crime: Implications for Offender Rehabilitation." *Journal of Criminal Law and Criminology,* 72:1055–71.

Ortner, Sherry B. 1984. "Theory in Anthropology since the Sixties." *Comparative Studies in Society and History,* 26:126–66.

Osterman, Paul. 1980. *Getting Started: The Youth Labor Market.* Cambridge, Mass.: MIT Press.

Patterson, Gerald R., and Thomas Dishion. 1985. "Contributions of Families and Peers to Delinquency." *Criminology,* 23:63–80.

Phillips, Llad, Harold L. Votey, Jr., and Darold Maxwell. 1972. "Crime, Youth, and the Labor Market." *Journal of Political Economy,* 80:491–504.

Piore, Michael P. 1979. *Birds of Passage: Migrant Labor and Industrial Societies.* Cambridge: Cambridge University Press.

Piven, Frances Fox, and Richard A. Cloward. 1971. *Regulating the Poor: The Functions of Public Welfare.* New York: Random House.

Polanyi, Karl. 1957. "The Economy as Instituted Process." In Karl Polanyi, Conrad M. Arensberg, and Harry W. Pearson, *Trade and Market in Early Empires.* Glencoe: Free Press.

Polanyi, Karl, Conrad M. Arensberg, and Harry W. Pearson. 1957. *Trade and Market in Early Empires.* Glencoe: Free Press.

Preble, Edward, and John J. Casey. 1969. "Taking Care of Business—The Heroin User's Life on the Street." *International Journal of the Addictions,* 4:1–24.

Quinney, Richard. 1974. *Criminal Justice in America.* Boston: Little, Brown.

——. 1977. *Class, State and Crime.* New York: David McKay.

Reinarman, Craig, and Jeffrey Fagan. 1988. "Social Organization and Differential Association: A Research Note from a Longitudinal Study of Violent Juvenile Offenders." *Crime and Delinquency,* 34 (no. 3):307–25.

Reiss, Albert J. 1986. "Why Are Communities Important in Understanding Crime?" In Albert J. Reiss and Michael Tonry, eds., *Crime and Justice: A Review of Research,* vol. 8, *Communities and Crime.* Chicago: University of Chicago Press.

Reiss, Albert J., and Michael Tonry, eds. 1986. *Crime and Justice: A Review of Research,* vol. 8, *Communities and Crime.* Chicago: University of Chicago Press.

Rich, Thomas F., and Arnold I. Barnett. 1985. "Model-Based U.S. Prison Population Projections." *Public Administration Review,* November, pp. 780–89.

Rodman, Hyman. 1963. "The Lower Class Value Stretch." *Social Forces,* 42:205–15.

Rogers, David. 1968. *110 Livingston Street: Politics and Bureaucracy in the New York City School System.* New York: Random House.

Roseberry, William. 1983. *Coffee and Capitalism in the Venezuelan Andes.* Austin: University of Texas Press.

Rosenberg, Terry J., and Robert W. Lake. 1976. "Toward a Revised Model of Residential Segregation and Succession: Puerto Ricans in New York City, 1960–1970." *American Journal of Sociology,* 81:1142–50.

Sampson, Robert J. 1987. "Urban Black Violence: The Effect of Male Joblessness and Family Disruption." *American Journal of Sociology,* 93 (no. 2): 348–82.

Sassen-Koob, Saskia. 1979. "Immigrant and Minority Workers in the Organization of the Labor Process." *Journal of Ethnic Studies,* 8:1–34.

——. 1981. *Exporting Capital and Importing Labor: The Role of Caribbean Migration to New York City.* Occasional Paper No. 28. New York: Research Program in Inter-American Affairs, New York University.

Schwendinger, Herman, and Julia Siegel Schwendinger. 1985. *Adolescent Subcultures and Delinquency.* New York: Praeger.

Sennet, Richard, and Jonathan Cobb. 1972. *The Hidden Injuries of Class.* New York: Vintage.

Sharff, Jagna. 1981. "Free Enterprise and the Ghetto Family." *Psychology Today,* March, pp. 41–48.

Shaw, Clifford. 1931. *The Natural History of a Delinquent Career.* Chicago: University of Chicago Press.

Shaw, Clifford R., and Henry D. McKay. 1931. *Social Factors in Juvenile Delinquency.* Report to the National Commission on Law Observance and Enforcement (Wickersham Commission), vol. 13, no. 2. Washington, D.C.: Government Printing Office.

Short, James F., Jr., and F. Ivan Nye. 1958. "Extent of Unrecorded Delinquency: Tentative Conclusions." *Journal of Criminal Law, Criminology, and Police Science,* 49:296–302.

Short, James F., Jr., and Fred L. Strodtbeck. 1965. *Group Process and Gang Delinquency.* Chicago: University of Chicago Press.

Silberman, Charles. 1978. *Criminal Violence, Criminal Justice.* New York: Random House.

Simon, Carl P., and Ann D. Witte. 1982. *Beating the System: The Underground Economy.* Boston: Auburn House.

Simon, Herbert. 1973. "Hierarchy and Organization." In Howard Pattee, ed., *Hierarchy Theory: The Challenge of Complex Systems.* New York: Brazillier.

Spergel, Irving. 1964. *Racketville, Slumtown, Haulberg: An Exploratory Study of Delinquent Subcultures.* Chicago: University of Chicago Press.

Stack, Carol B. 1974. *All Our Kin: Strategies for Survival in a Black Community.* New York: Harper & Row.

Stafford, Walter. 1985. *Closed Labor Markets: Underrepresentation of Blacks, Hispanics, and Women in New York City's Core Industries and Jobs.* New York: Community Service Society.

Steward, Julian H. 1950. *Area Research.* Bulletin No. 63. New York: Social Science Research Council.

Sullivan, Mercer L. 1979. "Contacts among Cultures: School Desegregation in a Polyethnic New York High School." In Ray Rist, ed., *Desegregated Schools: Appraisals of an American Experience.* New York: Academic Press.

Susser, Ida. 1982. *Norman Street: Poverty and Politics in an Urban Neighborhood.* New York: Oxford University Press.

Sutherland, Edwin. 1937. *The Professional Thief.* Chicago: University of Chicago Press.

Sutherland, Edwin H., and Donald R. Cressey. 1955. *Principles of Criminology.* 5th ed. Chicago: Lippincott.

Suttles, Gerald D. 1968. *The Social Order of the Slum: Ethnicity and Territory in the Slum.* Chicago: University of Chicago Press.

Sviridoff, Michele, with Jerome E. McElroy. 1984. *Employment and Crime: A Summary Report.* New York: Vera Institute of Justice.

Sviridoff, Michele, and James W. Thompson. 1983. "Links between Employment and Crime: A Qualitative Study of Rikers Releasees." *Crime and Delinquency,* 29 (no. 2): 195–212.

Sykes, Gresham M., and David Matza. 1957. "Techniques of Neutralization: A Theory of Delinquency." *American Sociological Review,* 22:664–70.

Tabb, William K. 1982. *The Long Default: New York City and the Urban Fiscal Crisis.* New York: Monthly Review Press.

[265]

Tannenbaum, Frank. 1938. *Crime and the Community.* New York: Columbia University Press.

Thompson, James W., James Cataldo, and George Loewenstein. 1984. *Employment and Crime: A Survey of Brooklyn Arrested Persons.* New York: Vera Institute of Justice.

Thompson, James W., Michele Sviridoff, and Jerome E. McElroy, with Richard McGahey and Orlando Rodriguez. 1981. *Employment and Crime: A Review of Theories and Research.* Washington, D.C.: National Institute of Justice.

Thrasher, F. M. 1927. *The Gang.* Chicago: University of Chicago Press.

Tittle, C., W. Villmez, and D. Smith. 1978. "The Myth of Social Class and Criminality." *American Sociological Review,* 43:643–56.

Tobier, Emanuel. 1984. *The Changing Face of Poverty: Trends in New York City's Population in Poverty, 1960–1990.* New York: Community Service Society.

U.S. Bureau of the Census. 1983. *1980 Census of Population and Housing, Census Tracts, New York, N.Y.–N.J. Standard Metropolitan Statistical Area.* Washington, D.C.: Government Printing Office, 1983.

Valentine, Charles A. 1968. *Culture and Poverty: Critique and Counterproposals.* Chicago: University of Chicago Press.

Vera Institute of Justice. 1979. "Employment and Crime: A Research Design." Mimeo.

Wallerstein, Immanuel. 1974. *The Modern World-System: Capitalist Agriculture and the Origins of the European World-Economy in the Sixteenth Century.* New York: Academic Press.

Wenger, Morton G., and Thomas A. Bonomo. 1981. "Crime, the Crisis of Capitalism, and Social Revolution." In David Greenberg, ed., *Crime and Capitalism.* Palo Alto, Calif.: Mayfield.

West, William Gordon. 1974. "Serious Thieves: Lower-Class Adolescent Males in a Short-Term Deviant Occupation." Ph.D. diss., Northwestern University.

Whyte, William F. 1943. *Street Corner Society.* Chicago: University of Chicago Press.

Wilkinson, Karen. 1974. "The Broken Family and Juvenile Delinquency: Scientific Explanation or Ideology?" *Social Problems,* 21 (no. 5): 726–39.

Williams, Terry, and William Kornblum. 1985. *Growing Up Poor,* Lexington, Mass.: Lexington Books.

Willis, Paul. 1977. *Learning to Labour.* Farnborough, Eng.: Saxon House.

Wilson, James Q. 1975. *Thinking about Crime.* New York: Basic Books.

Wilson, James Q., and Richard J. Herrnstein. 1985. *Crime and Human Nature.* New York: Simon & Schuster.

Wilson, William Julius. 1986. "Social Policy and Minority Groups: What Might Have Been and What Might We See in the Future?" Paper presented at conference on Poverty and Social Policy: The Minority Experience, cosponsored by Ford Foundation, Rockefeller Foundation, and Institute for Research on Poverty, Airlie, Virginia, November 5–7.

——. 1987. *The Truly Disadvantaged: The Inner City, the Underclass, and Public Policy.* Chicago: University of Chicago Press.

Wolf, Eric R. 1982. *Europe and the People without History.* Berkeley: University of California Press.

Wolfgang, Marvin E., Robert M. Figlio, and Thorsten Sellin. 1972. *Delinquency in a Birth Cohort.* Chicago: University of Chicago Press.

Index

Acosta, Julian: factory job for, 67; noninvolvement in crime, 139; reasons for losing jobs, 71–72; reasons for seeking employment, 64, 70; role of father and employment, 61, 67; transfer payments for support, 62; withdrawal from school, 37

Acosta family, employment in the, 63

Adams, Arvil V., 58

Addicts, social control and, 132–33

Adult-recruited youth crime, 202, 204–5

Age, criminal involvement and, 222, 224

Ageton, Suzanne S., 6, 224

Akers, Ronald L., 6

Aliens and employment, 66–67, 94–95

Allan, Emilie A., 224

Amin, Samir, 227

Anderson, Elijah, 7

Andrews, Zap: burglaries and, 151, 152; decrease in criminal involvement, 154, 155; employment agencies and, 80; messenger job for, 86; muggings and, 153–54; parents' attitudes toward schooling, 40; racial confrontations in school, 42; relevance of schooling for, 41; role of father and employment, 73; running errands, 77; service sector job for, 84–85; withdrawal from school, 43–44, 45

Arensberg, Conrad M., 9, 11, 232, 233, 244

Auto theft: in Hamilton Park, 182–83; in La Barriada, 140–47; of parts, 114; in Projectville, 165; reasons for, 19, 115

Baker, Juice: auto theft and, 165; drug selling and, 166–67; factory job for, 82; lack of family connections to jobs and, 80; messenger job for, 86; prison time for, 87; relevance of schooling for, 40; role of family and employment, 74; trial period for employment, 85; type of crimes committed by, 165–66

Banfield, Edward, 10, 242, 243

Barnes, Jerry: court appearances and effects on schooling, 44; effects of family on, 219; employment opportunities for, 87; gold chain snatching and, 154, 157, 158, 159–60; prison time for, 79, 161; relevance of schooling for, 41; role of parents' employment, 73; summer youth job for, 78; withdrawal from school, 45

Barnett, Arnold I., 2

Beck, E. M., 58

Becker, Gary, 5, 10, 29, 58, 107, 223

Becker, Howard S., 242

Bell, Daniel, 241

Bivins, Ben: affiliation with a clique, 111; burglaries and, 151; clerical job for, 86; court appearances and effects on schooling, 44; employment opportunities for, 76, 82; GED and, 46; gold chain snatching and, 154, 157, 163; prison time for, 79, 87, 161; reasons for turning to crime, 114–15; relevance of schooling for, 40; role of family and employment, 74; shoplifting and, 153

Bivins, Harold, 77

Blacks: economic position of, 22, 23; residential segregation of, 25. See also Projectville

Block, Michael K., 5, 107, 235

Blue-collar jobs. See Employment entries

Bluestone, Barry, 10, 58, 227

Blumer, Herbert, 9

Morales, Arturo, 14; arrested for theft, 133–34; auto theft and, 141–42; building superintendent job for, 65–66, 68; burglaries and, 127, 130, 132; clerical employment for, 71; disposal of stolen goods, 129; GED program and, 37; parents' attitudes toward schooling, 36; reasons for losing jobs, 72; reasons for turning to crime, 115–16; reversion to crime, 138–39; robberies and, 136; role of father and employment, 61–62; schooling of, 33; social programs and employment for, 69; social rewards of schooling for, 36; transition from crime to employment, 68–69; truancy, 36–37; withdrawal from school, 37, 64
Morales family, employment in the, 63
Morgan Houses, 72–73, 148
Muggings: in Hamilton Park, 183; in Projectville, 149, 153–54
Murphy, Peter: burglaries and, 180, 181, 184–85; drug use by, 185; employment opportunities for, 90, 92; reasons for losing jobs, 91; role of parents and employment, 88, 219; withdrawal from school, 48

National Institute of Justice, 12
Neighborhoods: criminal involvement and ecology of, 118–19; local markets for illegal goods/services, 119
Neighborhoods used in research: age of residents and immigration patterns of, 26, 27; comparison of crime patterns in, 201–5; description of, 18–20; family structure of, 22–24; housing tenure of, 27–28; income of, 20–22; race/ethnicity composition of, 24–25; residential segregation in, 25. *See also* Hamilton Park, La Barriada, Projectville
Newspaper ads, use of, 80–81
New York City Planning Commission, 200, 263
New York Times, 156–57
Nye, F. I., 4

O'Brien, Bonnie, 47, 190
Off-the-books jobs. *See Employment entries*
Ohlin, Lloyd, 4, 6, 11–12, 246, 247
On-the-books jobs. *See Employment entries*
Organized crime, 192–94
Orsagh, Thomas, 5
Ortner, Sherry B., 231
Osinski, Jim, 49
Osterman, Paul, 58–59

Padilla, Jorge: aliens as workers, 66–67; arrests and, 136; auto theft and, 141; building superintendent job for, 65; decrease in criminal involvement, 138; disposal of stolen goods, 129; job-related theft, 138; reasons for turning to crime, 124–25; transfer payments for support, 62; withdrawal from school, 37
Parents from Hamilton Park, attitudes toward schooling, 46–47, 56
Parents from La Barriada: attitudes toward employment, 61, 62–63, 67, 68, 69; attitudes toward schooling, 36, 56; contact with schools, 36–37
Parents from Projectville, attitudes toward schooling, 39–40, 56
Patterson, Gerald R., 218
Pearson, Harry W., 11, 232
Peplinski, George: employment opportunities for, 89–90; role of mother and employment, 88
Personal connections and employment. *See Employment entries*
Phillips, Llad, 226
Picking pockets, 114, 151, 152
Piore, Michael J., 10, 58, 228
Piven, Frances Fox, 228
Polanyi, Karl, 11, 232, 233
Police, relationship with: drug selling and, 171–73, 187–89; in Hamilton Park, 187–89; in La Barriada, 128, 132, 134; in Projectville, 150, 166
Police statistics, ethnographic data and, 199–201
Pollini, Carl: drug selling and, 191; employment opportunities for, 93; employment through school, 52; fighting in school, 50; role of father and employment, 88
Preble, Edward, 7, 241
Pregnancy, schooling and effects of, 43–44
Projectville: age of residents and immigration patterns in, 26, 27; comparison of ethnographic and census data on employment, 97–100; comparison of ethnographic and census data on schooling, 52–54; crime in, 148–77; description of, 19–20; employment in, 72–87; family income in, 21; family structure in, 23, 24; housing tenure in, 27–28; race/ethnicity composition in, 24, 25; relevance of schooling and employment in, 55; schooling in, 39–46; wages vs. public assistance in, 21–22. *See also* Blacks
Public assistance. *See* Wages vs. public assistance

Library of Congress Cataloging-in-Publication Data

Sullivan, Mercer L., 1950–
 "Getting paid" : youth crime and work in the inner city / Mercer L. Sullivan.
  p. cm.—(Anthropology of contemporary issues)
 Bibliography: p.
 Includes index.
 ISBN 0-8014-2370-8 (alk. paper).—ISBN 0-8014-9598-9 (pbk. : alk. paper)
 1. Juvenile delinquency—New York (N.Y.)—Case studies. 2. Urban youth—
Employment—New York (N.Y.)—Case studies. I. Title. II. Series.
HV9106.N6S85 1989
364.3'6'097471—dc20   89-42882

CPSIA information can be obtained at www.ICGtesting.com
Printed in the USA
BVOW03s1205270314

348925BV00001B/1/P